M000306060

"This series promises to be spiritually ar
careful, solid biblical exegesis. The meth
helpful to teachers of the faith at different l..
to people seeking to deepen their knowledge and thereby nourish their faith. I
strongly recommend the Catholic Commentary on Sacred Scripture."

— **Cormac Cardinal Murphy-O'Connor**, Archbishop of Westminster

"This series richly provides what has for so long been lacking among contemporary scriptural commentaries. Its goal is to assist Catholic preachers and teachers, lay and ordained, in their ministry of the word. Moreover, it offers ordinary
Catholics a scriptural resource that will enhance their understanding of God's
word and thereby deepen their faith. Thus these commentaries, nourished on
the faith of the Church and guided by scholarly wisdom, are both exegetically
sound and spiritually nourishing."

— **Thomas G. Weinandy**, OFM Cap,
United States Conference of Catholic Bishops

"This new Bible commentary series is based on solid scholarship and enriched
by the church's long tradition of study and reflection. Enhanced by an attractive format, it provides an excellent resource for all who are serving in pastoral
ministry and for the individual reader who searches the Scriptures for guidance
in the Christian life."

— **Emil A. Wcela**, Auxiliary Bishop (retired), Diocese of Rockville Centre;
past president, Catholic Biblical Association

"The CCSS is a long-awaited addition to Catholic books on the Bible. It is clearly
written, sticks to the facts, treats the Bible as true history, and does not get lost in
idle speculation and guesswork about the sources of the Gospels and the other
books. Homilists will find here the pearl of great price and the treasure hidden
in a field. Laypersons who are looking for a truly Catholic interpretation of the
Bible will find it here. Those who want to know more about God's holy word in
the Bible will want to purchase the whole set."

— **Kenneth Baker**, SJ, editor, *Homiletics and Pastoral Review*

"This new commentary series appears to me to be a gift of the Holy Spirit to
Catholic clergy, religious, and laity at this historic moment. Pope Benedict has
effectively announced the rebirth of Catholic biblical theology, bringing together

Scripture, tradition, and the teachings of the Church. This commentary reflects not only biblical criticism but also the unity of the Word of God as it applies to our lives. This is a marvelous and timely introduction."

—**Benedict J. Groeschel, CFR**, author and preacher

"This new commentary series should meet a need that has long been pointed out: a guide to Scripture that will be both historically responsible and shaped by the mind of the Church's tradition. It promises to be a milestone in the recovery of a distinctively Catholic approach to exegesis."

—**Aidan Nichols, OP**, University of Oxford; Fellow of Greyfriars, Oxford

"The Catholic Commentary on Sacred Scripture employs the Church's methodology of studying Sacred Scripture in a faithful, dynamic, and fruitful way. It is now the go-to resource that I can enthusiastically recommend to all my students."

—**Jeff Cavins**, founder, The Great Adventure Catholic Bible Study System

"Mary Healy and Peter S. Williamson, with Kevin Perrotta, have launched an exciting and most promising Catholic Commentary on Sacred Scripture. I plan to read and use it as a basis for preaching and am already profiting from the advanced segments."

—**Michael Scanlan, TOR**, Franciscan University of Steubenville

"The Catholic Commentary on Sacred Scripture fills a great void by giving us a serious, scholarly, and orthodox commentary series. These volumes are deep and profound yet lucid, easy to read, and rich with detail. This set will fill a great void for Scripture students of all ages, levels of education, and experience."

—**Steve Ray**, lecturer; author of the Bible Study Guides for Genesis and Acts; and writer, producer, and host of the ten-part documentary series *Footprints of God: The Story of Salvation from Abraham to Augustine*

"The Catholic Commentary on Sacred Scripture affords its readers a helpful guide for encountering the books of the Bible in a way that respects both the whole of Scripture and the givens of Catholic faith. Many will discover in the volumes of this collection wellsprings of spiritual refreshment."

—**Romanus Cessario, OP**, St John's Seminary

First and Second
Timothy, Titus

Catholic Commentary on Sacred Scripture

First and Second Timothy, Titus

George T. Montague, SM

Baker Academic
a division of Baker Publishing Group
Grand Rapids, Michigan

Published by Baker Academic
a division of Baker Publishing Group
P.O. Box 6287, Grand Rapids, MI 49516-6287
www.bakeracademic.com

Printed in the United States of America

Library of Congress Cataloging-in-Publication Data
Montague, George T.
    First and Second Timothy, Titus / George T. Montague ; Peter S.
Williamson and Mary Healy, general editors.
        p.   cm. — (Catholic commentary on sacred scripture)
    Includes index.
    ISBN 978-0-8010-3581-4 (pbk.)
    1. Bible. N.T. Pastoral Epistles—Commentaries. I. Williamson, Peter S.
II. Healy, Mary, 1964- III. Title.
    BS2735.53.M66 2008
    227'.83077—dc22   2008021001

Nihil Obstat:
Rev. John A. Leies, SM, STD
Censor Deputatus

Imprimatur:
Most Rev. José H. Gomez, STD
Archbishop of San Antonio

March 27, 2008

The *nihil obstat* and *imprimatur* are official declarations that a book or pamphlet is free of doctrinal or moral error. There is no implication that those who have granted the *nihil obstat* and the *imprimatur* agree with the content, opinions, or statements expressed therein.

In keeping with biblical principles of creation stewardship, Baker Publishing Group advocates the responsible use of our natural resources. As a member of the Green Press Initiative, our company uses recycled paper when possible. The text paper of this book is comprised of 30% postconsumer waste.

12 13 14 15 16 17 18   8 7 6 5 4 3 2

Contents

Illustrations

Editors' Preface

The Church has always venerated the divine Scriptures just as she venerates the body of the Lord. . . . All the preaching of the Church should be nourished and governed by Sacred Scripture. For in the sacred books, the Father who is in heaven meets His children with great love and speaks with them; and the power and goodness in the word of God is so great that it stands as the support and energy of the Church, the strength of faith for her sons and daughters, the food of the soul, a pure and perennial fountain of spiritual life.

Second Vatican Council, *Dei Verbum* 21

Were not our hearts burning while he spoke to us on the way and opened the scriptures to us?

Luke 24:32

The Catholic Commentary on Sacred Scripture aims to serve the ministry of the Word of God in the life and mission of the Church. Since Vatican Council II, there has been an increasing hunger among Catholics to study Scripture in depth and in a way that reveals its relationship to liturgy, evangelization, catechesis, theology, and personal and communal life. This series responds to that desire by providing accessible yet substantive commentary on each book of the New Testament, drawn from the best of contemporary biblical scholarship as well as the rich treasury of the Church's tradition. These volumes seek to offer scholarship illumined by faith, in the conviction that the ultimate aim of biblical interpretation is to discover what God has revealed and is still speaking through the sacred text. Central to our approach are the principles taught by

Vatican II: first, the use of historical and literary methods to discern what the biblical authors intended to express; second, prayerful theological reflection to understand the sacred text "in accord with the same Spirit by whom it was written"—that is, in light of the content and unity of the whole Scripture, the living tradition of the Church, and the analogy of faith (*Dei Verbum* 12).

The Catholic Commentary on Sacred Scripture is written for those engaged in or training for pastoral ministry and others interested in studying Scripture to understand their faith more deeply, to nourish their spiritual life, or to share the good news with others. With this in mind, the authors focus on the meaning of the text for faith and life rather than on the technical questions that occupy scholars, and they explain the Bible in ordinary language that does not require translation for preaching and catechesis. Although this series is written from the perspective of Catholic faith, its authors draw on the interpretation of Protestant and Orthodox scholars and hope these volumes will serve Christians of other traditions as well.

A variety of features are designed to make the commentary as useful as possible. Each volume includes the biblical text of the New American Bible (NAB), the translation approved for liturgical use in the United States. In order to serve readers who use other translations, the most important differences between the NAB and other widely used translations (RSV, NRSV, JB, NJB, and NIV) are noted and explained. Each unit of the biblical text is followed by a list of references to relevant Scripture passages, Catechism sections, and uses in the Roman Lectionary. The exegesis that follows aims to explain in a clear and engaging way the meaning of the text in its original historical context as well as its perennial meaning for Christians. Reflection and Application sections help readers apply Scripture to Christian life today by responding to questions that the text raises, offering spiritual interpretations drawn from Christian tradition or providing suggestions for the use of the biblical text in catechesis, preaching, or other forms of pastoral ministry.

Interspersed throughout the commentary are Biblical Background sidebars that present historical, literary, or theological information and Living Tradition sidebars that offer pertinent material from the postbiblical Christian tradition, including quotations from Church documents and from the writings of saints and Church Fathers. The Biblical Background sidebars are indicated by a photo of urns that were excavated in Jerusalem, signifying the importance of historical study in understanding the sacred text. The Living Tradition sidebars are indicated by an image of Eadwine, a twelfth-century monk and scribe, signifying the growth in the Church's understanding that comes by the grace of the

Holy Spirit as believers study and ponder the word of God in their hearts (see *Dei Verbum* 8).

Maps and a Glossary are located in the back of each volume for easy reference. The glossary explains key terms from the biblical text as well as theological or exegetical terms, which are marked in the commentary with a cross (†). A list of Suggested Resources, an Index of Pastoral Topics, and an Index of Sidebars are included to enhance the usefulness of these volumes. Further resources, including questions for reflection or discussion, can be found at the series web site, www.CatholicScriptureCommentary.com.

It is our desire and prayer that these volumes be of service so that more and more "the word of the Lord may speed forward and be glorified" (2 Thess 3:1) in the Church and throughout the world.

Peter S. Williamson
Mary Healy
Kevin Perrotta

Note to Readers

The New American Bible differs slightly from most English translations in its verse numbering of the Psalms and certain other parts of the Old Testament. For instance, Ps 51:4 in the NAB is Ps 51:2 in other translations; Mal 3:19 in the NAB is Mal 4:1 in other translations. Readers who use different translations are advised to keep this in mind when looking up Old Testament cross-references given in the commentary.

Abbreviations

†	indicates that the definition of a term appears in the glossary
//	indicates where the same account can be found in other Gospels
1QS	*The Community Rule of Qumran* (Dead Sea Scrolls)
Catechism	*Catechism of the Catholic Church* (2nd edition)
JB	Jerusalem Bible
KJV	King James Version
Lectionary	*The Lectionary for Mass* (1998/2002 USA edition)
LXX	†Septuagint
4 Macc	4 Maccabees
NAB	New American Bible
NEB	New English Bible
NIV	New International Version
NJB	New Jerusalem Bible
NRSV	New Revised Standard Version
NT	New Testament
OT	Old Testament
RSV	Revised Standard Version

Books of the Old Testament

Gen	Genesis	Tob	Tobit	Ezek	Ezekiel
Exod	Exodus	Jdt	Judith	Dan	Daniel
Lev	Leviticus	Esther	Esther	Hosea	Hosea
Num	Numbers	1 Macc	1 Maccabees	Joel	Joel
Deut	Deuteronomy	2 Macc	2 Maccabees	Amos	Amos
Josh	Joshua	Job	Job	Obad	Obadiah
Judg	Judges	Ps	Psalms	Jon	Jonah
Ruth	Ruth	Prov	Proverbs	Mic	Micah
1 Sam	1 Samuel	Eccles	Ecclesiastes	Nah	Nahum
2 Sam	2 Samuel	Song	Song of Songs	Hab	Habakkuk
1 Kings	1 Kings	Wis	Wisdom	Zeph	Zephaniah
2 Kings	2 Kings	Sir	Sirach	Hag	Haggai
1 Chron	1 Chronicles	Isa	Isaiah	Zech	Zechariah
2 Chron	2 Chronicles	Jer	Jeremiah	Mal	Malachi
Ezra	Ezra	Lam	Lamentations		
Neh	Nehemiah	Bar	Baruch		

Books of the New Testament

Matt	Matthew	1 Tim	1 Timothy
Mark	Mark	2 Tim	2 Timothy
Luke	Luke	Titus	Titus
John	John	Philem	Philemon
Acts	Acts of the Apostles	Heb	Hebrews
Rom	Romans	James	James
1 Cor	1 Corinthians	1 Pet	1 Peter
2 Cor	2 Corinthians	2 Pet	2 Peter
Gal	Galatians	1 John	1 John
Eph	Ephesians	2 John	2 John
Phil	Philippians	3 John	3 John
Col	Colossians	Jude	Jude
1 Thess	1 Thessalonians	Rev	Revelation
2 Thess	2 Thessalonians		

Introduction to the Pastoral Letters

Readers come to Scripture commentaries from all sorts of backgrounds. At one end of the spectrum are the totally uninitiated, at the other the Scripture scholar. If you are a beginner, you may simply wonder what these letters to Timothy and Titus are all about. If you are already familiar with the letters and have done some study of them, you may wonder how this commentary differs from the dozens of others already published. For those less familiar with the Pastorals, this commentary proposes to be a reader-friendly introduction. For those further along the line, two characteristics of this book, like others in the Catholic Commentary on Sacred Scripture, make it of interest and, I would hope, distinctive.

Since the letters are properly called pastoral, it is that dimension that interests me first of all; that is, how these letters provide fruitful reflection for the Church today, especially for those who are in any kind of Church ministry. Just as we don't have to reinvent the wheel, we don't have to reinvent the Church. How often when we read Paul's letters to the Corinthians we smile and say of our experience of church today, "Well, we've been through this before." I seek to connect the churches of the Pastorals with our churches today in the Reflection and Application sections, at times by relating my personal experiences. I am not merely interested in what the word of God meant *then* but in what it means *now*.

Second, most commentaries rarely quote any of the early post–New Testament commentaries. Yet these commentaries were the first efforts to show how these texts applied to the churches that inherited them. The Fathers were the first to *use* the Pastorals pastorally. Thus, when one of these early commentaries illumines the meaning by way of illustration or application, I quote it—not only because it is appropriate but also as warrant for what I am doing in applying the text to the life of the Church today. These early interpretations belong to what recent scholars call the *effective history of the text*, a history that the text has made and is still making even now. These comments generally appear in sidebars.

But those two interests must remain subservient to the major one—an honest and faithful search for and exposition of the meaning the letters had for their author and for the leaders and the churches addressed. The bulk of this commentary will be concerned with that.

There, of course, we meet the question of who the author was and why he wrote these letters.

Authorship: Who Wrote These Letters?

Coming in the New Testament at the end of the thirteen letters traditionally attributed to Paul, the letters to Timothy and Titus have had a checkered history in the Church, and especially among scholars. Already in the early Church they were grouped together as letters addressed to individuals rather than to churches, along with Philemon, the briefest, at the end. Marcion in the early second century, otherwise a champion of Paul, knew of the Pastorals but rejected them from his canon, probably because of his disagreement with some of their teachings, notably God's will to save all people and the goodness of marriage and the created order. But they were quoted as authoritative by early Christian writers, notably Polycarp, in the early second century, and possibly by *1 Clement*, at the end of the first. At any rate, they were accepted into the canon of inspired Scriptures quite early, as the †Muratorian canon indicates. That judgment was later confirmed by the Council of Trent, which finalized the Catholic canon. The Reformers, too, agreed that these letters were an essential part of the New Testament canon.

It was only at the beginning of the nineteenth century that Friedrich Schleiermacher questioned the authenticity of 1 Timothy on the basis of its vocabulary, followed by F. C. Baur and the Tübingen school. In their wake, a majority of modern and contemporary scholars rejected the Pauline authorship of all three of the letters, holding that they are the products of either a second-generation (AD 70–100) or even a third-generation (AD 100–130) author, who wrote all of them as a single literary production and wished to shore up his ecclesiastical concerns by giving them Paul's authority. According to this view, neither the Paul nor the Timothy nor the Titus of the letters is an actual historical figure, but the apostle is portrayed as a hero, herald, and teacher and his delegates as models with which a later church is expected to identify. How we interpret these three letters, then, depends a great deal on whether the historical Paul wrote them. For that reason, I need to address the question in this introduction. I will bring little if anything new to the academic discussion, but will provide a necessary preface to the spiritual and pastoral message of the letters, which is the primary focus of this commentary.

The scholars all use the same data but come to amazingly different conclusions. Quite recently, well-known scholars Luke Timothy Johnson, William Mounce, and Ben Witherington III defend the letters' authenticity (see Suggested Resources for bibliographic details), while I. Howard Marshall rejects it. Even some of the commentators who call the letters †pseudonymous believe bits of the letters (especially in 2 Timothy) are from Paul himself.

Somebody Else Wrote Them?

What are some of the reasons many scholars today question the authenticity of the Pastorals? First, the writing of these letters and some of the events recorded in them are hard to reconcile with what we know of Paul's life from the rest of his letters and from the Acts of the Apostles. For example, when did Paul undertake his mission to Crete presupposed in the letter to Titus? The book of Acts ends with Paul in Rome but tells us nothing about his martyrdom there and certainly nothing about his release.

Second, in vocabulary and style the letters show a marked difference from Paul's earlier letters. Some three hundred words in the Pastorals do not appear elsewhere in Paul. Among them is †eusebeia, a Greek word for "piety," sometimes translated "godliness" or "religion" or "†devotion." Another word is "healthy," sometimes translated "sound," applied to doctrine. "Good †conscience" is another. Likewise unique to the Pastorals is the expression "this saying is trustworthy" (five times).

Third, Church offices are said to be more developed in the Pastorals than in the earlier letters. Besides "†bishops" (overseers) and "elders," the role of the †deacon is expanded; there are also women deacons and possibly an order of widows. The charismatic churches of Paul's day are replaced by a tightly controlled hierarchical order. Institution has replaced †charism. This speaks for a later situation in the early Church.

Fourth, doctrinally there is more emphasis on preserving a tradition than on the dynamic proclamation of it. There is no mention of the cross or the resurrection where we might expect it (e.g., 1 Tim 3:16), and there is a lack of emphasis on the †parousia. Unlike Paul's earlier letters, where he engages false doctrines by presenting arguments against them, the Pastorals merely condemn error with barely a hint of description of it. The author also has a positive attitude toward the Mosaic law, which stands in stark contrast to Paul's opposition to it elsewhere. And, unlike 1 Cor 7:29–31, where Paul speaks of living in this world as if not, in the Pastorals the author seems more concerned with living in the present world in a virtuous way, or, as some authors suggest, he is recommending a settled "don't rock the boat" Christianity lacking the radical fire of the early Paul.

From a canonical point of view, the Church has judged these letters to be inspired and a norm for Church life. But of itself that does not guarantee that the implied author of a text is necessarily the historical author.[1] The Proverbs and Wisdom literature in general were ascribed to Solomon, but this meant that they stood in the tradition of Solomon, not necessarily that he authored them all. Similarly, the book of Isaiah was completed by twenty-six chapters written by later authors who claimed Isaiah as their patron and perhaps thought of themselves as a continuation of his voice for a later period. The same could be said about David and the psalms.

A similar situation existed in the Hellenistic world. Writers would attribute their work to an earlier, well-known figure. Where later scholars have discovered this tactic, they attach the prefix "Pseudo-" (e.g., Pseudo-Clement, Pseudo-Demetrius, Pseudo-Isocrates). The sensitivity we have today to authenticity (and copyright!) was not so much a concern to the ancients. The prefix "pseudo-" in the word "pseudonymous" sometimes has the tint of "false" or "falsifier" to it, but that is to see it through modern spectacles.

Scholars today generally agree that the author of the Pastorals, if pseudonymous, was not aiming at deception. On the contrary, he was a disciple of Paul who wished to continue and apply the Pauline tradition, as if Paul himself were speaking, to a later situation in the Church. Some scholars thus propose another word, "allonymity," to describe the "other" authorship more precisely.

In the mind of the biblical authors, the Tradition was a living reality needing constant application to the developing experience of the people. If a later disciple of Paul wrote these letters, the letters would give us a window on what Church life was like at a later period, and that would be enlightening in its own right. The sheer number of scholars who judge the writings pseudonymous certainly suggests the plausibility of their case. But, as always, it is the reasons that must be addressed and not mere common opinion.

---

1. "Implied author" means the author presented or implied by the text itself. It can happen that the implied author is not the actual author, if the latter chooses to write in the name of someone else.

Paul Wrote Them?

There are some serious weaknesses in the argument for pseudonymity.

Situating the Pastorals into the Rest of Paul's Life

First of all, neither the letters nor Acts gives us a complete picture of Paul's life. Acts, for example, uses one or two typical scenes from a town Paul visits, but his stays in those towns sometimes covered months, sometimes years. What did he do with the rest of his time? As for the conclusion of Acts, Luke achieved his purpose when he got Paul to Rome, and Luke does not further describe the apostle's death. We are simply not told what happened after Paul's initial peaceful house arrest there. Less than thirty years after Paul's death, *1 Clement* speaks of Paul traveling "as far as the Western boundary," that is, Spain.[2] This corresponds to Paul's intention in Rom 15:28. Clement, an authoritative figure in Rome and probably its bishop, would certainly have been in a position to know whether Paul achieved his goal. Assuming that he did, the only time he could have done it was after his Roman imprisonment recorded in Acts. That tradition says nothing, however, about a mission to the East—to Crete, for example, as is presumed in the letter to Titus. But could the mission to Crete have occurred sometime during Paul's earlier ministry? Acts omits great portions of Paul's ministry, some facts of which we know only from the undisputed letters, for example, the mission to Illyricum. The mission to Crete could have been one of those omissions.

As for reconstructing the life of Paul, it is possible that the Pastorals do give us information not found in the other sources. Among the undisputed letters, that is, those letters that virtually all scholars agree were written by Paul, some give us considerable information not found in Acts or even in other undisputed letters. From 2 Corinthians, for example, we learn of other imprisonments that we would not have suspected from Paul's other letters. We also have problems putting together the information even in the undisputed letters, such as Galatians, Philemon, and Philippians.

Language and Style

The argument for pseudonymity loses much of its strength when we consider the wide range of vocabulary and style already in the undisputed letters. A

---

2. *1 Clement* 5.7.

great deal of the style of Galatians, Romans, and 1 Corinthians is due to Paul's use of diatribe, a debate with an imaginary opponent, of which we find none in the Pastorals. The contrast of language is not so evident if we compare the Pastorals with Thessalonians, Philippians, or Philemon. Computer analysis of the words, grammatical constructions, and style of Kierkegaard's writing concluded that his works were written by different authors, whereas it is well known that Kierkegaard wrote them all.[3]

Moreover, it is clear from both common sense and an examination of the undisputed letters that a change in subject matter occasions a change in vocabulary. The style of a business letter today differs from that of a letter to a friend. Furthermore, part of rhetorical education was to learn the technique of making one's style fit the subject matter about which one was writing. In the Hellenistic period, students learned rhetoric by imitating the style of earlier, well-known rhetoricians, varying their style according to the setting of their work. Luke, for example, imitates the style of the Pentateuch in the very Jewish family scenes in Luke 1–2, whereas, in his introductions and later historical information, he imitates the style of the Greek historians. Paul, who knew the Hellenistic world as well as the Jewish one, had learned the rhetorical techniques common in his day.

The undisputed letters show that Paul followed the form for letter writing in the Hellenistic world. The Pastorals differ from the undisputed letters in that they are personal letters in which he gives directives to his delegates. But here too, as Luke Timothy Johnson points out,[4] there was a rhetorical template for the kind of letter we find in 1 Timothy and Titus, the †*mandata principis*, the directives given by the emperor or other government official to his subordinate. Thus both the form of the Pastorals and their subject matter differ considerably from the letters to the churches. Of course, a later imitator could easily have followed the template, but it is a weak argument to claim that the change of style proves that Paul did not write the letters. Finally, it should be noted that no one in the ancient Church challenged the Pastorals on the question of vocabulary and style, though there was such criticism of the epistle to the Hebrews and though other works attributed to Paul or about him were judged spurious (e.g., *Acts of Paul, Epistles of Paul and Seneca, Apocalypse of Paul*) and did not make it into the canon.

But what about the word †*eusebeia*, translated "devotion" or "religion" in the NAB? The term appears ten times in the Pastorals, but elsewhere in the New

3. See Alastair McKinnon, *The Kierkegaard Indices* (Leiden: Brill, 1970–73).
4. Johnson, *Letters to Paul's Delegates*, 106–7; Johnson, *First and Second Letters to Timothy*, 97.

Testament only in Acts 3:12 and 2 Pet 1:3, 6, 7; 3:11 (the latter may be dependent on the Pastorals). Though *eusebeia* does not appear in the undisputed letters of Paul, it does appear numerous times in the †Septuagint in the verb and noun forms, and Paul would have known it from there. Opponents of authenticity would say this is a sign of another hand, an attempt to dress up the gospel and the message of Paul in Hellenistic attire. Defenders of authenticity would say that Paul found here a rich word from the Greek culture of his day. It had links to the Septuagint and corresponded to the Hebrew notion of covenant devotion to God. And it conveyed in terms more understandable to the increasingly Gentile membership of the Church and to his Hellenized delegates, Timothy and Titus, the mysteries he had expounded in his earlier letters. The same could be said of some of the other more Hellenized terms he uses.

Church Order

Was the author's purpose to give Pauline sanction to a more developed hierarchy of the writer's time? If such were a concern of the imitator who presumably wrote all three letters, why is there no discussion of Church order in 2 Timothy? And is the authority structure really that much more developed in the Pastorals than in the earlier Paul? According to Acts 14:23 Paul and Barnabas appointed elders (†presbyters) on their first missionary journey. The actual structure of authority reflected in the Pastorals resembles that in the Jewish synagogues of the †Diaspora, which is exactly what we might expect of a rabbi-trained organizer. The structure also resembles those found in the Greco-Roman assemblies called *collegia*, as well as in the Qumran community, where the Dead Sea Scrolls were found, which existed up to AD 68. Furthermore, even though Paul's early communities were under his direct supervision as the primary authority, we find in his very first letter, at least fifteen years before the Pastorals were written, a reference to those "who are over you in the Lord" (1 Thess 5:12). And he speaks of "overseers and ministers" (literally "bishops and deacons") already in Phil 1:1, where "bishops" appear to be the board of elders, equivalent to "presbyters," a situation hardly different from that in the Pastorals, for the two are equated in Titus 1:5–7. Paul had already spoken of a woman deacon in Rom 16:1, so his reference to women deacons in 1 Tim 3:11 is not an innovation.

As Luke Timothy Johnson remarks, the letters do not create an institutional order; they presume one.[5] And the author is more interested in promoting the

---

5. Johnson, *Letters to Paul's Delegates*, 15.

virtues of the office holders than in undergirding the divine origin of their authority. The order they presume is not at all developed with the reverential terminology we find in Ignatius of Antioch at the beginning of the second century, in whose letters the deacons represent Jesus Christ, the bishop God the Father, and the presbyters God's high council and the apostolic college (*To the Trallians* 3). In the Pastorals their roles are more functional, as indeed are the roles of the leaders in 1 Thess 5:13, where they are to be esteemed because of their *work*.

And concerning the disappearance of †charisms, the gift of prophecy had an important role in the ordination of Timothy (1 Tim 4:14), an indication that charisms (gifts freely distributed by the Spirit) and institution (Church structure and hierarchy) are happy teammates in Paul's communities.

Doctrinal Continuity

Themes in the Pastorals are found in the earlier Paul. And much of what seems to be new in the Pastorals actually can be found in less concentrated form in the undisputed letters. But in the Pastorals there is a concentration on elements that we do not find in the earlier Paul: the emphasis on healthy (or sound) versus sick teaching, the life of virtue versus vice, stigmatizing rather than answering opponents, and, as mentioned earlier, a more Hellenistic tone and style. The cross is less emphasized, yes, but the saving death of Christ is not absent (Titus 2:14), nor are the themes of eternal life (1 Tim 6:12, 19; Titus 1:2; 3:7) and resurrection (2 Tim 2:18). Paul's eager awaiting of the parousia is still present in the Pastorals, where Christ's coming is frequently described as *epiphaneia* ("appearance, epiphany").[6] Hence, waning of eschatological hope cannot be claimed as evidence of the lateness of the Pastorals. Paul's positive attitude toward the law is also found in the undisputed letters (Rom 2:25; 3:31; 7:12, 14). Those defending authenticity would claim that the new challenges that Paul faced in the Pastorals required his emphasizing certain truths, focusing his teaching according to the needs of the readers, just as he did in earlier letters.

An alternative solution should be noted. Much of the vocabulary and style resembles that of Luke. It is seriously suggested by some scholars that the letters were written by Luke, who, 2 Tim 4:11 says, was Paul's sole companion at the writing of that letter. It is indeed possible that Luke shaped the expression of Paul's thought, particularly if Paul gave the educated Gentile more freedom in expressing his thought than he would have given one who simply recorded

---

6. 1 Tim 6:14; 2 Tim 1:10; 4:1, 8; Titus 2:13.

his dictation. Luke certainly knew, even better than Paul, the rhetorical styles of the Hellenistic world and was certainly a master of imitative style, which could explain the similarities in style with Greek writings of the day. The Lukan hypothesis makes more sense if Luke had been commissioned by Paul to write each of these occasional letters under the apostle's supervision and authority. In his failing months, Pope John Paul II would often give the main ideas he wanted to express in a talk or letter to one of his secretaries, who would then develop his thought and submit the work for the Pope's approval. Might this have been what the elder Paul did with Luke?

The disproportionate attention I have given to the defense of authenticity should not be taken as incontrovertible proof. The bottom line is that absolute certainty is not available on either side, though I must admit I find the case for authenticity more probable. For the purposes of this book, to avoid rehashing all these issues every time I comment on a passage, I have chosen to assume that the letters are from the apostle Paul not only because the evidence, in my opinion, leans that way but also for *literary* reasons, namely, that Paul is the author whom the letters themselves present to us, so that readers who wish to experience what the author wants them to experience must in any case place themselves in the posture of listening to the apostle who writes to his real delegates. Thus, when I use "Paul" I am referring to the author whom the letters themselves claim, granted that the debate still rages whether this is the historical Paul or a later disciple speaking on his behalf to a later church.

Historical Context

From the above discussion we can draw alternative conclusions concerning the historical context of these letters. They reflect either the actual situation of the apostle Paul and the churches of Ephesus and Crete during his public ministry or a later situation envisaged by a disciple of Paul. In either case, there is opposition to Paul's gospel by a group engaged in teaching in homes and possibly in the churches themselves.[7] Whether their teaching is intentionally directed at Paul or is simply introducing into the gospel a mixture of extraneous, even outlandish, ideas, we cannot be sure. Some of their teaching has to do with genealogies (1 Tim 1:4; Titus 3:9). In any case they reject the truth (1:14) and combine this with a twisted asceticism (1 Tim 4:1–5), which is not an unknown hybridization at that time.

---

7. 1 Tim 6:3–5; 2 Tim 2:14–18, 23; Titus 1:10–11; 3:9.

However, if Paul is concerned about false teaching and practice in the three letters, each also envisages a different situation, as is pointed out by those who hold that Paul wrote the letters. First Timothy is addressed to a rather well-organized church, and some of its problems are severe, even among the leaders. The situation in Titus is very different: the church is just getting on its feet, presbyters need to be appointed, and much attention must be given to catechesis. Second Timothy is written in the shadow of the Roman sword, and its tone is different from the other two. There are good reasons, again, to understand the historical situations to be those of Paul himself, faced with quite different pastoral concerns in each letter.

What Order?

The order of books in our Bibles follows the general practice of putting a group of writings in order by length. But is that the order in which they were written? Obviously, Pauline authorship would mean that 2 Timothy would be last, since Paul sees his death as imminent. But what of the order of the first two? First Timothy is the longest of the three, so we are not surprised that it appears first in our Bibles. But the Muratorian canon puts Titus first, and so does the fourth-century Latin commentary called the †Ambrosiaster. This order has been followed by some recent commentators, including Jerome Quinn, who finds confirmation in Titus's unusually long address, suggesting that the imitator wrote it as an introduction to all three letters.[8] Scholars who opt for authenticity usually put Titus between 1 Timothy and 2 Timothy. The organization of the church in Titus's Crete is more primitive, but that could simply be because the mission there was later and the church less developed than in Ephesus, where Timothy is located. In the last analysis, it is impossible to tell whether Titus or 1 Timothy was written first. On the assumption that the letters come from a later hand, the order does not make a great deal of difference. I am persuaded that the most plausible chronological sequence is 1 Timothy, Titus, 2 Timothy. Though my commentary follows the canonical order, the reader may prefer to read the letters in this proposed chronological order.

The evidence does not support the proposition that the three letters were written at the same time or in tandem. Each visualizes a separate pastoral situation and should be read in the light of Paul's other letters, not only the other Pastorals. I leave the introductions to the letters and their addressees to the commentary itself.

8. Quinn, *Letter to Titus*, 19–20.

Theological Themes

The Pastorals' inclusion in the canon was due not only to their link to the apostolic Tradition via Paul. It was also because the letters provided important directives for the life of the Church. There is only one God and one mediator between God and the human race, Jesus Christ (1 Tim 2:5–6), and God's plan is for the salvation of all, even for the worst sinners (1:15–16; 2:4). Liturgy is of prime importance in the life of the Church, and it is the occasion of prayer for the entire world, especially for its leaders (2:1–3). Orthodoxy is essential to the mission and survival of the Church, which is the pillar and foundation of the truth (3:15). Jesus is the [†]mystery of salvation in person, from the incarnation to the heavenly glory of the elect with him (3:16; Titus 2:11–14). Holiness is demanded of the Church's ministers, and they must be carefully screened before being appointed or ordained (1 Tim 3:1–13; Titus 1:6–9). Church order is assured by the authority of the apostle and his delegates, and such delegation is given by a sacramental laying on of hands (1 Tim 4:14). Baptism is a rebirth and renewal by the Holy Spirit (Titus 3:5), and the gift of prophecy is an important light for the Church (1 Tim 4:14). God's gracious gift calls everyone to holiness (Titus 2:11–12), manifested in virtue and good works.[9] But each stage of life experiences this call to holiness in its own way (1 Tim 5:3–6:2a).

Not for Clerics Only—for Everyone!

Because the Pastorals have to do with directions given from one pastor, Paul, to another, Timothy or Titus, laypersons may be tempted to feel there is little to feed their spirituality here. Not so. Granted that Paul speaks about bishops, presbyters, and deacons in these letters, there is a wealth of doctrine, spirituality, and down-to-earth common sense that will feed everyone. Particularly those engaged in Church ministry of any kind will find these letters inspiring and practical. *Lay Parish Ministers*, a 2005 study published by the National Pastoral Life Center in New York, documents the recent exponential growth of lay ministries in Catholic parishes in the United States. In that survey, those who worked more than twenty hours a week in some role of service in the Church numbered thirty thousand, to say nothing of the uncounted number of volunteers who contributed less than twenty hours.

Paul's blueprint for these ministers is very important. Even more important is his grand view of the Church and the whole mystery of salvation in which all of us are caught up, those who receive ministry and those who give it.

9. 1 Tim 2:10; 5:10, 25; 6:18; 2 Tim 3:17; Titus 2:7, 14; 3:8, 14.

From the Text to the Reader

I have not attempted to break new ground or to come up with a new theory about the Pastorals. If there is any originality in this book, it is that I have digested and hopefully made reader friendly the work of many scholars before me and added comments from the Fathers of the Church where their insight is helpful. I am most grateful to my own mentor, Père Ceslas Spicq, OP, for his excellent French commentary on the Pastorals, and to Luke Timothy Johnson for his more recent works on them. Other recent commentaries have also been consulted.

The work of the scholar does not end with the mere exposition of the text. In the 1993 *Interpretation of the Bible in the Church* the Pontifical Biblical Commission stated that "Catholic exegetes . . . arrive at the true goal of their work only when they have explained the meaning of the biblical text as God's word for today." That document, as well as scholars like Bernard Lonergan,[10] maintains that the closer we experience the reality of what the text is talking about the better we will understand it. I hope that I have distilled the biblical scholarship into a form easily absorbed by the reader. My goal is to feed the spiritual hunger of the reader, particularly if that reader is engaged in or interested in ministry in the Church. In other words, this is a pastoral commentary on the Pastorals. While I have tried to be faithful to the direction suggested by the text, I am far from claiming that my applications are the only legitimate way to draw out the significance of the text for Christian life today. What I have tried to show is how applications can and should be legitimately derived from the text itself.

Where not otherwise indicated, translations of nonbiblical sources are my own. The following Church documents were quoted from *The Sixteen Documents of Vatican II*, translated by the National Catholic Welfare Conference (Boston: Pauline Books & Media, 1965):

Dei Verbum (Dogmatic Constitution on Divine Revelation)

Lumen Gentium (Dogmatic Constitution on the Church)

Sacrosanctum Concilium (Constitution on the Sacred Liturgy)

Finally, I wish to thank Oswald Sobrino for the Scripture and Catechism cross-references, Elizabeth Siegel for the Lectionary references, and Cathryn Torgerson for her help with the index of pastoral topics.

---

10. Bernard Lonergan, *Method in Theology* (Toronto: University of Toronto Press, 1971), 156–58.

The First Letter to Timothy

Timothy is Paul's number one collaborator. The Acts of the Apostles (16:1–3) tells us that on Paul's second missionary journey he recruited young Timothy from his native town of Lystra, in Asia Minor, and thereafter the two were rarely separated. We often think of Paul as single-handedly converting Asia Minor and Greece, like a Lone Ranger. Not so. It was team ministry from the start. The apostle mentions Timothy as cosender of six of his letters: 1–2 Thessalonians, 2 Corinthians, Philippians, Philemon, and Colossians. Three of these letters are written from prison, although we cannot be sure whether Timothy was in prison with Paul when he wrote any of them. In the list of persons who send their greetings with Paul to Rome, Timothy ranks first (Rom 16:21). Paul sent him on at least two important missions, one to Thessalonica (1 Thess 3:2) and the other to Corinth (1 Cor 4:17). In his plans to send him on a mission to Philippi, he writes, "I have no one comparable to him for genuine interest in whatever concerns you. . . . You know his worth, how as a child with a father he served along with me in the cause of the gospel" (Phil 2:20, 22). In 2 Tim 4:9–21 Paul, imprisoned in Rome, asks Timothy to come to him soon. If Timothy came and was also imprisoned, it may be about his release from prison that Heb 13:23 refers: "Our brother Timothy has been set free." More details of Timothy's life will emerge as the commentary unfolds. But this thumbnail sketch suffices to show that if anyone could be considered Paul's chief confidant, if anyone could carry on where Paul left off or replace him in his absence and speak with his authority, it would be Timothy, the recipient of this letter. The apostolic Tradition must carry on.

What elements of that apostolic Tradition may we expect to find in this letter? Among them are the following: (1) the critical importance of orthodox teaching, (2) the primacy of liturgy in the Church's life, (3) the oneness of God and the mediation of Christ, (4) the call of all to holiness, but especially those who have a ministry in the Church, (5) the ordination of presbyters, whom we call priests today, and (6) the second coming of Christ (called in this letter his "appearance").

What lies before us is a directive letter of Paul to his delegate and collaborator. It bears similarities with what was known in the Roman world as the *mandata principis*, a letter giving directives by a superior to his subordinate, of which the letters of Trajan to Pliny are good examples.[1] Although addressed to individuals, these letters were often to be read publicly, both as confirmation of the authority given to the delegate to carry out the superior's directives and also as warrant for the audience to hold the delegate to his assigned duties. This is exactly what we find in 1 Timothy and Titus, which conclude with a greeting to all who hear the letters read (1 Tim 6:21; Titus 3:15). Timothy, of course, is not a servant or an employee of Paul. He is his dear "child." And yet he is set in authority over the church of Ephesus, a church that was probably composed of various households, some of which may well have been outside the city itself. The Ephesian church has reached a certain level of maturity and organization, for there are deacons and presbyters under Timothy's authority, the widows are organized, and it is not a question of establishing those institutions but rather of strengthening them and setting standards for candidates to the offices. The primary qualifications are virtues that should be found in every Christian. Thus today we can find addressed to us the challenges Paul addresses to the candidates and to Timothy himself. This is particularly so if we have a ministry in the Church.

The reader will find numerous echoes of themes from Paul's earlier letters. The themes that stand out in this letter are (1) the importance of forming the faithful in sound doctrine and of disciplining those teachers who would lead the faithful astray, (2) the primary importance of the liturgy and of the demeanor it merits, (3) the qualifications needed for those who aspire to the various ministries, and (4) a warning against false asceticism. Timothy himself has to be told to take a little wine for his stomach's sake and because of his frequent sicknesses. Timothy needs to take his authority seriously, to be emboldened to act vigorously, and to find strength in the grace of his ordination.

With the possible exception of the fourth item, these are themes that in recent years have been stressed by Popes John Paul II and Benedict XVI. The

---

1. For further details, see Johnson, *Letters to Paul's Delegates*, 106–8. Johnson cites Tebtunis Papyrus 703, in which an Egyptian senior official instructs a subordinate in some of his responsibilities, a very close parallel to the literary form of 1 Timothy. Johnson also shows evidence of these letters as early as the first century BC.

Church cannot survive on a dilution of its doctrine or on a mixture of it with deceptive alloys like the New Age movement or on succumbing to the mire of relativism ("one religion is as good as another"). The liturgy has been renewed in the spirit of Vatican II, giving it pride of place and stressing more active participation of the laity. And candidates for the priesthood and diaconate have been given greater scrutiny, to help avoid the kind of scandals that surfaced at the end of the last century.

But it would be a mistake to judge that this letter is all about discipline. Placed at its very center (3:16) and shedding its light on the entire letter is a lyrical celebration of the "mystery of devotion," the union of Christ and his Church in the drama of salvation history, from the incarnation of the Word to the exaltation of all the faithful with him in glory. Discipline and moral expectations are not legalistic chains. They are simply the natural consequences for a community that has been superabundantly graced by the love of God in Christ Jesus.

Timothy's First Charge

1 Timothy 1

Why does Paul write this letter? He is not in prison, as he will be in his second letter to Timothy, so there is no need for him to dwell on his own situation. Rather he is very concerned that his blueprint for the church in Ephesus guide Timothy's building of it while Paul is away. "Living the truth in love" was the foundation for all growth when Paul wrote to the Ephesians (4:15), and now the first part of that principle seems to be threatened: the pure truth of the gospel. What should Timothy do about it? And whose example should he follow?

Address and Greeting (1:1–2)

> [1]Paul, an apostle of Christ Jesus by command of God our savior and of Christ Jesus our hope, [2]to Timothy, my true child in faith: grace, mercy, and peace from God the Father and Christ Jesus our Lord.

OT: Isa 43:3; Jer 14:8
NT: Acts 16:1; 1 Cor 9:1; Phil 2:20, 22; Col 1:27–28
Catechism: Jesus as Savior God (594)

1:1   **Paul** begins most of his letters by underlining his title as **apostle**. It was a title dear to him because, although he had not known Jesus during the Master's earthly life, his vision of the glorified **Christ Jesus** accredited him with authority equal to that of the Twelve (1 Cor 9:1). Only in Philippians and Philemon does he omit the title, probably because he wishes to appeal there to bonds

Fig. 1. Artemis, the major deity of Ephesus, was the nurturing mother-goddess represented with multiple breasts. Paul clashed with her worship there.

of affection more than to his authority. Why, then, in this letter to his cherished disciple, should he use such strong affirmations of his divinely given authority? The answer lies in this letter, like the other Pastorals, being not merely a personal one. Like the "Chief's Orders" (*mandata principis*), it was a letter to be read publicly, authorizing and commanding Paul's representative to do or not do certain things. When Timothy executes Paul's directives, the listeners will know he is exercising not merely his own authority but that of Paul himself. In fact, the authority comes from God, for Paul is an apostle by order of **God**. The Greek word used here for **command** (*epitagē*) means more than simply the will (*thelēma*) of God, which he elsewhere invokes to ground his apostolate (1 Cor 1:1; 2 Cor 1:1; Eph 1:1; 2 Tim 1:1). *Epitagē* connotes a published decree, command, or injunction that countermands any other custom or order, used often in secular Greek for a mandate of the highest authority, in some cases that of a god or goddess.

The God who thus authorizes Paul is **savior**. This title appears in the Pastorals ten times (only fourteen times in the rest of the New Testament). It was a designation that would sound familiar to both Jew and Gentile. To the Jew it would evoke the whole history of Israel, rooted in God's saving act in the exodus and experienced by the Israelites individually and collectively throughout their history (Ps 24:5; 95:1; Sir 51:1). It is especially favored in the book of Isaiah, where it appears eight times, describing the Lord as the savior of Israel,[1] besides whom there is no other (Isa. 43:11), and one who will send a savior even to non-Jews who cry out to him "to defend and deliver them" (19:20). Paul's Gentile readers had heard the term since childhood applied to emperors, kings, and divinities. It was common throughout the empire, and Ephesus, the destination of this letter, was the center of the worldwide worship of the goddess "Artemis the Savior."

1. Isa 43:3; 45:15, 21; 49:26; 60:16; 63:8.

Zev Radovan/www.BibleLandPictures.com

In perfect parallel with "God our savior," **Christ Jesus our hope** shows the way God has been savior, that is, through Jesus. In Paul's earlier epistles, hope is usually directed toward Christ's second coming. Far from having abandoned interest in the parousia in these later years of his ministry, Paul is still looking for "the appearance of our Lord Jesus Christ" (1 Tim 6:14) and finds in it a powerful motive for living a life of Christian witness (2 Tim 4:8). While the time of that coming is unknown, Christ is in any case the basis of Christian "hope of eternal life" (Titus 1:2), which the faithful may attain already upon their death, a prospect that Paul faced early in his ministry (Phil 1:21–23) and will face once again near the end (2 Tim 4:6). The theme of hope is so strong in the Pauline literature that "hope" can stand for the very message of the gospel itself: the mystery that Paul proclaims is "Christ in you, the hope for glory" (Col 1:27–28). Nonbelievers are those "who have no hope" (1 Thess 4:13). Hope's connection with salvation, which we see in these opening lines of the letter, builds on a long Jewish tradition, of which perhaps the best expression is Jer 14:8: "O Hope of Israel, O Lord, / our savior in time of need!"

1:2   Paul had earlier described **Timothy** as his brother (1 Thess 3:2) and coworker (Rom 16:21), but in the Pastorals he calls him his **child** (1 Tim 1:2, 18; 2 Tim 1:2; 2:1). The Greek word used throughout is *teknon*, which is different from *huios* ("son"). To our modern egalitarian mind, for Paul to address a grown man as his "child" may seem condescending, if not excessively sentimental. It may seem to depart from Jesus' admonition about equality and the avoidance of titles ("you are all brothers"; Matt 23:8) and even from Paul's own statement in Gal 3:28 that in Christ the old distinctions disappear. But the model for Christian community is not the colorless, classless society of Marxism or the heedless individualism that political democracy can sometimes spawn. The Christian community is a family. If the new birth is a spiritual begetting from on high (John 3:5, 8), it also creates a family relationship with Jesus and with one another: "'Who is my mother? Who are my brothers?' And stretching out his hand toward his disciples, he said, 'Here are my mother and my brothers. For whoever does the will of my heavenly Father is my brother, and sister, and mother'" (Matt 12:48–50). Within the equality given by baptism in the Christian community, relationships of love, respect, and affection are often colored by the titles one uses in one's natural family.

This is the kind of sentiment we find in Paul here. Since one is born again not only of the Spirit but of the word of God (1 Pet 1:23), preaching the word and bringing others into the faith is like a spiritual procreation, one in which Paul sees himself as an instrument of the life-giving activity of God (2 Tim 1:1). Thus the apostle can call the Galatians his little "children" with whom, like a mother, he is "in labor" (Gal 4:19), the Corinthians his "beloved children" (1 Cor 4:14), and his presence among the Thessalonians "as a nursing mother" who "cares for her children" (1 Thess 2:7). This is why Paul already in an earlier letter could refer to Timothy as his child (Phil 2:22). Although probably not converted by Paul (Acts 16:1; Timothy seems to have received the faith from his grandmother and mother according to 2 Tim 1:5), Timothy was his most trusted collaborator from an early hour: "I have no one comparable to him for genuine interest in whatever concerns you. . . . As a child with a father he served along with me in the cause of the gospel" (Phil 2:20, 22). Thus the Greek word *teknon* ("child") suggests the tenderness parents might have for their offspring in infancy, an emotion that comes out more clearly in 2 Tim 1:2, where Paul calls Timothy "my *dear* child." As Paul faces his twilight years, is he thinking, as the elderly do, of his own survival in the person of his offspring? The relationship, of course, is a spiritual one, **in faith**. And by calling his child **true** (NAB, JB, and RSV; "own" in KJV; "loyal" in NRSV), Paul no doubt wishes to underline the authenticity of this long-lasting relationship that will hopefully accredit Timothy to the Ephesians as Paul's delegate. Behind the word "true" is likely the meaning of Hebrew *'emunah* ("truth") as faithfulness (e.g., Isa 25:1). Paul has experienced the treachery of disciples whom he will name in this letter (1 Tim 1:19–20). In contrast to them, Timothy has remained faithful.

As with his other letters, Paul has transformed the usual greeting of the Greek letters of his day, *chairete* ("rejoice") to *charis* (**grace**), evoking the biblical image of God as loving giver of gifts, especially the grace of salvation. **Mercy** adds the nuance of forgiveness bestowed freely upon the sinner (Eph 2:4). Perhaps Paul uses the word here to prepare for the testimony of his own experience of God's mercy in 1 Tim 1:12–17. Some might think God would confer his blessing and peace upon those who really deserve it, but Paul knows better, and he said so dramatically in Romans: "All have sinned and are deprived of the glory of God" (Rom 3:23; cf. 5:12). **Peace**, the traditional Jewish greeting, is more than the absence of war or peaceful coexistence; even less does it mean a psychological tranquility. It is rather an abundance of good things, and in the New Testament context that means the whole mystery of reconciliation with God and with one another (Rom 5:1; Eph 2:14–17). Notice, finally, how closely God the Father and the Lord Jesus Christ are joined in the bestowal of this blessing.

Reflection and Application (1:1–2)

Would you ever think of writing a letter or email using the kind of formal address Paul uses here? Probably not. We often simply write "Dear," a word that has become routine. We may think of the bonds of family or friendship that unite us with the recipient, but do we think of the spiritual bond in Jesus the Lord that we have with that person? Do we invoke a blessing on them as Paul does here? Every letter can be an evangelizing moment, provided it is based on real bonds of affection. In that sense we can "parent" the recipient by being an instrument of life, whether we have the title Father or Brother or Sister or Doctor. In Nepal, I was director of novices for six years. We did not insist on using formal titles like "Father," but on the day I said goodbye to return to the States, one of my novices, who had lost his father during the novitiate year, with tears in his eyes gave me a hug and said, "You have been a real father to me."

Urgent Agenda (1:3–7)

³I repeat the request I made of you when I was on my way to Macedonia, that you stay in Ephesus to instruct certain people not to teach false doctrines ⁴or to concern themselves with myths and endless genealogies, which promote speculations rather than the plan of God that is to be received by faith. ⁵The aim of this instruction is love from a pure heart, a good conscience, and a sincere faith. ⁶Some people have deviated from these and turned to meaningless talk, ⁷wanting to be teachers of the law, but without understanding either what they are saying or what they assert with such assurance.

OT: Ps 24
NT: 1 Cor 1:18–25; 4:4; 13:1–13; 2 Tim 2:14; Titus 1:14; 3:15; 1 Pet 1:22
Catechism: myths (285), magisterium (890–92), purity of heart (2518)

1:3   From the warm greeting, Paul now turns to a primary concern of his: the false teachings that have been circulating in Ephesus even prior to his departure.

Usually Paul adheres to the letter-writing practice of his day by following the greeting with a thanksgiving. That he does not, and instead plunges into his directives to Timothy, signals the seriousness of this commission. Why was it necessary for Paul to repeat his **request** that Timothy remain in Ephesus? From the description of what follows we may assume that his work was difficult, that some of the faithful were intransigent, and that Timothy may have been tempted to abandon the work in search of more fertile fields. He had, after all, been a traveling missionary with Paul and done very well. But there is a difference between initial success, with the enthusiasm it engenders, and the more laborious effort it takes to lead a community to growth and maturity. Paul casts his desire

Fig. 2. One pillar is the only standing remains of the gigantic Temple to Artemis in Ephesus. In Paul's and Timothy's day it had 127 columns, each over 60 feet high. Paul's preaching of the gospel caused a riot of the silversmiths who made images of the goddess and her temple (Acts 19:23–40).

as a request, though doubtless it would come across to his devoted Timothy as little short of a command. The word **stay**, too, probably has a tone of "standing firm" in the face of these difficulties. And what Timothy is to do is more than request. He is to **instruct** the troublesome individuals. He is to "instruct" or "charge" (RSV) or "insist" (JB) or "order" as a military commander would direct his subordinates. These individuals are **not to teach false doctrines**. Paul here creates an otherwise unknown Greek word ("alien-teach") that suggests that the teachings were not so much a direct attack on the gospel as a mingling of distracting irrelevancies with the pure gospel. This assumes that there is already a deposit of faith, a "pattern of teaching" to which the faithful are committed from the moment of their baptism (Rom 6:17).

What kind of deviation is at issue here? If Paul had mentioned **myths** only, we might have thought of those of the Greek world, which had permeated every level of the Mediterranean culture. But 1 Tim 1:7 speaks of "teachers of the law," and similar controversies about the law are faced by Titus (Titus 3:9). The addition of **endless genealogies** points instead to Jewish speculations, of which there are many examples from this period, allegorizing the lives of the patriarchs and even the events of creation, for example, in the writings of Philo,

1:4

35

the Jewish philosopher of Alexandria, in the book of *Jubilees*, and in the Dead Sea Scrolls. Philo wrote a whole book on Abraham, using the events of his life as allegories for the values of Stoic philosophy. It would have been tempting in Greek cultural centers like Ephesus to embellish the gospel message with Greek myths and Jewish allegories, with the hope of converting more of the Gentiles.[2] Second-century †gnostics carried on speculations about genealogies, as we know from Irenaeus quoting our passage.[3] So what we have here may refer to an early form of Jewish gnosticism.

The great danger, in any case, was reductionism—the gospel being just a new form of mythology, as some of the New Age movement today would have it. Whether a new form of religion or a system of ideas, it draws attention away from the death and resurrection of Jesus, the true source of our salvation. Such teaching is the wolf in sheep's clothing. Paul had confronted a similar love of empty speculation at Corinth. To this "wisdom of the world" in Corinth he had opposed the wisdom and power of the cross (1 Cor 1:18–25). To the speculations circulating in Ephesus he opposes **the plan of God that is to be received by faith**. This is a dense expression intended to achieve two purposes: (1) The word "plan" (*oikonomia*) literally refers to the administration and arrangement of a household, the suggestion being that God's order for the world and for his people stands in substantial contrast to the illusory and elaborate network of relationships in the "genealogies." (2) This plan is available only to those who have faith. Faith is an act of obedience (Rom 16:26) that opens the eyes of the soul to God's revealed word, his plan of salvation. Without this preliminary obedience, a foundation in faith, one may speculate endlessly or even study world religions, but one is not doing authentic theology.

1:5   **The aim of this instruction** is not suppression of Christian freedom or of that kind of wisdom of which the spiritually mature are capable (1 Cor 2:6–16). Its aim is **love**, which builds up ("knowledge inflates with pride, but love builds up"; 1 Cor 8:1). Heresy can only weaken and divide; God's truth, his light, engenders love (13:6; Eph 4:15). In our text the emphasis is on what charity can achieve over against the banal discussions that lead to dissensions rather than unity. This text influenced Augustine, who hailed love as the ultimate principle for biblical interpretation.[4]

Three conditions form the soil in which *agapē* can flourish—**a pure heart, a good conscience, and a sincere faith**. Jesus had promised that only those with

---

2. Paul himself allegorizes the story of Sarah and Hagar in Gal 4:21–31, but the allegorizing targeted in 1 Timothy seems to be of the kind that waters down or confuses the basic gospel.

3. *Against Heresies* preface.1–2.

4. *On Christian Doctrine* 1.26.41.

Divine Love

Agapē ("love, charity") appears ten times in the Pastorals, an indication of how central it is in the administration of the Church. When there is a crisis in the Christian community, the intervention of proper authority is not—or should not be—tyranny but the preservation and promotion of love, which "rejoices with the truth" (1 Cor 13:6) and is indeed its embodiment (Eph 4:15). The community of Ephesus later in Rev 2:4 was in danger of losing its lampstand (i.e., ceasing to be a church) because of the withering of its charity.

The word agapē, very rare in secular Greek, came into the New Testament via the Septuagint. There it translates Hebrew 'ahabah, which covers various kinds of love—for spouse, for kin, for friends. But in the New Testament agapē is reserved for the highest form of love—divine love—in which by grace human beings can participate.

How is love related to authority in the Church? The *General Instruction of the Roman Missal* (299) notes that at the Eucharist the priest should wear his stole, the symbol of authority, *beneath* the chasuble, the symbol of charity, which covers all (Col 3:14), including office and authority.

---

pure hearts could see God (Matt 5:8; see Ps 24), purity here meaning single-hearted desire to please God, in the line of the commandment to love the Lord with one's whole heart (Matt 22:37). In Matthew the stress is on interior cleanliness as opposed to the ritual cleanliness so important to the Pharisees. The heart, biblically speaking, is not primarily the seat of the emotions. It stands for all one's interior dispositions, including those of mind and will. When *agapē*, God's own love, is poured into the heart by the Holy Spirit (Rom 5:5), it initiates a process of purification, so that the first letter of Peter can say, "Love one another intensely from a [pure] heart" (1 Pet 1:22). The book of Wisdom says that God's wisdom does not dwell in a soul that plots evil or in a body in debt to sin (1:4). Many of the traits of this wisdom Paul applies to divine love.

†Conscience, the exercise of judging right and wrong, is part of every human being's decision-making process (Rom 2:15). But it can be distorted by lies (1 Tim 4:2), or, as is said more mildly today, it can be malformed or false. Even when it is right, one can reject its demands (1:19). The Christian's conscience is enlightened by supernatural faith (1:19; 3:9), and that seems to be the meaning here. When one's natural moral judgment is clear of error ("a clear conscience" in 3:9) and is enlightened by faith, it bears fruit in divine love.

1:6–7   Those who **have deviated** have done so because they cast aside these conditions and have ended up in a profusion of meaningless words. They are would-be Scripture scholars or theologians, **teachers of the law**, but they are incompetent, and their self-assurance implies that they would gladly impose their views as authoritative—as an alternative and self-appointed magisterium!

Reflection and Application (1:3–7)

There are two ways the human mind can approach the gospel. One is to examine it in the light of the Holy Spirit, who explores the very depths of God (1 Cor 2:9–15)—an approach by which one gains ever deeper insight into what God has revealed. The other approach is to import foreign or distracting elements that blur the clarity of the word of God by a kind of hybrid teaching that is half Christian and half something else. This kind of hybrid Christianity is more dangerous than out-and-out opposition, because it can be seductive. Its fruits are ultimately confusion, disunity, and sometimes immorality. †Gnosticism was a mixture of this sort, as is New Age teaching today and any theology that does not respect the teaching authority of the Church. Paul does not mean, of course, that we can exclude all subsequent tradition and theological reflection on the deposit of faith; indeed, these are absolutely necessary to confront precisely the mixture of the truth with falsehood that he is discussing. Only the full truth of the gospel can engender unalloyed love, and the three elements that Paul presents—a pure heart, a good conscience, and a sincere faith—are crucial conditions for anyone who would understand the word of God and even more so for those who would teach it.

The Law Is Good (1:8–11)

⁸We know that the law is good, provided that one uses it as law, ⁹with the understanding that law is meant not for a righteous person but for the lawless and unruly, the godless and sinful, the unholy and profane, those who kill their fathers or mothers, murderers, ¹⁰the unchaste, sodomites, kidnapers, liars, perjurers, and whatever else is opposed to sound teaching, ¹¹according to the glorious gospel of the blessed God, with which I have been entrusted.

OT: Gen 19:5; Lev 18:24–30; 20:23
NT: John 1:14; Rom 3:19; 7:12; Gal 5:19–21
Catechism: fulfillment of the law (2052–55), homosexuality (2357–59), the new law (1972)

We know that is a typical Pauline way of introducing arguments to support a   1:8
previous statement.[5] These "teachers of the law" (1:7) are using the Torah in the
wrong way. Paul states repeatedly in Romans that **the law is good** (Rom 7:12, 14,
16, 18), and Rom 3:19 provides a parallel to Paul's statement here: "We know that
what the law says is addressed to those under the law." But the law must be used
as law ("properly," NIV; "legitimately," NRSV, NJB; "like any law," JB). There is a
strong emphasis on the word **provided**, meaning that the law is good *if* it is used
in keeping with its purpose. Thus, possibly responding to the old accusation that
Paul is doing away with the law, the apostle says he is doing nothing of the kind.
But the purpose of the law was not to hatch speculations about genealogies. Its
purpose was to reveal sin (Rom 7:7) and to lead to Christ (Gal 3:23–25). The
righteous who live by faith (Rom 1:17) and love escape the condemning power
of the law by transcending it (Gal 5:16–25). But to suppose that the law can escape its own condemning power is to expect more than it can give (Rom 3:20).
Particularly, to use it to spin irrelevant genealogies is to abuse its nature.

Paul then elaborates what kind of sins the law is meant to expose or, more   1:9–10
exactly, what kind of sinners it is meant to identify. The list resembles others
by Paul (1 Cor 5:11; 6:9–10; Gal 5:19–21). It is not exhaustive (**and whatever
else is opposed to sound teaching**) and roughly follows the order of the Ten
Commandments. It begins with the **lawless**, then mentions the **unruly**. There
is only a slight difference between these two traits. Paul applies the first to the
Gentiles who lack the Mosaic law (1 Cor 9:21), but most often it simply means
those who disregard the law even though they know it. The law then becomes
a reminder, even a condemnation, of their rejection of God. Hence, being "lawless" in this sense is equivalent to **godless** (frequently in the Septuagint). The
second term, "unruly," sometimes translated "rebellious" or "undisciplined,"

Christ and the Law

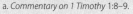 

LIVING TRADITION

Ambrosiaster, the earliest commentary on 1 Timothy in the West (late
fourth century), says that the only correct ("lawful") reading of the
law is in the light of Christ.[a] And St. John Chrysostom writes: "The law,
if you use it rightly, sends you to Christ. For since its aim is to justify,
though it cannot do so, it sends you to the one who can."[b]

a. *Commentary on 1 Timothy* 1:8–9.
b. *Homilies on 1 Timothy* 1:8–9.

---

5. Rom 2:2; 8:28; 1 Cor 8:1, 4; 2 Cor 5:1.

suggests a more confined ambient for the behavior, such as spoiled children who disobey their parents (Titus 3:2) or even those who rebel against authority in the Church (1:10).

English translations of the Greek word *arsenokoitai* are varied enough to confuse the modern reader: "males who engage in sexual activity w[ith] a pers[on] of his own sex,"[6] "sodomites" (NAB, RSV, NRSV), "them that defile themselves with mankind" (KJV), "perverts" (NEB), "those who are immoral . . . with boys or with men" (JB). "Practicing homosexuals" is probably a better translation, given the understanding today of the difference between attraction and behavior. Even more exact would be "those who practice homosexuality," since anyone who engages in homosexual activity would be included, whatever their predominant inclinations may be. There is no reason to limit the meaning here to pederasty. Homosexual behavior is condemned in the Old Testament (Gen 19:5; Lev 18:24–30; 20:23) and in the New (Rom 1:26–27; 1 Cor 6:9).

1:11   The preceding instructions derive from the gospel itself. Such is the meaning of **according to the glorious gospel** in the concluding verse. What Paul has just said about the law is an integral part of the whole gospel message, which demands and produces holiness. This verse provides a rhetorical flourish and much more. God's glory is his self-manifestation both in creation and in the events of salvation history, climaxing in his Son, Jesus Christ, proclaimed now by Paul. If Paul began this section with a positive reference to law but nuanced by its limitation (1 Tim 1:8), he concludes by highlighting the gospel, for it is first of all good news and grace, which go beyond the demands of the law. Finally, Paul invokes the moment of his calling, when Christ **entrusted** him with the gospel. English usage cannot capture the final emphatic position of the pronoun *egō* ("I")—unless we would translate "the glorious gospel . . . which has been entrusted to *me*"—affirming once more for Timothy and his flock the apostolic authority with which Paul lays down these instructions. This provides a transition to the next section, which will elaborate on Paul's call.

Reflection and Application (1:8–11)

Does the law still apply, or doesn't it? It is a question any reader of Paul will ask, for in some places he says positive things about the law and in other places negative things, even saying that reliance on the law brings a curse (Gal 3:10,

---

6. W. Bauer, F. W. Danker, W. F. Arndt, and F. W. Gingrich, *A Greek-English Lexicon of the New Testament and Other Early Christian Literature*, 3rd edition (Chicago: University of Chicago Press, 2000), 135.

13). Even some of his first readers interpreted his gospel of freedom as licensing sexual promiscuity, a misinterpretation that he hastened to correct (1 Cor 6:12–17). Briefly put, when he thinks of the law as circumcision and the food laws, he sees it as meaningless for justification, and he is particularly adamant that Gentiles should not be circumcised (see the whole letter to the Galatians). The law as God's moral expectations does not bring justification either, but Paul does see it as good for two reasons. First, like a mirror, it set an ethical standard that showed the people how sinful they were and how much they needed God's grace (Rom 3:20; 5:20). Second, it prepared the way for Christ (Gal 3:24). That the moral injunctions of the law were still in force is evident from Paul's lists of vices, like the one above.

But that is not the whole story, for like Jesus, Paul sees the whole law fulfilled by love (Gal 5:14), and love is no longer merely a law. It is God's own love poured into our hearts by the Holy Spirit (Rom 5:5), enabling us to do all that the law demands, not because it is law but because the Holy Spirit empowers us to go beyond it: "If you are guided by the Spirit, you are not under the law" (Gal 5:18). Think of a high bar that no athlete has been able to jump over. This would represent the old situation, God's expectations, the law, which no one was able to fulfill. Then comes a runner who not only leaps over the bar but reaches even higher, as if flying. This is what happens when one is empowered by the Holy Spirit. The righteous demands of the law are "fulfilled in us, who walk not according to the flesh but according to the Spirit" (Rom 8:4 RSV). Does that mean that all Christians are perfect? No, but when we fail, we fall short not of the expectations of the law but of the power of the Holy Spirit. We fail to use what we were given.

Paul as a Supreme Example (1:12–17)

¹²I am grateful to him who has strengthened me, Christ Jesus our Lord, because he considered me trustworthy in appointing me to the ministry. ¹³I was once a blasphemer and a persecutor and an arrogant man, but I have been mercifully treated because I acted out of ignorance in my unbelief. ¹⁴Indeed, the grace of our Lord has been abundant, along with the faith and love that are in Christ Jesus. ¹⁵This saying is trustworthy and deserves full acceptance: Christ Jesus came into the world to save sinners. Of these I am the foremost. ¹⁶But for that reason I was mercifully treated, so that in me, as the foremost, Christ Jesus might display all his patience as an example for those who would come to believe in him for everlasting

life. ¹⁷To the king of ages, incorruptible, invisible, the only God, honor and glory forever and ever. Amen.

OT: Lev 5:18; 22:14; Num 15:22–31
NT: Acts 8:3; 9:5; 1 Cor 15:8; Gal 1:13; Phil 3:6
Catechism: mercy (1846–48), ignorance and sin (1860)

1:12   The thanksgiving that was delayed until now differs from the usual ones in Paul's letters. Instead of thanking God for some good in the readers, Paul here thanks the Lord for the grace of his own ministry, a topic easily introduced by the mention of himself at the end of the previous verse. It also provides a contrast of his own life under the law, just discussed, with his present life under grace. As such it is a powerful demonstration of the effect of God's saving love over the vain speculations just targeted. It is as if Paul were saying to the heterodox teachers, "Can your teachings change lives the way the true gospel has changed mine?" Changed lives are the seal of the gospel's authenticity, and no change is more remarkable in the New Testament than that of Paul. The gospel for Paul was first of all a personal experience, an encounter with the savior, enabling the apostle thereafter to proclaim the good news with utter conviction. This section also reinforces his authority, and that of Timothy his delegate, as coming from Jesus.

Paul refers to the moment of his conversion as a strengthening. The Greek word could also be translated "enabling," indicating that in addition to strength it also gave him competence. Not only was he humanly weak, like Peter, he was the worst of sinners. Yet Christ empowered him with all that he needed to fulfill the task. Even more appreciated in this grace of investiture was that Christ deemed him **trustworthy**. The Greek word *pistos* can mean "faithful" or "worthy of trust." It was common in the Greek world as a designation of soldiers, delegates, or judges, even citizens or friends, whose loyalty could be counted on. A task so exalted as that of apostle requires even greater fidelity.

1:13   Paul had been a **blasphemer**. How can he say that, if indeed he had thought he was acting in God's behalf in rounding up and imprisoning Christians and even approving the stoning of Stephen (Acts 8:1)? In retrospect, and in the light of his conversion, he now sees how mistaken and blind he was. The Pharisees believed in the resurrection of the just but thought it would happen only at the end of the age, whereas Christians were proclaiming that it had already begun in Jesus. The Holy Spirit too, according to Pharisaic expectations, would be given at the end but not now; for now, the law was sufficient. But the disciples of Jesus were claiming that they—all of them—had already received the Holy Spirit. Furthermore, they were actually worshiping Jesus as *mara* ("Lord"), and to Paul's monotheism this was blasphemous. They even claimed to be eating his flesh and drinking his blood! So from a human point of view it is understandable that he had persecuted the Church with "zeal" (Phil 3:6), "beyond measure and tried to destroy it" (Gal 1:13). But his conversion had turned his understanding of blasphemy on its head— it was blasphemous of him to deny that Jesus is Lord, risen from the dead and giver of the Holy Spirit. Even to persecute the disciples of Jesus was now blasphemy, for that meant persecuting Jesus himself—as we read in Luke's account of Paul's encounter with Jesus on the road to Damascus (Acts 9:5).

Fig. 3. Mosaic of St. Paul handing letters to Timothy.

    Arrogant has the note of excess, of extreme violence. The book of Acts describes Paul's violence as imprisoning men and women and voting in favor of their death (Acts 8:1; 9:2; 22:4; 26:10). But he received mercy because he **acted out of ignorance**. The Old Testament already acknowledged the difference between sins done in ignorance and those done with evil intent (Lev 5:18; 22:14; Num 15:22–31), the former being capable of atonement. Yet the apostle is appalled at the objective evil he has done. It is not diminished but made understandable by his subjective blindness. It is characteristic of converts to see their past sins as having an enormity that they did not realize when they were committing them, even if they were excusable, or partly so, on the grounds of ignorance or malformed conscience.

    Where sin abounded, grace has abounded all the more (Rom 5:20). Paul loves words that begin with "super" (Greek *hyper-*): Rom 5:20; 8:26, 37; 2 Cor 7:4; 10:14; 2 Thess 1:3. All the forms used in those passages appear in the Bible only in Paul. So too here, **abundant** already means an overflowing fullness, but Paul's adding the prefix "super" means "without measure," accentuated by placing it at the beginning of the sentence in Greek: "Superabundant has been. . . ." Paul is still thinking of his own experience of this unspeakable grace, in contrast to the law and even more so to the fruitless speculations on it. Since **faith and love** are parallel to **the grace of our Lord**, we can paraphrase 1 Tim

1:14

1:14 this way: "What incredible trust the Lord showed me in calling me to be his apostle! Indeed, what love he showed me!" Of course, Jesus' trust and love evoked a response of faith and love on Paul's part. Even that response was grace!

1:15   **This saying is trustworthy** appears five times in the Pastorals, twice with the complement **and deserves full acceptance.** Like Jesus' frequent "amen, amen, I say to you," Paul uses the formula to introduce an article of faith or a liturgical statement or in any case a truth universally accepted by all Christians. Similar phrases occur twice in the book of Revelation: "These words . . . are trustworthy and true" (Rev 21:5; 22:6). They have roughly the same meaning as the English idiom "you can count on this" or "this word shall surely come to pass" or "this prophecy is true." The object of the saying here is an article of faith, equivalent to Matt 9:13 (Jesus came to call not the righteous but sinners) and John 3:16 (God so loved the world that he sent his only Son to save it). That Christ "came into the world" (a favorite Johannine expression) suggests that his entire life, ministry, and death was not merely for the Jews but for all humankind.

1:16   Paul calls himself the **foremost** among all sinners. Not the first in time, surely, but the first as type. He is not really comparing himself to anyone (Judas, for example), but simply expressing his overwhelming sense of being the proto-typical sinner, much like the publican who said, "O God, be merciful to me a [literally *the*] sinner" (Luke 18:13). But the other side of the coin is that Paul's sin reveals God's **patience,** the Lord's longsuffering mercy for those who would follow Paul in receiving it. If God could show his mercy to a sinner like Paul, how could he refuse it to anyone else who would believe in Christ? Such faith not only brings forgiveness of sins but **everlasting life.**

1:17   Paul concludes with a doxology. Israel often hailed God as king and occa-sionally as **king of ages** (Tob 13:7; Sir 36:17). The Greek word for "of ages" is *aiōnōn,* a word related to "everlasting" at the end of the preceding verse, thus making a rhetorical link. The eternal life received by believers is not merely an endless life; it is the very life of the eternal God. If incorruptibility is the mark of the resurrected body (1 Cor 15:52) and of the crown won by those faithful unto death (9:25), it is the gift of the God who is incorruptibility itself. Being pure spirit, he is **invisible** to mortal eyes (John 1:18). His glory he will not share with idols, for he is **the only God;** "there is no other" (Isa 44:6; 45:21). **Honor and glory** were part of an early revered doxology, as we see in Rev 5:13. Thus, although Paul began the letter with a call for discipline, he concludes this sec-tion by hailing the God of grace who has worked powerfully in his own life and promises to do so in the lives of all who believe.

Reflection and Application (1:12–17)

This section invites a deep reflection on the dynamics of conversion and what the conversion of one person can do for himself and for the Church. Paul had been a violent man. He had witnessed and approved the stoning of Stephen (Acts 8:1) and persecuted the early Christian community. His conversion was so cataclysmic that many Christians had difficulty believing it. But Jesus called him even to be an apostle. Paul's example shows that those who have done the worst things—blasphemy, persecution, and violence—can be forgiven and even be called to ministry.[7] Some of the most fervent and evangelizing Christians have come, like Paul, from a life of violence to holiness and zeal. Paul's conversion opened his eyes to see the enormity of what he had done, even though he had done it in ignorance. How often I have seen this happen with women who in the confusion of an unwanted pregnancy and ignorance of the truly lethal nature of an abortion chose it and only later came to realize the enormity of what they had done. Often they have trouble believing God could forgive them or accepting that forgiveness, because they cannot forgive themselves. But in forgiving Paul and calling him to be an apostle, God has shown that his mercy is infinitely greater than any person's sin.

There is a further inference from this text. We speak often of believing in God, less often of the reverse: God believing in us! Yet that is what also amazes Paul, that God would believe in Paul and his potential in a way that Paul had never dreamed. Like a parent who never loses faith in a wayward child, God believes in our potential, our future. We too can say that the grace of God has been superabundant through the faith and the love shown us in Christ Jesus.

Recalling the Prophecies (1:18–20)

---

[18]I entrust this charge to you, Timothy, my child, in accordance with the prophetic words once spoken about you. Through them may you fight a good fight [19]by having faith and a good conscience. Some, by rejecting conscience, have made a shipwreck of their faith, [20]among them Hymenaeus and Alexander, whom I have handed over to Satan to be taught not to blaspheme.

NT: Acts 13:1–3; 1 Cor 5:5; 14:1; Eph 6:10–13
Catechism: prophecy as a special grace (2004), conscience (1777–78)

---

7. Not every ministry in the Catholic Church is open to those guilty of public crime. Ordination to the priesthood, e.g., is forbidden to those who have deliberately committed murder or certain other crimes (Canons 1040, 1041).

1:18   Paul returns now to the directive he gave in 1:3–5. He reminds Timothy
that his call to the ministry was from God and encourages him to "hang in
there" in the struggles that this vocation now involves. That will require him
to exercise a number of virtues. The verb **entrust** here has the sense of handing
on something to be carefully kept and handed on in turn, like a sacred Tradition (2 Tim 2:2). In the same vein, **Timothy, my child** is less an expression of
affection here than that of a father solemnly handing on a precious heritage to
his son. In the Greek there is a charming similarity of sound between the verb
paratithemai ("I entrust") and *Timothee* ("Timothy"). Timothy's appointment
was designated by prophecies (the plural suggests that several were spoken),
hence by divine intervention. Who spoke the prophecies we do not know, just
as we do not know who spoke the prophecy by which Paul and Barnabas were
designated for their first mission to Asia Minor (Acts 13:2). The real speaker
was the Holy Spirit, and that is why prophecy is held in high esteem in the
Pastoral Letters. The words inspired by the Holy Spirit are taken seriously and
recalled (1 Tim 4:1), especially those connected with the appointment to office
(here and 4:14). As in Acts 13:1–3, designation by prophecy is followed by the
laying on of hands (1 Tim 4:14; 2 Tim 1:6–7).

It is not clear when or how this designation or ordination of Timothy took place.
According to Acts 16:1–3 it was at Lystra that Paul first met Timothy (see also 2 Tim
3:10), who was highly recommended by the faithful there. Paul chose him as a
companion on his journeys. Since it was customary to lay hands on those sent out
on mission (Acts 13:1–3), it is likely that both the prophecies and the laying on of
hands took place at that time. This ritual was accompanied, it seems, by Timothy's
public profession of faith or oath of fidelity (1 Tim 6:12; see Rom 10:10).

Discipleship and leadership are spiritual combat for which God has supplied
the necessary armor (Eph 6:10–17). Here, encouraging Timothy to **fight a good
fight**, Paul uses precise military language ("wage the good warfare," RSV; "fight
like a good soldier," JB; or "launch the campaign"), more appropriate, perhaps,
for one who is to lead a battle than for an individual boxer who trains for a
bout (1 Cor 9:26–27). **Through them** suggests that in the challenges of his office Timothy will find strength and courage in being commissioned through
prophecies as an officer of the King of kings and, through the laying on of hands,
in being endowed with a charism of the Holy Spirit. This gift is always available
and needs only to be fanned into flame (2 Tim 1:6–7).

1:19   **Faith and a good conscience**, paired three times in 1 Timothy (here and
1:5; 3:9), are Timothy's armor (Eph 6:16). The leader is first of all a disciple,
and he must therefore be outstanding in his faith in Jesus Christ, since he is

to form and teach other disciples. His own conscience must be formed by this faith if he is to model discipleship for others and make the sometimes difficult decisions that his office requires.

A teaching technique arises out of the †chiasm faith-conscience-conscience-   1:20
faith. Timothy has faith and a good conscience. Others who reject conscience make a "shipwreck" of their faith. Consider, Paul says, those who have brought this fate on themselves. They are two who are probably the leaders of a group that opposed Paul in Ephesus: **Hymenaeus,** mentioned again in 2 Tim 2:17, and **Alexander,** who may be the coppersmith who "did me a great deal of harm" in 4:14–15. These two Paul has **handed over to Satan,** a technical term for excommunication. In 1 Cor 5:5 Paul had prescribed such excommunication for the incestuous man who refused to repent. There it was a moral issue, and the discipline was aimed at his reform ("that his spirit may be saved"). Here the issue appears to be a matter of doctrine and of direct opposition to the authority of the apostle. When all attempts to correct an erring member of the Church fail and there is danger that others will be led into sin, heresy, or disbelief, then the apostolic authority, with the power to bind and loose (Matt 16:16–19; 18:18), merely confirms what the individual has in reality chosen: withdrawal from the community. Within the Christian community, the individual enjoys multiple protections against Satan, but outside it he or she is vulnerable to the devil's attacks or the chastisements of "the angel of the abyss" (Rev 9:11). This therapy of privation, like the prodigal son's hitting bottom, should be a wake-up call to return to the Father's house. Here in 1 Timothy this medicinal purpose is less evident but is implied in the verb **to be taught,** that is, "that they may learn," as a disobedient child might learn from punishment by his or her parent. "Blasphemy" means desecration of something sacred, even a direct insult to God. Such, in Paul's view, is the sin of those who obstinately reject the faith and the discipline handed on to them by the apostles.

Reflection and Application (1:18–20)

Note how prominent prophecy is here. So it is likewise in the Acts of the Apostles, Revelation, and elsewhere in the New Testament. This raises the question of its role in the Church today. Peter's Pentecost sermon hailing the coming of the Spirit to "all flesh" (Acts 2:17), Jesus' saying in Matthew implying that the disciples are prophets (Matt 5:12), and Paul's discussion of the gift of prophecy (1 Cor 14) indicate a dissemination of prophecy among the people of God that is without parallel in the Old Testament (Num 11:29). The underlying assumption was that this gift of the prophetic Spirit is part of the essential nature of the Church for all time. Church Fathers such as Justin Martyr pointed to the charisms and especially prophecy as indications of the superiority of the New Testament over the Old, of Christianity over Judaism. Though there are false prophets today just as in the early Church, nevertheless, the boat of Peter moves forward not only by the rudder of discernment and authority but by the wind of the Holy Spirit manifesting itself in hundreds of new ways in every age. Pope John Paul II upon awaking every morning prayed that he might not resist any movement of the Holy Spirit that day.

Paul uses the image of the "good fight" to inspire Timothy in his struggle. The spiritual combat is not the only image in the Bible for spiritual growth, but it is a frequent one. The enemy is not human beings but "the principalities, . . . the powers, . . . the world rulers of this present darkness, . . . the evil spirits" (Eph 6:12). And sometimes, as Pogo said, "We have met the enemy, and it is us." The New Testament constantly warns us to "watch," lest we suffer a surprise attack of temptation or the evil one. Spiritual lethargy can be perilous. But as Timothy drew strength from the living word of God, so we too may do so. At one moment in my life I was on the point of resigning from a very difficult assignment. In fact, I had written a letter to my Provincial asking him to relieve me. But then after fasting and prayer, I sensed very clearly the Lord saying to me, in the words of Isaiah, "I . . . have called you for the victory of justice" (Isa 42:6). I continued the ministry, and it was blessed as never before.

Liturgy and Conduct

1 Timothy 2

What are Paul's priorities for the growing church of Ephesus? And does this have anything to say about priorities in the Church of today? It may surprise us, but he begins with the liturgy. Although Paul does not mention the Eucharist in what follows, we may assume that such is the setting for these directives on prayer and proper conduct during the Eucharistic assembly.

First Things First (2:1–4)

¹First of all, then, I ask that supplications, prayers, petitions, and thanksgivings be offered for everyone, ²for kings and for all in authority, that we may lead a quiet and tranquil life in all devotion and dignity. ³This is good and pleasing to God our savior, ⁴who wills everyone to be saved and to come to knowledge of the truth.

OT: Isa 43:3; Jer 14:8; 29:7; Ezek 18:23, 32
NT: John 8:32; Acts 12:5; Rom 13:1–7, 13–14; James 5:14–15; 1 Pet 2:13–14; 2 Pet 3:9
Catechism: intercession (2636), respect for civil authority (1880), hell (1035, 1037)
Lectionary: (2:1–8) Mass for the Evangelization of All Peoples
Lectionary (Byzantine): (2:1–7) Beginning of the Liturgical Year

First of all, then indicates that Paul is now getting to the substance of his   2:1
mandate to Timothy. But the word "first" also indicates primacy in importance. The first duty of the Church is to pray, and the first duty of the shepherd is to organize the worship of the Church. Luke notes that the apostles realized this

Vatican II on the Liturgy

The Second Vatican Council gave primacy of excellence to the Church's public worship: "Every liturgical celebration . . . is a sacred action surpassing all others; no other action of the Church can equal its efficacy by the same title or to the same degree" (*Sacrosanctum Concilium* 7). "The liturgy is the summit toward which the activity of the Church is directed; at the same time it is the font from which all her power flows" (10).

This text of Paul had a profound effect on the liturgy of the Church from the earliest times. A gloss, a marginal comment added by another hand, quotes the fourth-century Ambrosiaster thus: "This prescription is for the Church; *given by the Teacher of the Gentiles, it is followed by our priests*, that they should make supplication for all, praying for the rulers of this world."[a] *Sacrosanctum Concilium* 53, referring to our text, directs that intercessions "be made for holy Church, for the civil authorities, for those oppressed by various needs, for all mankind, and for the salvation of the entire world." In the Catholic Church, this prayer for authorities and for all humankind and for the Church forms a major part of the Good Friday liturgy, is prescribed for the General Intercessions at every Sunday liturgy, and is expressed in the prayer of the Sacramentary for the eighth Sunday of the year: "Lord, guide the course of world events and give your church the joy and peace of serving you in freedom."

a. *Commentary on 1 Timothy 2:1.*

primacy very early in Jerusalem and took steps to keep first things first when they appointed other ministers so they could devote themselves to prayer and preaching (Acts 6:4). Here Timothy must realize he is more than a teacher of truth (1 Tim 1:3–7); he is above all a minister of worship.

There are only slight differences in the four types of prayers listed. **Supplications** are prayers occasioned by some concrete circumstances or pressing need. **Prayers**, frequently associated with supplications, is a more general term for prayer. It was in answer to his disciples' request to "teach us to pray" that Jesus taught them the Lord's Prayer (Luke 11:1–13). **Petitions**, sometimes translated "intercessions," comes from a verb used to describe the favor a subject enjoys in being admitted to the presence of the king so as to present a request. For the Christian this means to beseech the "king of ages," whom Paul just mentioned (1 Tim 1:17). The series climaxes (with no connecting "and" in the Greek) with **thanksgivings**. A plural word for "Eucharist," here the meaning is simply expressions of gratitude for past benefits bestowed

St. John Chrysostom on Praying for Everyone

LIVING TRADITION

Two benefits derive from [this prayer]. Hatred toward those who are outside is cleared away, for no one can feel hatred toward those for whom he prays. And those for whom we pray are made better and lose their ferocious disposition by the prayers that are offered for them. For nothing is so apt to draw men under training as to love and be loved. Think what it was for those who persecuted, scourged, banished, and slaughtered the Christians to hear that those whom they treated so barbarously offered fervent prayers to God for them.[a]

a. *Homilies on 1 Timothy* 2:1.

on those for whom prayers are offered. In Phil 4:6 Paul tied three of these terms (prayers, supplications, and thanksgivings) together, suggesting in both places that thanksgiving should always accompany what Christians ask for in prayer.

This prayer is not just for one's family or the local congregation or even for the Church. It is **for everyone**. Christians considered prayer for one another and for the Church a sacred duty (Acts 12:5; James 5:14–15). This was not difficult and sprang spontaneously from the Jewish soul schooled in the value of intercessory prayer. But Jesus had also told his disciples to pray for their *enemies* (Matt 5:44), and the Church could never forget that he himself

Our Spiritual Ancestors and the State

BIBLICAL BACKGROUND

In the theocracy of ancient Israel, prayer for public authorities was not an issue, because, in spite of abuses, there was a basically understood unity of religion and public life. In the Babylonian exile, however, problems arose. Were the Jews to carry on an active, political resistance against their captors, or were they to promote the public welfare in the hopes thereby to preserve their religious freedom and one day merit repatriation? Jeremiah 29:7 answered the question thus: "Promote the welfare of the city to which I have exiled you; pray for it to the LORD, for upon its welfare depends your own." Inscriptions and the writings of Philo and Josephus confirm this attitude among the Jews and the practice of prayer for public authorities. In the first century, Jews prayed for the emperor, offering sacrifices for him in the temple until they rejected the practice at the beginning of the revolt of AD 66.

The Prayer of Clement

LIVING TRADITION

Around AD 96 Pope Clement sent a long letter to the Corinthians urging obedience not only to the authorities in their community but also to civil rulers. At the end of the letter Clement concludes with a prayer for "our rulers and governors on earth." On March 7, 2007, Pope Benedict XVI, recalling the prayer, said: "After the texts of the New Testament, it represents the most ancient prayer for political institutions." Here is the prayer that the fourth pope of Rome sent to the Corinthians: "Grant to them Lord, health, peace, concord, and stability, so that they may exercise without offense the sovereignty that you have given them. Master, heavenly King of the ages, you give glory, honor, and power over the things of earth to the sons of men. Direct, Lord, their counsel, following what is pleasing and acceptable in your sight, so that by exercising with devotion and in peace and gentleness the power that you have given to them, they may find favor with you."[a]

a. *1 Clement* 61 (translation from Catechism 1900).

had done so as he was dying on the cross (Luke 23:34), thus fulfilling the prophecy of the suffering Servant (Isa 53:12). The Christian's prayer must extend as far as his charity (Matt 5:44). Luke, who records Jesus' prayer for his enemies from the cross, also tells us that Stephen prayed for those who stoned him, and therefore for Paul himself, who approved of his execution (Acts 7:58–60).

2:2　　The first beneficiaries of these prayers are **kings**. This would apply particularly to the emperor (*basileus*, "king," was his common title in the East). If indeed our letter is from Paul's own hand, this would specifically mean Nero, to whom tradition assigns the responsibility for Paul's death. But "kings" would also apply to local monarchs to whom were delegated considerable powers in Roman times; for example, the Herods. The converted pagan would no longer pray *to* the emperor but *for* him. **All in authority** meant any dignitary in the government, from high office to low. It would apply with all the more reason to those in authority in the Church.

Jesus had said to render to Caesar the things that are Caesar's (Mark 12:13–17), and Paul himself, who, according to Acts, generally came off well at the hands of his Roman judges, could write in his letter to the Romans a theology of obedience to legitimate authority as obedience to God (Rom 13:1–7; compare John 19:11; 1 Pet 2:13–14). Prayer for such authorities is an essential element of Christian worship for all times and circumstances.

If this prayer includes persecutors, it is not wholly disinterested. The great **2:3** good it seeks is in the first place "peace," the needed calm and tranquility without war and persecution, so that the Church may lead its life without harassment (Acts 24:2). But this freedom is not merely freedom *from*. It is freedom *for*. "Devotion" translates the Greek word *eusebeia*. Other translations render it "godliness" or "piety" or "religion." In the Septuagint the noun regularly stands for "fear of God," that religious awe and reverence felt before the transcendent presence of God. The adjective form, "devout" or "godly" (*eusebēs*), regularly translates Hebrew *saddiq* ("righteous") or *hasid* ("devoted"). In the Pastorals it refers to a godly Christian lifestyle. In our text it suggests that the external peace just prayed for facilitates the kind of holiness the Church wishes all its members to pursue. If persecution fans the flame of heroism in the martyrs, it often quenches the flickering flame of faith in the weak (Matt 24:12). Similarly, in times of peace Christians can live as good citizens with "dignity" and are not compelled to resist with their blood. This is worth praying for. Like the offering of an acceptable sacrifice, it is **pleasing to God** as well.

In the Old Testament, intercession was an important responsibility given **2:4** to the priests. In the New Testament, it is the responsibility of the priesthood of all the faithful, joined as they are by baptism to the constant intercession of Jesus the high priest (Heb 7:25). He is "our savior" and also wants to save all people, and the intercessory prayers of the Church enter into this saving will of God. To paraphrase St. Thomas Aquinas, although God does not need our prayers in order to act, he wishes to act because we have prayed.

In the context of Paul's earlier concern about right doctrine, salvation means coming **to knowledge of the truth**. Biblically speaking, religious knowledge is not merely intellectual; it involves one's whole being—mind, heart, and will. Truth here is not philosophical truth but revealed truth, the gospel message, the truth that leads to eternal life, which is God and his Son Jesus Christ. "I am . . . the truth" (John 14:6; see 1 Cor 1:21).

Reflection and Application (2:1–4)

If God wills that everyone be saved, does that mean that everyone will be saved? Very early in the history of exegesis the Church Fathers perceived a theological problem raised by this text: if God wills all people to be saved and not all are saved, doesn't this mean either that God's will is not all powerful or that he really doesn't want all people to be saved? It seems that either the omnipotence of his will or the universality of his will is at stake. Tertullian sought a way out

On the Existence of Hell

The Catechism makes a clear statement on hell. "The teaching of the Church affirms the existence of hell and its eternity. Immediately after death the souls of those who die in a state of mortal sin descend into hell, where they suffer the punishments of hell, 'eternal fire.' The chief punishment of hell is eternal separation from God, in whom alone man can possess the life and happiness for which he was created and for which he longs" (1035).

by specifying the *people* as "those he adopted,"[1] but this is contrary to the text, which says he wants *all* to be saved. Augustine sought to render justice to the word "all" by saying that the whole human race somehow exists in those who are saved,[2] but this too seems to be an escape from the obvious meaning of the text. Origen maintained that all people would necessarily be saved (*apokatastasis*),[3] but this teaching was rejected by the Church on the basis of Jesus' repeated warnings about the possibility of damnation (e.g., Mark 9:43–48).

The Greek Fathers stood closer to the text by understanding the Greek verb "wills" (*thelō*) as a real will-act extending to all people, but conditioned on our free response. *Thelō* is a favorite word of Paul (used more than sixty times), frequently employed for a desire of the heart, a strong and sincere wish, whereas another Greek word, *boulomai*, is preferred for an absolute determination, a fixed and irreversible decision (1 Tim 2:8; 5:14). Matthew uses *thelō*, as Paul does here, to translate Jesus' sad recognition that his own will to gather the children of Jerusalem like a hen her chicks has not succeeded (Matt 23:37). Yet there are other divine decrees that are absolutely unconditioned by the will of human beings (Luke 10:22; 1 Cor 12:11). The awesome reality, then, behind Paul's use of *thelō* here is this: here is a will of God *whose accomplishment depends on the cooperation of the human party.* If it did not, what use would there be in Paul's pleading for the prayers of the Church? Certainly the prayer of the Church does not guarantee the salvation of those for whom it prays, but it is not a mere gesture. It is a participation in Christ's intercession before the Father. And as such it is a real contributing factor in God's plan for the salvation of the world!

1. *On Prayer* 4.
2. *Admonition and Grace* 44.
3. *On First Principles* 1.6.2; 2.10.4–8.

God's Will and Our Free Will

Saint John Damascene explains: "God wills by a primary and antecedent will that all be saved. . . . This primary will is called antecedent
and it marks God's desire. The cause of this will is in God. The other
will is called consequent; it is only a permission, and it has its roots in
our acts."[a] In other words, God's "Plan A" is that all be saved, but human
beings' free will can reject that salvation, and God permits that ("Plan
B") because he will not take back the gift of free will that he has given
to humankind.

a. *De Fide Orthodoxa* 2.29.

One God, One Mediator for All (2:5–7)

> [5]For there is one God.
> There is also one mediator between God and
> the human race,
> Christ Jesus, himself human,
> [6]who gave himself as ransom for all.
>
> This was the testimony at the proper time. [7]For this I was appointed
> preacher and apostle (I am speaking the truth, I am not lying), teacher of
> the Gentiles in faith and truth.

OT: Deut 6:4
NT: Matt 20:28; Rom 1:3; 15:16; 1 Cor 8:6; Gal 1:11–12; 2 Tim 1:11; Heb 8:6
Catechism: monotheism (201), Christ the one mediator (618, 1544), Christ died for all (605)
Lectionary: (2:5–8) Mass for the Unity of Christians

The foundation of our prayer for the salvation of all people lies in there   2:5
being only one God. The **one God** contrasts with "everyone" of the preceding
verse. In a world in which each people or tribe had its particular god who took
care of that people's interests, to state that there is only one God "and there is
no other" (Isa 45:5) is to proclaim revolutionary consequences. The one God
is the God of all nations, the God of the Gentiles as well as of the Jews (Rom
3:29–30; 1 Cor 8:4–6; Eph 3:4–21; 4:6). This religious conception, then, affects
the Christian view of the human race—it is one (Eph 4:6; Acts 17:26). Accordingly, there can be no plurality of mediators. Obviously national priesthoods
or local divinities are excluded. Now, with the appearance in the flesh of God's
only Son, there also is no longer place for the mediatorship of Moses (Gal 3:19)

Dominus Jesus

On August 6, 2000, the Vatican Congregation for the Faith published a document, *Dominus Jesus*, that echoes the "one God, one mediator" statement of 1 Timothy. The document states (13):

> In his discourse before the Sanhedrin, Peter, in order to justify the healing of a man who was crippled from birth, which was done in the name of Jesus (cf. Acts 3:1–8), proclaims: "There is salvation in no one else, for there is no other name under heaven given among men by which we must be saved" (Acts 4:12). . . .
>
> Paul . . . writes: ". . . There is one God, the Father, from whom are all things and for whom we exist, and one Lord, Jesus Christ, through whom are all things and through whom we exist" (1 Cor 8:5–6). . . . In the New Testament, the universal salvific will of God is closely connected to the sole mediation of Christ: "[God] desires all men to be saved and to come to the knowledge of the truth. For there is one God; there is also one mediator between God and men, the man Jesus Christ, who gave himself as a ransom for all" (1 Tim 2:4–6).

or of any Jewish high priest (Heb 8:6; 9:15; 12:24) or of any angel (Col 2:18; Heb 2:16). The **one mediator** is **Christ Jesus, himself human**. Acceding to the desire for inclusive language, the NAB loses the impact of the Greek, which could be more precisely translated: "One mediator of God and *men*, the *man* Jesus Christ." Unlike English, Greek has two words for "man": *anthrōpos*, meaning man as "human being," and *anēr*, man as the gender-specific male. It is the former, generic word, that Paul uses here. Being one with the human race, Jesus can represent it before God, for he is Second Adam containing in himself, like Adam, the whole of humanity (Rom 5:15; 1 Cor 15:47; Phil 2:7–8). Irenaeus says concisely, "He shows God to human beings and human beings to God."[4]

Obviously Paul does not mean to exclude the mediation of the Church or of himself as an apostle or of any other ministry or channel of grace, as long as it serves the mediation of Christ, which is alone sufficient. Paul himself is a minister of the word of God (1 Thess 2:13); he intercedes for his readers (Phil 1:4); he is called and appointed by Jesus as his apostle to the Gentiles (Rom 11:13); the Church is the pillar and foundation of the truth (1 Tim 3:15); the saints intercede before the throne of God (Rev 5:8; 6:9–10; 8:3–4). And the prayers of the faithful, just mentioned in this letter to Timothy, like those of the martyrs and other saints in heaven, can be effective mediation for the Church and the world, as long as they are "through Jesus Christ our Lord."

4. *Against Heresies* 4.20.

If the first motive for this intercessory prayer is that there is only one God,   **2:6** who is God of all, the second is the self-sacrifice of Christ, **who gave himself as ransom for all**. In the Gospel tradition that Paul surely knew, Jesus gave his life "as a ransom for many" (Mark 10:45). "Many" was not meant to be restrictive, but lest his Greek readers take it that way, Paul spells out "many" as "all." Thus Christians are inspired to pray that the self-gift of Christ on the cross not have been in vain, but that its fruits be manifested in the effective salvation of all. Parallel to this self-gift of Christ is a cryptic, verbless phrase that literally says "the witness at the proper time." Although conceivably this could be the Father's witness of Christ, the more likely meaning is that it is Christ's witness not only of his love but of his and the Father's intense desire to save all of humankind. See to what lengths our God went to save the human race!

This "testimony" took place at the "time" willed by God, under Pontius Pilate,   **2:7** and the proclamation of it continues through Paul's ministry. For this, Paul has been constituted **preacher and apostle**. The Greek word for preacher here is *kēryx*, from which we get our term "kerygmatic": it means "herald." It is easy to see how fitting this image is for the role of the preacher of the gospel. He is a herald of the "king of ages" (1 Tim 1:17), charged with transmitting the good news in its integrity to those to whom it is destined, a function of faithful and totally obedient service and also a religious function of the highest sort. Those to whom he is to transmit the message, however, are the **Gentiles**, all people.

Kēryx in the Greek World

BIBLICAL BACKGROUND

In classical times the *kēryx* served as a diplomatic messenger, not having the rank of ambassador but simply serving as a "hotline" for his master to whomever he might be sent. His job was to deliver the message in its integrity, nothing more, nothing less. For this reason, the *kēryx* enjoyed diplomatic immunity everywhere and was considered to be under the protection of the god of any locality where he appeared. To dishonor him was considered an act of impiety that would bring down the wrath of the gods. The herald also had a role to play in public worship: he began the prayers before the people assembled, prayed for the common good, got everything ready for the sacrifice. Acting as speaker for the assembled community, he presented to the divinity the prayers and requests of the people. At Ephesus the sacred herald was charged with reciting litanies and prayers during the sacrifice or public assemblies. Finally, the herald at times is said to bring the message of the gods to humans.

Two other words complete Paul's description of his ministry. He is an **apostle**, not one of the Twelve but appointed by direct intervention of Jesus Christ (1 Cor 9:1), authorizing him to introduce most of his letters with this badge of authority. There may have been some dispute over Paul's authority in Ephesus, as there were some Corinthians who seemed to have preferred Apollos or Peter (1:12). And there was early dispute as to the extent and the conditions under which Gentiles should be admitted to the Church. In other words, some questioned whether God had really called Paul to open wide the gate to the Gentiles—"for all" (1 Tim 2:6)—and make their admission as easy as he did. In the face of such questions, **I am speaking the truth, I am not lying** (a typical Pauline expression; see Rom 9:1; 2 Cor 11:31; 12:6; Gal 1:20) is meant to reinforce what he has just said about God's calling everyone to salvation and Paul's own divinely bestowed mission in that plan. Because Paul is apostle to the Gentiles (1 Tim 3:16; 2 Tim 4:17), he is also their **teacher**, emphasizing that he understands the message and is competent to unfold its meaning. **In faith and truth** is a way of saying "in the true faith."

Reflection and Application (2:5–7)

The bishops of the Second Vatican Council found our text highly relevant for the renewal of the Church today, and they said so in the opening paragraphs of *Sacrosanctum Concilium*. One of the four goals of the council was "to strengthen whatever can help to call the whole of mankind into the household of the Church." There follows a sentence of jolting impact: "The council *therefore* sees particularly cogent reasons for undertaking the reform and promotion of the *liturgy*" (1, emphasis added). The Church understands that there is a profound link between her mission of bringing everyone to salvation and her liturgical practice, that is, her prayer and worship. This is precisely what Paul is saying in 1 Tim 2:1–7, a text to which Vatican II's document on the liturgy refers three times, twice in the first five paragraphs. If the liturgy "is the outstanding means whereby the faithful may express in their lives, and manifest to others, the mystery of Christ and the real nature of the true Church" (2), its inclusion of common prayer for all people expresses God's universal love, the value of Christ's sacrifice for all, and the awesome responsibility laid upon Christians to exercise their royal priesthood by interceding for the grace of salvation and bringing it to all people. Of course, Christians exercise this responsibility not only at the liturgy but whenever they pray for the needs of others, particularly for their acceptance of the gospel and conversion to Christ.

Fig. 4. The ruins of the theater in Ephesus, where the crowd ran, rioting over Paul's threat to the goddess Artemis.

The doctrinal basis for this vocation of intercession is that there is only one God for all people and only one mediator, Jesus Christ. While God surely has a plan for those who have never heard of the gospel or who have a faulty understanding of it, the objective plan revealed by God is Jesus Christ, the way, the truth, and the life. The rampant relativism of today's world has obscured this fact and led many Christians to excuse themselves from evangelization.

Protestants often question Catholics about their invoking Mary and the saints in prayer, and they quote 1 Tim 2:5 as basis for their objection to the practice. A Catholic response is that if we ask the saints on earth to pray for us, why should we not ask the saints in heaven? Our glorified brothers and sisters do pray for the Church, as we see in the book of Revelation (5:8; 8:3–4). Mary, the mother of Jesus, the Messiah, Davidic king, does not enjoy any less rank than the queen mothers in the Davidic dynasty preceding her, who were honored by their sons, the kings, and had the right to intercede with them (1 Kings 2:19–20). The Second Vatican Council put Mary's role in relation to Christ's unique mediatorship this way:

> There is but one Mediator, as we know from the words of the Apostle . . . [1 Tim 2:5–6]. The maternal duty of Mary toward men in no wise obscures or diminishes this unique mediation of Christ, but rather shows His power. For all the salvific

influence of the Blessed Virgin on men originates, not from some inner necessity, but from the divine pleasure. It flows forth from the superabundance of the merits of Christ, rests on His mediation, depends entirely on it and draws all its power from it. In no way does it impede, but rather does it foster the immediate union of the faithful with Christ. . . .

Just as the priesthood of Christ is shared in various ways both by the ministers and by the faithful, and as the one goodness of God is really communicated in different ways to His creatures, so also the unique mediation of the Redeemer does not exclude but rather gives rise to a manifold cooperation which is but a sharing in this one source.

The Church does not hesitate to profess this subordinate role of Mary. It knows it through experience of it and commends it to the hearts of the faithful, so that encouraged by this maternal help they may the more intimately adhere to the Mediator and Redeemer. (*Lumen Gentium* 60, 62)

Holy Hands, Holy Hearts, Holy Deeds (2:8–10)

[8]**It is my wish, then, that in every place the men should pray, lifting up holy hands, without anger or argument. [9]Similarly, [too,] women should adorn themselves with proper conduct, with modesty and self-control, not with braided hairstyles and gold ornaments, or pearls, or expensive clothes, [10]but rather, as befits women who profess reverence for God, with good deeds.**

OT: Ps 119:48; 143:6; Isa 3:16
NT: 1 Cor 14:40; 1 Thess 5:17; 1 Pet 3:2–5
Catechism: fashion (2286), immoderate love of riches (2445)

2:8   We continue here to be in the context of worship. Although the NAB appears to assign praying only to men and proper attire only to women, the structure of the Greek puts praying first, before it mentions men or women, so that the sense can also be: "I wish them to pray, the men lifting up holy hands . . . the women with proper attire." In this understanding, Paul qualifies the praying of the community with dispositions particularly needed by the men and those particularly needed by the women, given the kinds of temptations they were subject to either by nature or in that culture. Men were prone to anger and aggression, women to excessive preoccupation with how they looked.

Women's Fashions in the Roman Empire

BIBLICAL BACKGROUND

Paul's counsel to women about their manner of dress must be understood in the context of the Roman culture of the day, which had penetrated widely into Asia Minor. "You are as you dress" was a principle taken for granted. Women who appeared in public unveiled or immodestly dressed were seen as offering the same availability as prostitutes, who also used lavish dress and jewelry to add to their attraction. But in the first century there was in the Roman world a movement of "new women" who were beginning to flaunt this type of dress.[a] In the first century, modest dress of a married woman would be a full-length garment with a discreet neckline. "The way that wives dressed in public sent clear signals to men, thereby presenting themselves as either modest or promiscuous women."[b]

The Pythagorean and Neo-Pythagorean philosophers counseled:

> A wife's adornment [is] . . . with quietness, white and clean in her dress, plain but not costly, simple but not elaborate or excessive. For she must reject garments shot with purple or gold. For these are used by hetairai [courtesans, prostitutes] in soliciting men generally. . . . The ornament of a wife is her manner and not her dress. And a free and modest wife must appear attractive to her own husband, but not to the man next door, having on her cheeks the blush of modesty rather than of rouge and powder, and a good and noble bearing and decency and modesty rather than gold and emerald.[c]

a. See Bruce W. Winter, *Roman Wives, Roman Widows: The Appearance of New Women and the Pauline Communities* (Grand Rapids: Eerdmans, 2003).
b. Ibid., 108.
c. Papyrus Graecae Haunienses 13.6–29, quoted in ibid., 107.

Paul first addresses the men. They are to lift up **holy hands**. Jews would regularly lift up their hands in prayer,[5] and this practice continued in the early Church, as we see in our text and in the *Orantes* in the catacombs.[6]

The women were also to pray. The note in the NAB is quite misleading here: "Women are not to take part in the charismatic activity of the assembly." This certainly does not square with what Paul says in 1 Cor 11:5, 13, where he takes for granted that women pray and prophesy during the community's worship. We are not sure exactly to what degree this was innovative on Paul's part. On the one hand, in the synagogue of Elephantine, in Egypt, women took part in the prayers. But the Jewish Talmud, which may reflect a practice going back to

5. Ps 28:2; 44:21; 63:5; 119:48; 134:2; 141:2; 143:6.
6. The *Orantes* are paintings of a woman, representing the Church, lifting up her hands in prayer.

the first century, dispenses women, along with slaves and children, from saying even the Shema, the daily Jewish prayer, beginning, "Hear, O Israel" (Deut 6:4). In the Roman world, women were often active in the pagan liturgies. Paul was strongly convinced that "in Christ Jesus . . . there is neither male nor female" (Gal 3:26–28 RSV), and the gift of the Spirit meant that both men and women would prophesy (Acts 2:17–18; 21:9 [the four daughters of Philip prophesy]). Paul also has a remarkable number of female collaborators (Priscilla, Julia, Phoebe, Euodia, Syntyche, Tryphena, Tryphosa, Persis). If we are to understand women's role here in tandem with 1 Cor 11:5, women are equally charged to intercede for the world.

2:9–10   Paul counsels women to **adorn themselves with proper conduct, with modesty and self-control** rather than with elaborate dress and jewelry. These virtues in women were highly recommended by the Greek writers of the day. To this general cultural principle, Paul adds the context of worship, where an even greater reverence and respect should reign supreme. In addition, Paul's directive is an application of his principle of equality, this time not between men and women but between rich and poor. In 1 Cor 11:22 he corrects wealthy members of the Church for putting their poorer brothers and sisters to shame by eating lavishly before those who had nothing. Many Christians in Asia Minor belonged to the wealthier class, as we can judge from the letters to the churches in the Apocalypse. Rich dress and adornments would be a mark of the ruling class or those who aspired to it. Well-to-do women would be inclined to dress in their finest for worship. **Pearls**, for example, brought from the Persian Gulf or the Indian Ocean, could command an exorbitant price. In the context of worship, there would be a striking inequality between the rich and the poorer women, who were equals in Christ. Women who **profess reverence for God** (probably a reference to their baptismal promises) should want to be adorned with **good deeds**. "Adorning" suggests that good deeds give the Christian woman a beauty that jewelry or cosmetics can never produce.

Reflection and Application (2:8–10)

If this section of the letter is taken seriously by Christians today, the consequences are many. We are called to be intercessors for the entire world—an exercise of the royal priesthood of all believers (1 Pet 2:5)—not just for our friends, our families, or our neighbors. God's passionate love for all people—which led to the sacrifice of his own Son—calls for our collaboration in intercession for the salvation of all, including our enemies. Such prayer is not the private domain of women. Tempted today, as many men are, to leave spiritual leadership in family and Church to the women, they are called by this text to set an example in prayer.

Liturgy demands both reverence and moral purity. A very practical part of that reverence is appropriate dress. "Is That a Naked Woman in That Pew?" ran the headline of a column by the editor of *Today's Catholic* of the Archdiocese of San Antonio. The author went on to tell of her shock at seeing a woman in a pew ahead of her, bare shoulders, back, and legs—the rest being blocked by the back of the pew. She could see no clothes whatever on the woman, and that was a perfect lead-in to her complaint about immodest dress in Church.

Receptivity and Motherhood (2:11–15)

> [11]**A woman must receive instruction silently and under complete control. **[12]**I do not permit a woman to teach or to have authority over a man. She must be quiet. **[13]**For Adam was formed first, then Eve. **[14]**Further, Adam was not deceived, but the woman was deceived and transgressed. **[15]**But she will be saved through motherhood, provided women persevere in faith and love and holiness, with self-control.**

OT: Gen 2:22–25; 3:1–6, 16, 20
NT: Acts 18:24–26; 1 Cor 11:3–16; 14:33b–36; Gal 3:28; Eph 5:21–32; Titus 2:3–5
Catechism: equality of men and women (369), children in marriage (2366–67)

We now come to what many consider the most offensive text of the New   2:11
Testament. In recent times this text has occasioned more literature than any other passage in the Pastorals.[7] The difficulties involved in interpreting this passage are one reason that it is omitted in the Lectionary of the Roman Rite and therefore is never proclaimed publicly at the Eucharist.[8] Anyone aware of the advancement of women in modern times can easily see why. Yet the text does belong to the canon that the Church accepts as inspired Scripture, so in justice we need to look at the text in light of the historical circumstances in which it was written and only then raise the question of what principles underlie it and what implications they might have for the contemporary Church. Many interpreters today regard Paul's instructions here as a matter of Church discipline

---

7. A review and critique of scholarly literature is given by Mounce, *Pastoral Epistles*, 117–49.
8. It should be noted that there are a variety of reasons for omitting passages from the Lectionary, including space constraints. The daily and Sunday Lectionary readings in the Roman Rite cover only about 70 percent of the New Testament.

that applied to a particular moment in the Church's life but no longer apply as stated, due to a different cultural situation, like the kosher rule in Acts 15:29. However, we need first to try to understand Paul on his own terms.

Switching from the plural to the singular **woman**, Paul says that she must first of all **receive instruction**. In the Mediterranean culture of the day, although there were notable exceptions,[9] women were generally not as well educated as men. This was probably true in the Judeo-Christian communities as well. Some rabbinic doctrine held that women should not be instructed in the Torah. In this atmosphere, it was likely that men would be more knowledgeable about the Scriptures than were women. If that was so, it goes a long way toward explaining why Paul would want women to "receive" teaching. Quite the opposite of some rabbinic doctrine that women should not be instructed in the Torah, Paul insists that women should learn and come to understand the gospel more fully. **Silently and under complete control**, then, does not mean that the woman is never to speak. The NJB captures the sense well and less provocatively: "During instruction, a woman should be quiet and respectful."[10] Even less does it mean that women are to be submissive to all men. It simply means that a woman is to be submissive with a quiet demeanor to the one who is teaching with authority in the Church.[11]

2:12   Those official teachers are men. First Timothy 2:12 repeats the same thought as 2:11 but goes farther. A woman is not merely to receive instruction but she is not to teach. **I do not permit a woman to teach. . . . She must be quiet.** Some scholars think that Paul here has in view only the situation in Ephesus, where there was heretical teaching (1:3–8; 4:1–5) and where some women were creating a disturbance (5:13). The context, however, suggests otherwise, especially in the scriptural appeal later to Adam and Eve as prototypes. Furthermore, the same principle is laid down in 1 Cor 14:33b–36, that women are not to teach and are to keep silent. Both texts, of course, stand in some tension with what Paul assumes in 1 Cor 11:5, 13, where women pray and prophesy in the assembly. How to resolve the tension? There is a difference between prayer and prophecy, on the one hand, and teaching, on the other. Praying and prophesying, of a spontane-

---

9. Bruce W. Winter, *Roman Wives, Roman Widows: The Appearance of New Women and the Pauline Communities* (Grand Rapids: Eerdmans, 2003), 116.

10. Elsewhere in the New Testament, these same Greek words (or their verb forms) are used to describe virtuous conduct to be embraced by all Christians, whether in civil society (Rom 13:1, 5; 1 Thess 4:11; 2 Thess 3:12; 1 Tim 2:2; Titus 3:1; 1 Pet 2:13) or within the community (1 Cor 16:16; Eph 5:21; 1 Pet 5:5).

11. Obviously, men other than the teacher should also listen with respect. It seems, though, that in Ephesus some of the women were causing difficulties in the community and would therefore need to be taught restraint (1 Tim 5:13).

ous nature, are subject to the subsequent discernment of the community and its authorities, whereas teaching is done by those recognized by prior discernment as qualified to do so, that is, those who have an official teaching function in the Church. In 1 Cor 12:28 and Eph 4:11 the noun "teachers" is used rather than "teaching," and these teachers are closely associated with the offices of apostle, prophet, or pastor. It is a question therefore of public teaching with apostolic authority,[12] as is suggested by the immediately following **or to have authority**, not that of private instruction.

Obviously there were women among Paul's fellow workers who fulfilled some kinds of teaching roles, if we are to accept the remarkable number of women coworkers whose names are scattered throughout Paul's letters, especially in Rom 16, and the witness of Acts that Priscilla, with her husband Aquila, instructed Apollos in the faith (18:24–26). And in Titus 2:3–4 women are instructed to teach younger women. Timothy himself, in his younger years was taught by his mother and grandmother (2 Tim 1:5). This distinction between official and unofficial, or domestic, teaching corresponds to the culture of the day, where we find no evidence of women ever serving as professional teachers, but they did have important roles of teaching in the domestic sphere.[13]

Paul's prohibition of official teaching is reinforced by his statement that he does not permit a woman **to have authority over a man**. It is possible to translate "woman" as "wife" and "man" as "husband." If that were the case, the thought would be that in the public forum a woman should not be in a position where she would be exercising authority publicly over her husband. This position receives some support from the immediate reference to Adam and Eve. However, the context suggests that Paul is speaking of submission to a man who is teaching with authority in the Church, whether he is her husband or someone else.

But why should all of this be so? Many authors suggest that in the culture, particularly the Jewish culture of the day, the man's primary sphere of authority was in the public arena, the woman's sphere was in the home. Outside this domestic sphere, Paul was willing to accord women roles in public prayer and prophecy, but not in official teaching. Why? One reason was surely for the sake of order in the community, the same principle enunciated in 1 Cor 11:3–16 and 14:33. To do otherwise would be to unduly upset the domestic and civil order as it was understood in the day and thus to compromise the possibility of both Jews and Gentiles accepting the core message of the gospel. It was for

---

12. Notice the connection of apostle and teacher in 1 Tim 2:7.
13. Winter, *Roman Wives*, 116.

the same reason that Paul said that all Christians, including slaves, should remain in the civil state they found themselves when called (7:17–24).[14] The preaching of the gospel called for conversion and holiness first and foremost. It would take generations before the implications of the gospel regarding human dignity would lead to direct confrontation with the social stratifications of the ancient world.

2:13   But whatever we might presume to be the cultural justification of these directives, Paul now introduces the authority of the Bible in support of them. **Adam was formed first, then Eve.** The logic of this argument may escape our modern mind. Paul is basing his directive on his understanding of the relationship between the man and the woman depicted in Gen 2, before the fall. There God "formed" (Paul uses the same word as in Gen 2:7) Adam first and thereafter made from his flesh a helpmate or companion for him, Eve. Though named by him (as were the animals), she is his equal, bone of his bone and flesh of his flesh. The principle of the first being the superior was a rabbinic argument, but we do not know whether that was current in Paul's time. Perhaps Paul is applying to the creation story the common notion that precedence in relationships belongs to the person who is senior. According to this logic, husbands, heirs to Adam, have a kind of seniority in the order of the family.

Whatever reasoning lies behind Paul's explanation of this order, it needs to be understood and applied in light of other New Testament teaching about the purpose and nature of precedence or authority in Christ. Interpreted in this way, Paul's meaning is that Adam's authority is a responsibility of love and service aimed at the union of persons, their becoming one flesh; this was part of the caring he owed Eve and not a license for abuse or neglect, which is an effect of the fall (Gen 3:16). If so, that authority is something Eve participated in through love, seeking with him the common good. Certainly this is the picture that Paul draws of Christ in relation to the Church in Eph 5:21–32. For Paul as for the Bible in general, equality does not mean identity of roles. The ideal relationship willed by the Creator was a communion of persons, made possible by the complementarity of the man and woman. In the Trinity the Father is prior and the Son proceeds from the Father, receiving everything from the Father, yet is fully equal and one with him in love.

---

14. 1 Cor 7:21 is a problem text: "Were you a slave when you were called? Do not be concerned, but, even if you can gain your freedom, make the most of it." This NAB translation, with the word "even," seems to suggest that if the slave has the opportunity to gain freedom, he or she should nevertheless not make use of it. However, the slave had no choice in the matter; emancipation was not in the slave's control. And so Paul's thought would be that such a change of state would not alter his advice, for this change does not affect one's status as a Christian. Instead one should use the new state in the service of Christ.

Rejection of Motherhood in the Ancient World

BIBLICAL BACKGROUND

Contraceptives are not a modern invention. In the century after Paul, Soranos of Ephesus in his *Gynecology* lists and describes the contraceptives in use in his day. There were women in the first century who chose contraceptives or abortion in order to avoid having a child. Seneca says that some women in his day tried to hide their pregnancy, so preoccupied were they with the shape of their bodies.[a] Both contraception and abortion could be fatal. Ovid lashes out: "Often she who kills in the womb dies herself."[b] The †*Didache*, an early Christian catechetical manual, commands: "You shall not terminate the child by abortion and you shall not kill the child once born."[c] So there was sufficient need for Paul to strongly uphold the dignity and vocation of motherhood.

a. Winter, *Roman Wives*, 111.
b. *Amores* 2.38.
c. *Didache* 2.2.

In 1 Tim 2:14 Paul's thought turns to Gen 3, the story of the fall. Here Adam abdicates his responsibility in regard to Eve, for it was Adam who had received the commandment (Gen 2:17), and after the fall the Lord first addresses Adam, not Eve, indicating that Adam had the ultimate responsibility for the sin and therefore should have intervened at the moment of the temptation. Paul puts the responsibility for the fall on Adam in Rom 5:12–14, with no mention of Eve. However, the sin of each was different. **Adam was not deceived, but the woman was deceived and transgressed**. Paul's argument is not that Adam did not sin whereas Eve did, but that Eve failed by *being deceived*. And in yielding to that deception she broke her communion of will with Adam. Adam was not deceived; he just *did* it. That, morally speaking, was worse not only because he disobeyed God's explicit command but because he failed to exercise his responsibility to intervene with Eve at the moment of her weakness. Thus it is unlikely that Paul means that because of Eve's deception women are less fit than men to teach. If that were his meaning, he would also logically have to say that men are disqualified to lead because Adam sinned.

Thus, given that both were wounded by their sin, this verse must not be isolated from the preceding, which portrayed the couple's original grace. The prototype is not the couple's original sin (which would mean women were incompetent to teach and men incompetent to lead) but their original grace, the communion of persons in perfect accord with the will of God.

2:14

On the Maternal Role of Women

LIVING TRADITION

Pope John Paul II wrote: "The moral and spiritual strength of a woman is joined to her awareness that *God entrusts the human being to her in a special way*. Of course, God entrusts every human being to each and every other human being. But this entrusting concerns women in a special way—precisely by reason of their femininity—and this in a particular way determines their vocation" (*Mulieris Dignitatem* [*On the Dignity and Vocation of Women*] 30, emphasis original). "There is no doubt that the equal dignity and responsibility of men and women fully justifies women's access to public functions. On the other hand the true advancement of women requires that clear recognition be given to the value of their maternal and family role, by comparison with all other public roles and all other professions. Furthermore, these roles and professions should be harmoniously combined, if we wish the evolution of society and culture to be truly and fully human" (*Familiaris Consortio* [*On the Christian Family in the Modern World*] 23).

The responsibilities of Adam and Eve, though shirked through their sin, are prototypes of the relationship between man and woman in the exercise of authority in the Christian community. In the state of original grace Adam's authority, far from being a domination of Eve, was a responsibility in love, as both of them were united in loving obedience to God. Eve had a reciprocal responsibility for Adam's welfare, which she abdicated by giving him the fruit. The degeneration of this union into a domination by the man is the result of sin (Gen 3:16); it is contrary to God's plan. To apply God's original order for marriage to the restriction of official teaching to men may seem a leap, but this apparently is what Paul does.

It is helpful to remember that the text is concerned not with every teaching role in the Church but only those who teach with apostolic authority, what today we would call the hierarchy. But this does not let those with pastoral authority off the hook either. Their model for the care of the Church is not even Adam's original grace. It is Christ's loving care for his bride, for whom he laid down his life (1 Pet 5:3).

If this is the correct way to understand this difficult passage, it means that leadership and teaching authority in the Church is not modeled after secular society but on Christian marriage—and this within the context of the broader sacramental symbolism of the Church as the bride of Christ.

2:15   Paul now turns to the domestic roles of women. The initial **but** connects this thought to the preceding: "not teaching (see 1 Tim 2:12), but. . . ." The Greek word translated **motherhood** means literally "childbearing" (JB, NIV, NJB, NRSV).[15] He could hardly mean that women needed to be childbearers in order to be saved, since he commends virginity in 1 Cor 7:25–35. Rather, he is pointing to the more usual state of life of women. It is possible that Paul is responding to those heretics he mentions later in this letter who forbade marriage (1 Tim 4:3) or to contraception or the detestable practices of abortion and infanticide practiced in the Mediterranean world. Although the Greek word means literally "childbearing," it is hardly conceivable that Paul would have limited the woman's role to the biological function of procreation. Rather it would include, as the NAB suggests, the entire vocation of motherhood, with all that implies of raising children and running the home. It is precisely by carrying out well their great responsibilities in the family and home that women with this vocation will work out their salvation.

The virtues Paul commends confirm this. **Faith** and **love** are, of course, the foundation virtues of the Christian life. As in earlier letters Paul expects these virtues to be expressed by certain effects (1 Thess 1:3; Phil 1:9–10; Gal 5:22), especially **holiness** (1 Thess 3:12–13), so here. The word *sōphrosynē* (**self-control**) can also be translated "good judgment" or "moderation" or "decency" or "chastity." It is one of the marks of women who are pursuing holiness.

Reflection and Application (2:11–15)

Some may find it incredible that in the people of God only men should have the formal teaching authority in the Church partly on the basis of Paul's interpretation of Genesis, with its millennial antiquity. We can more easily understand, and therefore easily accept, the cultural argument: that's the way it was then, but it doesn't have to be that way today.

But the Church is not a secular society. It is modeled upon marriage, indeed on the prototype of marriage given in the creation of man and woman and on the fulfillment of that prototype in the marriage of Christ and the Church. The union in love, depicted in Genesis as "one flesh," can be, and often is, violated when one party or both abdicate their responsibilities toward their union in

---

15. An alternative literal translation is "by the birth of the child." On this basis, a few ancient and modern interpreters understand Paul to be saying that despite humanity's fall through the transgression of a woman, women will be saved (like the rest of the human race) through *the* childbirth, that is, through the birth of the Messiah as promised in Gen 3:15, if they **persevere in faith and love and holiness, with self-control.** By linking salvation to the *birth* of Jesus, this interpretation hints at the importance of Mary's (and womankind's) role in the redemption of the human race, offsetting a woman's role in the fall.

Diversity of Ministry but Unity of Mission

LIVING TRADITION

On the respective roles of the laity and the ordained clergy, the Catechism teaches:

> In the Church there is diversity of ministry but unity of mission. To the apostles and their successors Christ has entrusted the office of teaching, sanctifying, and governing in his name and by his power. But the laity are made to share in the priestly, prophetical, and kingly office of Christ; they have therefore, in the Church and in the world, their own assignment in the mission of the whole People of God. . . .
>
> From him [Christ], bishops and priests receive the mission and faculty ("the sacred power") to act *in persona Christi Capitis*; deacons receive the strength to serve the people of God in the *diaconia* of liturgy, word, and charity, in communion with the bishop and his presbyterate. (873, 875)

love. But that is not the structure God planned. Nor is it the relationship he established in the New Testament, where Christ is the New Adam and his bride, the Church, is the New Eve. We are in the realm of symbols, which the contemporary mind sometimes finds difficult to understand. But for the Church, the marital relationship between Christ and the Church is not mere metaphor; it is essential to the structuring of the Church. And one of the ways it is expressed is in the priesthood, where the priest in celebrating the Eucharist acts as male *in persona Christi*—that is, in the role of Christ. Similarly, the source, or authority, for apostolic teaching is vested in the successors of the apostles, the college of bishops in union with the pope, Peter's successor.

That said, what are we to make of the exponential explosion of women in ministry in the Church today, both in teaching and in roles of authority? Women with doctoral degrees are teaching not only in Catholic universities but in seminaries, where they participate in the formation of future priests. And women are serving as chancellors in dioceses, where they are the "right arm" of the bishop, exercising his delegated authority over the diocese. Women are serving as heads of offices in the Church at the national and international (i.e., the Vatican) levels. And what are we to make of the honor given by the Church to St. Catherine of Siena, St. Teresa of Ávila, and St. Thérèse of Lisieux with the title Doctor (or "teacher") of the Church, indicating the extremely valuable contribution of women's teaching to the life of the Church? The list could go on. This is surely a development that Paul, with his many women collaborators, would applaud. Are we to say that the Holy Spirit who inspired this text has not also been at work in bringing forth the contribution of women we see today to the building of the Church? But all of this teaching authority is done, as it was with Paul, within the parameters of a doctrinal Tradition that is ultimately the responsibility of those entrusted with apostolic teaching authority.

To see how the Church today deals with the question of the dignity and the role of women, one should read Pope John Paul's 1988 Apostolic Exhortation *Mulieris Dignitatem* and his earlier *Familiaris Consortio*. In both documents he stresses the original ideal of marriage as a communion of persons fulfilled in Christ and the Church. In our day, when women have assumed more public roles both in society and Church, the idea of "salvation by motherhood" may seem antiquated. Yet perhaps, after the advancement of women in professional fields formerly dominated by men, it is appropriate to recall that the role of mothers is crucial for the healthy psychosocial development of children and is more than a profession. It is a vocation divinely sanctioned and divinely blessed.

Celebrating the Eucharist, I have often wondered how women who spend half their time attending to their infants or young children, sometimes taking them to the cry room or the bathroom, manage to get anything out of the celebration. This text has helped me understand that motherhood is its own channel of grace and that the Lord must supply in some way what they might otherwise miss. After all, in Mary, the mother of Jesus, who tended to his childhood needs in the synagogue, the whole world was "saved through motherhood."

Qualifications of Ministers

1 Timothy 3

Now that Paul has given direction for the worship of the Church, he turns his attention to another vital question—the qualifications of its leaders. Although the Church of the first century differs in some respects from the Church today, the character traits that Scripture tells us are needed by men and women in key roles of leadership remain largely the same in every age. These qualities are helpful to keep in mind in considering whom we should encourage to become priests, deacons, or lay ecclesial ministers. Those of us who occupy these roles of ministry will benefit by reflecting on the kind of people we should seek to be.

Finally, at the end of this chapter, Paul concludes with what could be called the doctrinal centerpiece of the entire letter—a beautiful hymnic summary of the mystery of salvation in Christ.

Bishops (3:1–7)

[1]This saying is trustworthy: whoever aspires to the office of bishop desires a noble task. [2]Therefore, a bishop must be irreproachable, married only once, temperate, self-controlled, decent, hospitable, able to teach, [3]not a drunkard, not aggressive, but gentle, not contentious, not a lover of money. [4]He must manage his own household well, keeping his children under control with perfect dignity; [5]for if a man does not know how to manage his own household, how can he take care of the church of God? [6]He should not be a recent convert, so that he may not become conceited and thus incur the devil's punishment. [7]He must also have a good reputation among outsiders, so that he may not fall into disgrace, the devil's trap.

OT: Lev 21:7–8; Num 1:48–53
NT: Rom 15:16; Phil 1:1; 1 Tim 5:9–10; Titus 1:5–9; 1 Pet 5:1–4
Catechism: ministerial priesthood (1547), three degrees of Holy Orders (1554)

Paul now turns to those coworkers his delegate will need for the continuing   3:1
work of the ministry. What is striking is the ordinariness of the listed qualities.
Most of the virtues listed have to do with character to which every lay Christian
should aspire. In fact, these virtues are esteemed by the pagan world as well. It
is as if to say, if you are looking for a good bishop, look for a good Christian!
The bishop, for example, need not be a visionary or a prophet or one endowed
with other extraordinary charisms. He is going to be the focal point of unity
for the flock, and thus he should not be captive of any school or ideology, but
rather he is to be someone who can in some way hold his people together. This
will become evident as we examine the text.

Repeating the emphatic formula of 1:15, Paul first addresses **whoever aspires to the office of bishop.** Our English word "bishop" derives from the
Old English "bisceop," which came from the Greek word used here, *episkopos*
(literally "overseer"). The leadership of the early local Christian communities
seems to have been modeled on that of the synagogue, where a board of elders
was charged with the administration of the synagogue. In the Pastorals there
is not always a clear distinction between *episkopos* and *presbyteros* (literally
"elder"). In Titus 1:5–7 the terms appear to be synonymous. In Phil 1:1 Paul
addresses the "overseers" (*episkopoi*), or bishops, of the Philippian community
without mentioning presbyters, so it seems the bishops are members of a board
of elders who supervise the community, loosely corresponding to our parish
priests today. One of them, of course, could have been the head or coordinator
of the group.

We must be careful, therefore, not to assume that the term *episkopos* means
the same as bishop in today's Church. There is no evidence in the Pastorals, for
example, that these bishops could ordain or appoint other bishops or presbyters.
That prerogative belongs to Timothy and Titus (Titus 1:5). By the early second
century, the office of bishop would develop into what some scholars call the
monarchical episcopate, where one bishop, now understood to be, like Timothy
and Titus, successor to the apostles, presides over presbyters and deacons.

Paul is encouraging those men who are qualified to aspire to the office of
bishop. If the bishop has an office of authority, one held in high esteem in the
community, why wouldn't Christians aspire to it naturally, without having to be
encouraged to do so? This is a question that people of our day would normally
ask, since positions of prominence and authority are generally thought to be

more desirable. On the other hand, perhaps then, as now, there were sacrifices entailed in accepting leadership in the Church. Although honor is sometimes attached to such roles, so is much hard work, usually with modest financial compensation, if any. Besides that, there are conflicts and difficult people to deal with, as the Pastoral Letters and contemporary experience demonstrate. Add to that the real possibility of persecution in the early Church, demonstrated repeatedly in the life of Paul and others, and even outstanding Christians might well be wary.

In any case, the charisms that were thought to be greater even by Paul, with the exception of that of the apostle, were not administrative. In the hierarchy of gifts Paul puts administration, or pastoral oversight, as the second to last in Rom 12:8 and 1 Cor 12:28 and in last place in Eph 4:11. The †Didache also has to deal with the same low esteem of the offices of bishop and deacon: "Select for yourselves bishops and deacons worthy of the Lord . . . for they also perform the services of prophets and teachers for you. So do not despise them, for they are the persons who are honored [by God] among you, together with the prophets and the teachers."[1] Hence, in view of the need for sound leadership in a community whose members were not all eager to volunteer, Paul promotes the supervisory office.

3:2   But not just anyone who desires the office should be appointed. Now follows a series of qualifications, the first of which, **irreproachable**, is that the candidate have a good reputation both within the Church and with outsiders, for he will represent the Church in a way that others do not. What might be excused, overlooked, or dismissed as human weakness in an individual Christian will not so easily be ignored in one who is an official representative of the Church, one who is, in fact, charged with promoting the Church's adherence to truth and holiness. The bishop is a public person.

Accordingly, he should be **married only once**. This might surprise those of us in the Catholic Church. In light of our current practice and experience, we would be shocked that the bishop would be married at all! (But remember that we are not talking about bishops in our modern sense but most probably of "presbyters," like today's priests.) In the emerging Church things were different. The Greek expression means literally "husband of one wife," an ambiguous phrase that could mean (1) being monogamous rather than polygamous, (2) being faithful to one wife without a mistress, or (3) being married only once and if widowed or divorced not remarrying. Given the promiscuity in marriage in the Roman world (Pompey had five wives, Herod had nine!), the first

---

1. *Didache* 15.1–2.

two meanings would not be irrelevant to one who by public office would more closely represent the Church, faithful spouse of Christ. This kind of marital fidelity was, of course, an expectation of all Christians, just as were the other virtues listed here. So we cannot rule out the possibility that Paul simply means that, in the area of sexuality, the bishop should be a model of Christian marital chastity. But it seems more likely that the third, more traditional meaning is Paul's meaning here. That is, the bishop must be married only once. The same qualification is required of deacons (1 Tim 3:12), presbyters (Titus 1:6), and widows who are officially enrolled (1 Tim 5:9).

What is the reason for this restriction? It probably reflects the Jewish tradition of special rules of holiness, including sexual and marital restrictions, placed upon those engaged in sacred public service, whether military (the holy war; 1 Sam 21:6; 2 Sam 11:11) or priestly (Lev 21). Many of the pagan cults also had sexual restrictions for those engaged in sacred functions. Saint Thomas Aquinas's insight therefore is probably correct: "This [restriction] was made not merely for the sake of continence but because of the representation of the sacrament, because the spouse of the Church is Christ, and the Church is one."[2] Marriage is an image of the relationship between Christ and his one Church. Spouses who marry only once in their lifetime give a clearer reflection of this exclusive love than spouses who remarry after being widowed. While Paul allowed for remarriage (1 Cor 7:39) and even encouraged it under certain circumstances (1 Tim 5:14), he holds the bishops to a higher standard.

Paul's prescription here does not extend to celibacy (recommended by Jesus in Matt 19:12 and by Paul in 1 Cor 7:25–35), which is only a counsel. But that expectation would become the norm in both the West and the East for bishops and in the West eventually for priests as well. That development simply continued the trajectory already set by Paul when he said that the bishop should not marry a second time. Some Protestant churches interpret "married only once" to mean that he *should* be married, but that is not the question Paul is addressing, nor is it likely in view of Paul's celibate status (1 Cor 7:7)—and Timothy's, as ancient tradition holds.

The next qualification, *nēphalios* (**temperate**) means literally one who abstains from wine. But inasmuch as this is mentioned explicitly later in 1 Tim 3:3, and Paul recommends a moderate drinking of wine to Timothy in 5:23, the meaning here is the more general one of sobriety, temperance, moderation. This virtue is important not merely for example's sake but also to be clear minded and alert to the needs of the flock. The next two traits, **self-controlled**

2. *Commentary on 1 Timothy 3:1.*

and **decent**, often paired in secular Greek, are almost synonyms for a person who is prudent and judicious and also polite and courteous. **Hospitable:** there was hardly any virtue more demonstrative of *agapē* than hospitality (5:10; Rom 12:13; 1 Pet 4:9; 3 John 5).

Although the bishop in the Pastorals is a member of the board of elders, not all of these actually teach (1 Tim 5:17), but the *ability* to **teach** is a requisite for the bishop. He must have sufficient knowledge of the faith to be able to recognize and respond to false teaching (Titus 1:9). More importantly, he must be able to teach those in his charge. For this he does not have to be eloquent, just solid in his faith (1 Pet 5:9). If there are other gifted teachers in Timothy's church as there are elsewhere (1 Cor 12:28–29; Eph 4:11), this text would assume that the supervision of them is the responsibility of the bishop.

3:3 Now come two negative traits: **not a drunkard, not aggressive.**[3] Greek historian Xenophon remarked what common experience teaches—that drunkenness makes one forget duties and makes one incapable of ruling a household.[4] And drunkenness leads to quarreling and fighting, certainly the opposite of what is expected of a leader of unity. **Gentle** can also have the sense of "even tempered, inclined to compassion, approachable, welcoming"—important qualities in Christian leaders in every age. A bishop should not be one who hastily takes sides in a dispute or is **contentious**, and in difficult cases he should be inclined to solutions of mercy. One of the functions of the board of elders in the synagogue and in the Church was to care for the poor (Luke 12:42). A bishop therefore, who supervises the distribution of funds, must not be **a lover of money**, for the goods of the Church belong to God and to the poor. One cannot serve God and mammon (Luke 16:10–13; 2 Tim 3:2). Judas, one of the Twelve, was a lover of money (John 12:6). A bishop—priest or pastor—who stands in the apostolic Tradition must not be so.

3:4–5 Since it is assumed that the bishop is married, further evidence of his suitability to rule "the household of God" (1 Tim 3:15) is his ability to **manage his own household well**. A sign of this is the obedience of his children **with perfect dignity**, that is, the atmosphere of the home should be one of a loving order, for the household is a microchurch. It was a commonplace in the Greek world that those worthy of public office should show their ability to manage their own affairs: "Whenever you intend to consult with anyone about your affairs, look first to how he has managed his own; for the one who has shown poor judgment in conducting his own business will never give wise advice

---

3. Other versions read "violent" (NIV, NRSV) or "hot-tempered" (JB, NJB) for **not aggressive**.
4. *Economics* 12.9–12.

Hospitality in the Early Church

In the early Church there was constant travel by apostles, prophets, and evangelists seeking to spread or strengthen the faith. While they could stay in commercial hostels, if there were Christians in the town, these would welcome the travelers into their homes. The bishop should be outstanding in this kind of service, for he represents the Church, which in turn images the hospitality of God. The *Shepherd of Hermas*, a second-century Christian work, echoes this tradition: "Bishops . . . always gladly received into their homes the servants of God. . . . The bishops always gave shelter . . . to the needy and widows as part of their ministry. So all of them will be sheltered by the Lord forever."[a]

A decree of the Council of Macon, France, in 585, states the following: "The bishop's house, which was established for the purpose of receiving in hospitality everyone without exception, should not have dogs, lest those who trust to find relief in their miseries suffer instead injury to their bodies, being lacerated by the bites of hostile dogs. The bishop's dwelling should be guarded with hymns, not barking, with good works, not destructive bites."[b]

In Patna, India, I had the pleasure of being given a traveler's lodging and meals several times at the bishop's house, where it was obvious that other traveling missionaries were regularly housed and fed, for the rooms were many and the dining tables expansive.

a. *Shepherd of Hermas, Similitudes* 9.27.
b. *Decrees of the Council of Macon* (Corpus Christianorum: Series Latina 148A) 13.

about the business of others."[5] And the Jewish author Philo observes that Joseph was first placed in charge of Pharaoh's household and, when proven there, he was placed in charge of the management of the whole country, "for the future statesman needed first to be trained and practiced in house management; for a house is a city in miniature."[6] In our day we have seen in many cases the split between a politician's domestic life and his or her public life. In the Church at least it should not be so.

A recent convert should not be considered for this office. Why not? They often bring an enthusiasm that long-time Christians lack. But no, Paul says, because, like tender plants in God's field (1 Cor 3:9), they usually lack the maturity and stability needed to make experienced judgments, and, if they were known to have been public sinners, their previous life may be fresh in the memories

3:6

5. Pseudo-Isocrates, *To Demonicus* 35.
6. *On the Life of Joseph* 38.

of those who know them. It would be easy for one like this, placed in office, to become **conceited**, to lord it over his fellows, a possibility envisaged by 1 Pet 5:3: "Do not lord it over those assigned to you, but be examples to the flock." **The devil's punishment** has been interpreted in various ways. It could mean the devil's own punishment for his sin of pride, but, in light of the parallelism with 1 Tim 3:7, it more likely means the punishment that the devil could draw the leader into because of his pride. This punishment is probably not eternal damnation but the chastisements with which Satan afflicts the faithful (1 Cor 5:5; Rev 12:10), in this case the catastrophic results of pride-motivated despotism or stupidity in administration.

3:7   Concluding this section, Paul extends his concern for the uprightness of the candidate even to **outsiders**. Their estimation of the candidate is also important. **A good reputation** is not something to be despised (Sir 41:12–13). It is important for the Church's outreach in evangelization, as Paul often emphasizes (1 Cor 10:32–33; Phil 2:15; 1 Thess 4:12; Titus 2:5, 8). A candidate too fresh from conversion could easily fall back into his old ways (**the devil's trap**) and bring contempt upon himself and the whole Christian community.

Reflection and Application (3:1–7)

At the end of this section, one is struck by how much common sense it contains. Paul manifests long pastoral experience, made up possibly of both

What Qualities Are Needed in Priests?

LIVING TRADITION

In his pastoral exhortation on the formation of priests, *Pastores Dabo Vobis* (*I Will Give You Shepherds*), Pope John Paul II wrote:

> Of special importance is the capacity to relate to others. This is truly fundamental for a person who is called to be responsible for a community and to be a "man of communion." This demands that the priest not be arrogant, or quarrelsome, but affable, hospitable, sincere in his words and heart, prudent and discreet, generous and ready to serve, capable of opening himself to clear and brotherly relationships and of encouraging the same in others, and quick to understand, forgive and console (cf. 1 Tim 3:1–5; Titus 1:7–9). People today are often trapped in situations of standardization and loneliness, especially in large urban centres, and they become ever more appreciative of the value of communion. Today this is one of the most eloquent signs and one of the most effective ways of transmitting the Gospel message. (*Pastores Dabo Vobis* 43)

successes and failures in the appointment of Church leaders. He is also keenly aware of the Jewish tradition of leadership in the synagogues, as well as of the Hellenistic ideals for those worthy of public office.

Although the Church of today differs in many respects from the Church of the first century, similar qualities are necessary in Church leaders. Formation of men for the priesthood in the Catholic Church today has four dimensions: spiritual, intellectual, pastoral, and human. Paul's list of traits for the bishops of his day begins with a strong foundation in the human virtues.

In this regard it is easy to understand the relationship Paul sees between the *oikos* that is the household and the *oikos* that is the Church. Today, as Pope John Paul II stressed in *Familiaris Consortio*, we speak of the family as the domestic Church. There is no better way to strengthen the Church and equip present and future generations with the human qualities necessary for ministry than to strengthen its families.

Christians were a very small minority at the time this letter was written. In traveling to another city, they would naturally seek out a Christian household for lodging, if they knew of one. Such was the rule of hospitality then. Would we even think of doing something like that today? Would Christians be open to lodge other Christians *just because they are Christians*, even if they did not know them personally? Have we so absorbed the individualism of the surrounding culture that such a practice would be deemed an unacceptable intrusion on our privacy? There may be other issues, of course, like fear of violence or robbery and the fact that many today can claim to be Christian without showing evidence of it in their lives. But at some point trust involves risk.

Canon Law on the Holiness of Clerics

LIVING TRADITION

"In leading their lives clerics are especially bound to pursue holiness because they are consecrated to God by a new title in the reception of orders as dispensers of God's mysteries in the service of His people" (Canon 276).

Deacons (3:8–13)

[8]Similarly, deacons must be dignified, not deceitful, not addicted to drink, not greedy for sordid gain, [9]holding fast to the mystery of the faith with a clear conscience. [10]Moreover, they should be tested first; then, if there is nothing against them, let them serve as deacons. [11]Women, similarly, should be dignified, not slanderers, but temperate and faithful in everything. [12]Deacons may be married only once and must manage their children and their households well. [13]Thus those who serve well as deacons gain good standing and much confidence in their faith in Christ Jesus.

OT: Num 3:5–10
NT: Acts 6:1–7; 8:4–8; Rom 16:1; Phil 1:1
Catechism: diaconate (1569–71)
Lectionary: (3:8–10, 12–13) Mass for the Ordination of Deacons

3:8　　Although the word "deacon" (*diakonos*) is used broadly in the New Testament either for ministry in general or for service,[7] here it refers to a specific office within the community, as in Phil 1:1, where it is also mentioned with "overseers," that is, bishops. In Acts 6:1–7 the apostles appoint deacons to care for the needs of the Greek-speaking Christian widows, no doubt distributing to them food and other necessities.[8] One of them, Philip, appears as an evangelist in Acts 8, first in Samaria, then along the road from Jerusalem to Gaza, and finally in Caesarea, where he is named as an evangelist with four daughters gifted with prophecy (21:8–9).

Although much the same deportment is expected of the deacon as of the bishop, the two qualifications not mentioned here are hospitality and the ability to teach. Perhaps not much should be made of this omission, as the very function of distributing the Church's goods would demand hospitality, and the ministry of teaching might require a separate delegation by the bishop. Like the bishop, the deacon is to be **dignified**, not boorish. And especially he is not to be **deceitful**, that is, double tongued or saying one thing to one person and the opposite to another. His public role forbids this, for it is destructive of community: "Through the blessing of the righteous the city is exalted, / but

7. Various English words are used to translate *diakonos*: "servant" (Matt 20:26; Mark 9:35; John 12:26), "attendant" (Matt 22:13), "minister" (Eph 3:7), and "deacon" (1 Tim 3:8). Paul applies the term to secular rulers (Rom 13:4), to male and female ministers of the gospel (16:1; Col 1:7), to himself (1 Cor 3:5), and to Christ (Rom 15:8; see also Mark 10:45).
8. The title "deacon" is not used in Acts to describe the role of the seven who are appointed (though the verb *diakoneō*, "to serve," is used in 6:2), but tradition has always regarded this moment as the origin of the diaconate.

through the mouth of the wicked it is overthrown" (Prov 11:11). In a world where lying is commonplace, Christians are warned that their speech should be either yes or no (Matt 5:37) and that they will give an account even for every idle word (12:36).

Like the bishop, deacons are to observe moderation in drink, a counsel that would be especially meaningful if they are to serve at table. If the bishop is not to be a lover of money (1 Tim 3:3), the deacon must be even more detached: **not greedy for sordid gain**, since he handles the community's resources and their distribution (Acts 6:3). These traits should come not from constraint but from within, because he holds the gospel in his heart.

Paul uses the word †**mystery** about twenty times with various shades of meaning. Derived from the Greek word *myō*, meaning "to keep the lips sealed," it was used in the Greek mystery religions for certain rituals that only the initiated were privy to and that they were obliged by oath to keep secret. For Paul, the mystery was hidden in God from all eternity but has now been publicly made known. It was encoded in the Scriptures, but its meaning is now revealed in the person and work of Jesus Christ (Rom 16:25–27). The mystery is the person and the work of Jesus Christ; it is identical with the gospel. In Romans, as here, it is connected with faith: "My gospel and the proclamation of Jesus Christ, according to the revelation of the mystery kept secret for long ages but now manifested through the prophetic writings and . . . made known to all nations to bring about the obedience of faith" (16:25–26). Today we often call it the paschal mystery, the whole sweep of God's plan culminating in the passion, death, and resurrection of Jesus, the sending of the Holy Spirit to the Church, and the bringing of it to glory. This mystery was, of course, revealed to the Twelve. Paul could not claim their prerogative, but he did receive the same revelation by a direct encounter with the risen Lord, and the aspect of the mystery revealed to him in a special way was the role of the Gentiles as equal partner with the Jews (1 Tim 2:4).

It is something that one holds **with a clear conscience**, with "clear" or "pure" being substituted for "good," used in 1:5. The mystery of faith is not just revealed doctrines, nor is it merely an ethic that excludes the vices just mentioned. First Timothy 3:16 tells us that the mystery is the person of Jesus Christ. As a chalice holds the Eucharistic blood of Christ, so the deacon must hold the mystery; and as pure gold befits the divine contents of the chalice, so must the deacon's conscience be pure because of the one he holds. At times "holding" means "clinging," especially in time of temptation.

But the true character of candidates may not be evident at first. Just as today doctors and other professionals need to be certified on the basis of training and

3:9

3:10

supervised experience, so it was in the Hellenistic professional world: judges, priests, even those considered worthy of citizenship were expected to undergo scrutiny before being accredited for service. The candidates in the community at Qumran were expected to undergo two years' probation before being admitted to the community. The Church later extended the catechumenate even longer. With all the more reason, then, someone who is destined to a sacred ministry **should be tested**. This prescription is not mentioned for the bishops probably because it is assumed that their longer experience in the community has made their upright character evident. If the deacons are appointed through the laying on of hands, this is not to be done hastily (5:22). It is not clear whether being tested refers to a consultation of the community, to a reasonably long period of the candidates' honorable membership in the community, or to a specific kind of additional probation.

3:11   **Women** here is taken by some to refer to the wives of deacons. The Greek word *gynē* can sometimes mean "wife." But if such were the case here, we would expect the text to read "*their* wives," and the word **similarly** seems to parallel them perfectly with the men deacons just mentioned, whose role is picked up again in the very next verse (3:12). Furthermore, we know that Phoebe was a deacon of the church at Cenchreae (Rom 16:1). Thus we can be relatively certain that there was, in the Pauline communities at least, an order of women deacons. What functions they performed we do not know, though the parallel with the men and the use of the same masculine form of the noun in the case of Phoebe suggest that some of their functions were similar. However, we can rightly assume that certain needs of women in the community could be more fittingly met by women deacons. Post–New Testament practice, which plausibly continues the Pauline discipline, indicates that these women were consecrated virgins or widows and that their primary duty was to prepare women for baptism by instructing them, anointing their entire bodies in preparation for immersion, and otherwise ministering to their needs.

3:12–13   A single marriage and the ability to manage their family and household are expected of deacons as of bishops. First Timothy 3:13 may appear to the modern reader like belaboring the obvious, until we recall that in the highly stratified Greek world not only the work of slaves but trades such as bakers, cooks, and wine merchants were considered "slavish, menial, and unworthy of the free person."[9] In the Church of Jesus Christ, however, even the most menial service is honorable, for the Lord washed the feet of his disciples and told them to do so for one another (John 13:3–17). He told them that he had not come to be

---

9. Plato, *Gorgias* 518a–b.

Women Deacons?

There is an interesting confirmation of the existence of female ministry in the Church from an unusual source at the beginning of the second century. Pliny the Younger, an able administrator under Emperor Trajan, was appointed commissioner of the province of Pontus-Bithynia in Asia Minor in AD 110. Among the letters he wrote to the emperor reporting his disposition of various cases and asking Trajan's advice, one discusses his treatment of Christians. Those who, upon repeated questioning, professed to be Christians he executed, while those who recanted he excused. Among the persons he tortured in order to gain information were "two female slaves [Latin *ancillae*] who were styled deaconesses [*ministrae*]."[a]

In the East there was an order of deaconesses, usually fulfilled by widows or consecrated virgins, until the Middle Ages. The fourth-century *Apostolic Constitutions* has a prayer for the ordination of deaconesses (8, 20). It seems their functions were primarily related to the baptism of women in a period when baptism not only required proper instruction but the anointing of the entire body and immersion. Although the order of men deacons appeared to be open to further ordination to the priesthood, there is no evidence that such was the case for the women. Even if the Greek word for ordination (*cheirotonia*) of priests and male deacons is at times used for the ordination of women, the purpose for which they were ordained was for ministry to women. There is no indication they ministered at the altar. As the practice of baptizing infants became the norm, the need for the baptismal ministry of women deacons diminished.

In 2003 the International Theological Commission, reporting to the Congregation of the Doctrine of the Faith, concluded:

> The present historical overview shows that a ministry of deaconesses did indeed exist, and that this developed unevenly in the different parts of the Church. It seems clear that this ministry was not perceived as simply the feminine equivalent of the masculine diaconate. At the very least it was an ecclesial function, exercised by women, sometimes mentioned together with that of subdeacon in the lists of Church ministries. (*From the Diakonia of Christ to the Diakonia of the Apostles* 11)

It is likely that the rise of anchorites (women hermits) and religious orders of women fulfilled the need originally met by women deacons, though in the West the requirement of cloister was an inhibiting factor until St. Vincent de Paul (1581–1660) found a way around it for the Daughters of Charity. But it was not until the nineteenth century that women's communities generally were allowed to pursue service outside the cloister. In any case, we should be careful not to assume that the functions fulfilled by today's deacons were the same back then. Today, women religious and laywomen minister in the Church in ways quite beyond what the women deacons did.

a. *Letters* 10.96.

served but to serve (Mark 10:45) and that he who would be the greatest must be the servant of all (Matt 20:26; Luke 22:26). Those who fulfill this office well **gain good standing**. The most likely interpretation of this pregnant phrase is that as they fulfill their duties well and in holiness, the deacons will be all the more appreciated by the community they serve. But that is not all, for they gain **much confidence in their faith in Christ Jesus**; that is, as they serve well, their own faith will grow and they will come closer to the Lord Jesus Christ, whom they serve in his members.

Reflection and Application (3:8–13)

The restoration of the permanent diaconate in the Roman rite since Vatican II has recovered aspects of diaconal ministry that were present in the early Church. This text is read at the ordination of deacons and describes well the necessary qualities for the selection and the reward that comes to those who serve the Church as permanent deacons. The considerable space that Paul gives to the qualifications of ministers alerts us to the importance of ministries and offices in the Church. Whether these be pope, bishop, priest, deacon, teacher, administrator, evangelist, or catechist, each is necessary for the upbuilding of the body of Christ. One must be well grounded in the faith but also be a person of mature judgment and virtue. None of us is perfect, of course, but living in a Christian community should be a formative experience in which leadership skills and virtues may be honed. It is also in such an environment that vocations can be fostered.

The Church—Pillar and Foundation of the Truth (3:14–15)

[14]I am writing you about these matters, although I hope to visit you soon. [15]But if I should be delayed, you should know how to behave in the household of God, which is the church of the living God, the pillar and foundation of truth.

OT: Num 12:7; Jer 1:18
NT: 2 Cor 6:16; Eph 1:22–23; 2:19–22; 1 Pet 4:17
Catechism: three meanings of Church (752), the Church as house of God (756)

3:14–15   This passage, central to the letter, is, with 3:16, the linchpin between the matters that Paul has just discussed in a general way—doctrine, prayer, and ministry— and the practical directives that follow concerning Timothy himself, widows, and presbyters. Paul wants to motivate Timothy and the community with a vision: ministry is not just jobs to be done; it is a sacred service to God's household and the mystery of his revelation. **You should know how to behave** can be understood as applying to Timothy himself ("how *you* should behave") or in a more general sense ("how *one* should behave"). The latter is more probable, because Paul does not imply that Timothy's behavior has been unsatisfactory. Rather, to all those who hear the letter it serves as a reminder of how they should act in the holy assembly. And it gives Timothy the authority to intervene should it be necessary.

Although **household** is one of the metaphors for the Church here, Paul is not discussing an individual house-church. The church in Ephesus is considerably developed (much more so than the Cretan church in the letter to Titus), and Timothy has responsibility for more than one house-church. *Oikos* ("household") here is a striking metaphor for the community of believers: like a household in the first-century Mediterranean world, the Church is an extended family bonded by a central life together, with its members having different roles and functions. Although the whole world belongs to God, the Church is his house, his sanctuary (1 Cor 3:16), and those who live there are the householders or family members "of the faith" (Gal 6:10) or **of God** (also Eph 2:19). Paul could have used his earlier "temple" metaphor (1 Cor 3:16–17; 2 Cor 6:16), and it is surprising that he did not, given that Ephesus boasted its world-renowned temple of Artemis and the Church could be portrayed as its Christian counterpart. But the pagan *temple* did not convey the sense of community and interpersonal relationships the way *household* did. Moreover, household suggests an ongoing lifestyle requiring daily virtues, not the kind of occasional worship one does in a temple. Similarly, the New Testament (except for James 2:2) avoids calling the Christian community a "synagogue" and chooses instead **church** (Greek *ekklēsia*, "assembly"). It evokes the *qahal yahweh* ("the assembly of the Lord") in the desert, that is, the people called out of the land of darkness and slavery into covenant union with the Lord (Num 16:3; 20:4; Deut 23:2–9; Mic 2:5). In his earlier epistles Paul used the word "church" for the local assembly; for example, his first letter is addressed to "the church of the Thessalonians" (1 Thess 1:1). But in the later epistles it comes to stand for the universal Church, and that surely is the meaning here. Already in the earlier letters it is clear that Paul expects the same standard of behavior to apply to all his churches (1 Cor 11:16).

The living God is an Old Testament title (Ps 84:3; Hosea 2:1) used frequently by Paul.[10] It contrasts the God of Israel with the idols that cannot move or speak, found in abundance in Ephesus, especially in the temple of Artemis.

---

10. Rom 9:26; 2 Cor 3:3; 6:16; 1 Thess 1:9; 1 Tim 4:10.

The Church as Pillar and Mainstay of Truth

LIVING TRADITION

The bishops at Vatican Council II wrote:

This is the one Church of Christ which in the Creed is professed as one, holy, catholic and apostolic, which our Saviour, after His Resurrection, commissioned Peter to shepherd [John 21:17], and him and the other apostles to extend and direct with authority [cf. Matt 28:18–19], which He erected for all ages as "the pillar and mainstay of the truth" [1 Tim 3:15]. This Church, constituted and organized in the world as a society, subsists in the Catholic Church, which is governed by the successor of Peter and by the Bishops in communion with him, although many elements of sanctification and of truth can be found outside of its visible structure. These elements, as gifts belonging to the Church of Christ, are forces impelling toward catholic unity. (*Lumen Gentium* 8)

Two other metaphors complete the picture of the Church. **Pillar** was used metaphorically in ancient Greek literature for persons who were strong supports for institutions, cities, or families. In the Bible, likewise, God promised to make the fearful Jeremiah a pillar of iron (Jer 1:18). The figure is used in the rabbinic literature for Abraham, Aaron, Rabbi Yohannan ben Zakkai, or simply the just person, who is the pillar on which the whole world rests.[11]

The second metaphor, **foundation** (NAB, NIV), is variously translated "support" (NJB), "bulwark" (NRSV), "buttress."[12] The Qumran community considered itself to be "the foundation of truth for Israel,"[13] a close parallel with Paul's understanding of the role of the Church here. Pillars can also be foundations: the earth rests on its pillars (Job 9:6). The combination of these figures suggests the stability and the permanence of the Church. They evoke the promise in Matt 16:18 of the Church founded on rock that the powers of death cannot overcome. Here, in the midst of Paul's concerns about orthodoxy, the specific reference is to the **truth** of the gospel that the Church solidly upholds. It is the Church, rather than the Bible, that is the pillar and mainstay of the truth. When this letter was written, there was no New Testament as we know it today; but there was the Church. The selection of books judged to be inspired took several centuries, and it was the Church that discerned which books belonged to the Bible and which did not. That did not mean that the Church was above

11. Babylonian Talmud, tractate *Hagigah* 12b.
12. The JB combines "pillar" and "foundation," thus reading: "which upholds the truth and keeps it safe."
13. *Rule of the Community* (1QS 5.5).

the word of God. No, it lives under the authority of the word of God and is fed by it, but it also knows what is good food and what is not. In that sense one looks to the Church's authority when there is doctrinal dispute involving the meaning of biblical texts.

Reflection and Application (3:14–15)

From the earliest times in the Church, as we can tell from this letter of Paul, there was controversy over teaching as well as behavior. In the midst of this, Paul appeals not only to his authority as an apostle but to the authority of the universal Church. In the light of the multiplication of churches today with contradictory doctrines, all claiming to be based on the Bible, this word of Paul points to the Church as the location of right teaching. Several years ago I met a young man, son of a Protestant minister, who had converted to the Catholic Church. I asked him what prompted him to do so. He replied that he heard so many different interpretations of Scripture among the myriad of Christian denominations that he asked himself, "Is this what Jesus wanted to happen to his truth? Jesus must have provided some other way to protect his word from error. That led me to the Catholic Church." That man is a professor in a Catholic seminary today.

Heart of the Letter: The Mystery (3:16)

> [16]**Undeniably great is the mystery of devotion,**
>   **Who was manifested in the flesh,**
>   **vindicated in the spirit,**
>   **seen by angels,**
>   **proclaimed to the Gentiles,**
>   **believed in throughout the world,**
>   **taken up in glory.**

NT: John 1:14; Acts 1:2; Rom 1:4; 8:11; 16:25; Eph 3:3–10; 1 John 1:1–3
Catechism: summaries of faith (186), mystery of Christ (1075)

"Great is Artemis of the Ephesians!" cried the rioting crowd of Ephesus when Paul challenged their idolatry with the gospel (Acts 19:34). Whether intentionally or not, in this letter to Ephesus, Paul counters that cry with: **Great is the mystery of devotion!** Devotion (*eusebeia*) is sometimes translated "piety,"

3:16

Mystery in the Ancient World

BIBLICAL
BACKGROUND

In the Jewish tradition of which Paul was heir, the mystery (*sod* or *raz*) referred to the plan of God or the heavenly council revealed to the prophets for the sake of the people (Jer 23:18, 22; Amos 3:7). Hence it was a secret because it originated in God; but God wanted it to be known, and he made it known through his human spokespersons. The members of the Qumran community wrote often of the *raz* ("mystery") hidden in the writings of the prophets but now revealed in the interpretation given by their founder, the Teacher of Righteousness. Similarly, in Paul, the Christian mystery is God's plan of salvation, the "secret" of his heart, but a secret now revealed in the gospel (Rom 16:25–26; Eph 3:3–10).

This availability of the mysteries of God to everyone also appears in the writings of Philo, an Alexandrian Jew, when he contrasts Jewish contemplatives with those who practice the pagan mysteries. The prayerful Jew, unlike the initiate into pagan mystery cults, is "initiated into the mysteries of the sanctified life" but that means being immersed in the Laws, the Prophets, the Psalms, "and anything else that fosters and perfects knowledge and piety [*eusebeia*]."[a] Jewish historian Josephus adds another element when he contrasts pagan initiation mysteries with Jewish theocracy, where religion (*eusebeia*) is "the end and aim of the entire community"—not of the select few!—and "the priests are entrusted with the special charge of it."[b]

This background helps us understand why for Paul the mystery is not esoteric or individualistic, as in the mystery religions of his day (and in much New Age theosophy today); it is open for all, and it is served by public ministers like Paul and the other ministers he has been discussing.

a. *On the Contemplative Life* 25.
b. *Against Apion* 2.188–89.

"religion" (JB, NRSV, NIV), or "godliness" (NIV). It was a common word in the Greek world for reverence for the gods and things religious. We met the word "†mystery" in 1 Tim 3:9, where it was called "the mystery of faith." In the Greek mystery religions, the mysteries were divine secrets associated with certain rituals. They were not to be divulged to anyone under pain of sacrilege.

After the mention of mystery, we would expect the next clause to begin with "which," but it begins with **who**. The mystery, then, is not a thing but a person, Jesus Christ. Now follows a hymn that Paul may have taken from the Church's liturgy at the time. It takes us out of discussion and into celebration. In a series of three contrasts it celebrates the mystery like a seesaw of God's actions from the earthly to the heavenly. Although the first member, **manifested in the flesh,** is taken by some scholars as referring to the appearances of the risen Christ, the more obvious meaning is Christ's earthly life, including his suffering "in the flesh" (Heb 5:7; 1 Pet 4:1). It reinforces the intended contrast with the second member, **in the spirit**, which does refer to his risen state.

What does it mean that Jesus was **vindicated in the spirit**? Some translations read "justified" for "vindicated." In biblical usage, to be justified is to be vindicated. God's justice is his fidelity to his own sworn word, his covenant promise (Rom 1–5). Why was it important to speak about *vindicating* Jesus? It is not easy for us, at two millennia's distance, to appreciate the early Christians' discomfort at professing faith in a God who was a human failure, who was condemned by the supreme court of the Jews and executed as a public criminal by the most shameful death imaginable. Both Jew and Gentile found this hard to accept (1 Cor 1:23). So it was important to show that the cross was not the end. God was faithful to Jesus by raising him from the dead and enthroning him as Lord of heaven and earth, thus reversing in a resounding way the verdict of the Jewish court. "In the spirit" could mean "in power," contrasted with Jesus' weakness "in the flesh." But more likely the reference is to the role of the Holy Spirit, "the Spirit of the one who raised Jesus from the dead" (Rom 8:11). In Rom 1:3–4 Jesus' earthly existence "according to the flesh" is contrasted with his existence now "according to the spirit of holiness through resurrection from the dead." Acts 2:33 says that by his resurrection and exaltation at God's right hand Jesus not only received the Holy Spirit from the Father but it was he who poured the Spirit out upon the Pentecostal community. Once poured out, what does the Spirit do? According to John 16:8–11 the Spirit-Paraclete's role is precisely to continue to vindicate Jesus, to prove where justice really lies, to confirm Jesus' glorification by even greater works done now through the disciples (14:12).

Angels were not only witnesses to the resurrection of Jesus; they welcomed their Lord into heavenly glory. The closest parallel to this is found in Heb 1:3–14, where the risen Lord takes "his seat at the right hand of the Majesty on high, / as far superior to the angels / as the name he has inherited is more excellent than theirs," and "let all the angels of God worship him." The appearance to the angels in heaven is paralleled by the proclamation of this mystery to the nations on earth—**proclaimed to the Gentiles**. This aspect of the mystery was particularly dear to Paul, "apostle to Gentiles" (Rom 11:13). **Believed in throughout the world**: by the time of the writing of this letter, the gospel had been planted "throughout the world," perhaps as far as Spain (Col 1:6; Rom 16:26). Certainly the early Church must have been astounded at the rapid spread of the gospel in the whole world (Col 1:6) and must have seen this as a further vindication of its truth. Addressing Timothy in Ephesus, Paul may intend a retort to the vaunted universality of the cult of Artemis, "whom the whole province of Asia and all the world worship" (Acts 19:27). Unlike the Ephesians who worship Artemis and her "statue that fell from heaven" (19:35 NRSV), Christians worship the living Christ who indeed came from heaven and has now returned there.

The hymn climaxes with the glorification of Christ and the promised glorification of all those with him. If we understand **taken up in glory** only of Jesus' personal resurrection and return to the Father, this happened before the proclamation to the world. But the mystery is not only Jesus' personal glorification but the union of all believers with him (Eph 2:4–6). Thus the hymn celebrates the triumphant close of history with the glorification of the whole Christ, head and members.

The movement of the mystery of Christ and his Church can be illustrated thus:

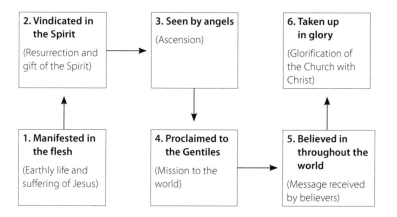

Reflection and Application (3:16)

If this hymn is the theological center of the letter, then all ministers, bishops, deacons, presbyters, and widows need to understand the sublime dignity of their office. The Church is the household of God himself, the place where God dwells. More than that, it is the locus of the mystery of mysteries, God's plan of salvation in Jesus Christ, a human being now glorified and, like the head of a comet, bearing others to glory in his train. To serve the unfolding of this mystery demands the noblest and holiest deportment.

False Teaching and Advice to Timothy

1 Timothy 4

From here on the letter alternates between general pastoral advice and Paul's personal concern for Timothy, young and in delicate health. The apostle, unable to be present himself to deal with the issue of false teachings, insists to his disciple, sometimes repetitively, that he must be strong in his personal spiritual life and in his dealing with deviant teachers and other matters of discipline. The text has all the marks of a dictated letter. We can imagine Paul pacing up and down, pausing to capture a thought, returning and repeating a previous counsel, concerned to strengthen Timothy, who seems to be embattled by false teachings on all sides.

False Teachings Are Predicted (4:1–5)

¹Now the Spirit explicitly says that in the last times some will turn away from the faith by paying attention to deceitful spirits and demonic instructions ²through the hypocrisy of liars with branded consciences. ³They forbid marriage and require abstinence from foods that God created to be received with thanksgiving by those who believe and know the truth. ⁴For everything created by God is good, and nothing is to be rejected when received with thanksgiving, ⁵for it is made holy by the invocation of God in prayer.

OT: Gen 1:31; 9:3–4
NT: Acts 10:9–16; 1 Cor 7:36–38; 14:1; Col 2:16–23; 1 Thess 5:1; 1 John 2:18–28
Catechism: the Church's ultimate trial (675), the new law (1972), thanksgiving (2638)

4:1   One of the strikingly new characteristics of the first Christian communities was the outbreak of the spirit of prophecy, which had virtually disappeared in Judaism and which Jewish tradition tended more and more to assign either to the past, as sufficiently contained in the Scriptures, or to the end times yet to come. But for Paul, the end times had already begun with the resurrection of Jesus, and the gift of the Spirit was a further sign of this fact. The purpose of prophecy in the Christian community was to build up, encourage, and console the faithful (1 Cor 14:3). This would not exclude warnings about hard times to come, as in the case of Agabus predicting a famine (Acts 11:28) or Paul's impending imprisonment (21:10–11), since even these would serve to strengthen the faithful in the face of coming adversity. By **the Spirit** is Paul referring to any specific prophecy or to the Gospel warnings about hard times to come and especially about the debilitating effects of false prophecy (Matt 7:15; 24:11–12; Mark 13:5–6; see also 2 Thess 2:2)? Perhaps both. In any case, the Spirit's message was explicit and clear: the final times will be marked by false teachings that could lead astray, if possible, even the elect (Matt 24:24; Acts 20:29–30).

Prophecy in the New Testament

BIBLICAL BACKGROUND

New Testament prophecy is not to be confused with the kind of crystal-ball predictions or astrology or palm reading or tarot-card reading that certain people today peddle for profit. Nor is it the work of psychics. In the New Testament it is a gift of the Holy Spirit bestowed to build up, strengthen, and console the faithful (1 Cor 14:3). Occasionally the prophetic word concerns the future, as when Jesus foretold the destruction of the temple (Mark 13:2) or Agabus an impending famine (Acts 11:28) and Paul's future detention in Jerusalem (21:10–11) or the Apocalypse foretelling the fall of Rome (Rev 18). Often too it is tied to a prophetic witness in the face of persecution (Matt 5:11–12). In Acts 13:2 a prophecy designates Paul and his companions for their first mission to Asia Minor. And in the Pastorals prophecy designated or accompanied the ordination of Timothy (1 Tim 1:18; 4:14). But most often prophecy is simply a spontaneous word under the inspiration of the Holy Spirit expressing, as Paul said, encouragement to the community. Luke also attributes Zechariah's spontaneous hymn at John the Baptist's birth to the gift of prophecy (Luke 1:67–79). It is quite different from the gifts of teaching, healing, administration, or service. Because of the spontaneous nature of prophecy, and because there can be false prophecy (Matt 7:15–20), the gift must be discerned (1 Thess 5:19–21) according to its congruence with faith in Jesus Christ (1 Cor 12:1–3). The Church is both hierarchic and charismatic. Without the former, the Church would be chaotic; without the latter, it would be dead.

Such lies and temptations to infidelity can come only from Satan (2 Cor 4:4; James 3:15), who in the guise of false teachers can sometimes masquerade as an angel of light (2 Cor 11:13–14).

It is not merely demonic origin that accounts for the straying of Christians **4:2** into error; it is the human agents who put on the actor's mask. The original meaning of the Greek word *hypokritēs* was "actor," easily suggesting fake identity, since the Greek actors wore masks. They are the kind that Jesus described as wolves dressed like sheep (Matt 7:15). Their **consciences** may bear the brand of Satan, as military deserters, convicts, or fugitive slaves were branded. However, such brands are easily recognizable, so this may not be the image that Paul has in mind here when he speaks of **branded consciences**, since he is concerned with a problem of deception. Thus some translators prefer "seared" (NIV, NRSV); an alternative translation would be "cauterized." That is, just as in the medical practice of the ancient world flowing blood would be dried up by burning, the consciences of these teachers have become hardened so much that they have come to believe that what they are doing is right, even perhaps giving glory to God (John 16:2). Like some of the terrorists of our day, they believe they are doing God's work.

Who precisely are these people who **forbid marriage** and impose **abstinence** **4:3** **from** certain **foods**? Some commentators see here an early form of †gnosticism, which considered the material world a mistake of the creator god. They despised matter, condemned marriage, and required various forms of asceticism. Others conjecture that the teachers belonged to a movement similar to that at Qumran, where a Jewish Essene community of celibates observed certain dietary restrictions. But the Essenes did not condemn marriage, and the discovery of animal bones in the monastery environs attests to their eating meat. If the false teachers were demanding abstinence from only certain foods, we might conclude that they were Judaizers, but the condemnation of marriage puts them outside the pale of orthodox Judaism.

Paul himself had commended celibacy (1 Cor 7:25–35), though only if it was voluntary; and he supported marriage (7:1–24). He respected those who preferred to eat only vegetables (Rom 14:2), though he refused to make this a norm for all. In 2 Cor 11:27 Paul refers to his own "frequent fastings." The error of these false teachers is in making abstinence from marriage and certain foods a universal *law*. Although the promoters of this extreme asceticism may be those who claim that the resurrected life they are already living demands these measures, in our present text Paul does not say that their error is based on a false timetable for the resurrection but rather on their total misconception of the goodness of creation.

Gnosticism

BIBLICAL
BACKGROUND

Although it had earlier roots, gnosticism flourished in the second century and even beyond. It took various forms, but a common element was the belief that the creator of the world was not the supreme god but a lesser god, that material creation was a mistake, matter itself being evil, and that through certain ascetic practices one could get back to the supreme god. When it adopted Christian elements, gnosticism reinterpreted them in its own terms and hence denied or despised the incarnation. Gnosticism provided the greatest religious challenge to the Church in the second century. Irenaeus was the greatest opponent of this heresy.

Everything that God created God called good, and he blessed the union of male and female (Gen 1). Foods are God's gift and are therefore to be taken with joy (Acts 2:46) and thanksgiving (Rom 14:6; 1 Cor 10:30; Phil 4:6).

Believers who **know the truth** will not be taken in. The Greek word for **know** here refers to a precise knowledge, often used in either verb or noun form for recognizing something or someone and distinguishing that object or person from a counterfeit or a false identity. Thus Rhoda *recognized* Peter's voice (Acts 12:14). Paul frequently uses the noun for an exact knowledge of the gospel, a knowledge that is the fruit of charity but also has objective content (Phil 1:9). Thus Paul implies the importance in the Church of theology and religious instruction as a bulwark against deviant ideologies.

4:4–5   And what is the truth that the believers know? Here specifically it is that **everything created by God is good**—and it is thanksgiving that acknowledges that goodness and its source. Jesus gave thanks before each meal (Mark 6:41; 8:6–7; 14:22; Luke 24:30). What is already naturally good is **made holy** by this thanksgiving. Food thus becomes a "sacramental," an occasion of grace, for it is sanctified by **the invocation of God in prayer** (literally "by the word of God and prayer"). "Word of God" may refer to a scripture passage read before the meal or simply to the blessing God gives when the human party "blesses" God. Or it may refer to the word of God in creation, which made everything good (Gen 1). The prayer then would be the grateful human acknowledgement of the goodness of the food, and this acknowledgement "makes it holy." In any case, the closeness of **thanksgiving** in the previous two verses indicates that the prayer is not so much a petition as it is a prayer of thanks. This text is the oldest witness of the Christian practice of praying before meals.

Reflection and Application (4:1–5)

Our consumer society seems to have little appreciation of creation as *gift*. From purchase to consumption to trash, speed and haste rule our lives: fast food, faster cars, instant foods—all to save time. But for what? What is happening to the contemplative approach to creation? Can we stop and realize that all that surrounds us—and, yes, our very selves—is gift? Pausing for prayer in the midst of our busy day, or at the end of it, helps us to remember.

Advice to Timothy—Part 1 (4:6–10)

> [6]If you will give these instructions to the brothers, you will be a good minister of Christ Jesus, nourished on the words of the faith and of the sound teaching you have followed. [7]Avoid profane and silly myths. Train yourself for devotion, [8]for, while physical training is of limited value, devotion is valuable in every respect, since it holds a promise of life both for the present and for the future. [9]This saying is trustworthy and deserves full acceptance. [10]For this we toil and struggle, because we have set our hope on the living God, who is the savior of all, especially of those who believe.

NT: Rom 15:16; 1 Cor 9:24–27; 2 Tim 2:15–16; 4:3
Catechism: hope (2090)
Lectionary (Byzantine): (4:9–16) Sunday of Zacchaeus

Paul now turns to pastoral counsels for Timothy. The Church is the family of God (3:15), and thus all its members are brothers and sisters (5:1; 2 Tim 4:21). The Greek word *adelphoi*, translated **brothers** here, includes women as well. **These instructions** refer to the immediately preceding teachings concerning the gravity of the final times in which Timothy and his church are living and the importance of being on guard against misleading influences. If Timothy so teaches, he will show that he is **a good minister of Christ Jesus.** *Diakonos* here is used not in the specific sense of "deacon" but in its general sense of "minister" or "servant." Such a minister is continually nourished by **the words of the faith.** If Paul had used the singular "word" instead of the plural, we would assume he meant simply the message of the gospel. But the plural suggests something more specific. Does he mean the words of Scripture? "Scripture" back then ordinarily meant the Old Testament, since the New Testament writings were still in process. When Paul speaks of Timothy's learning the sacred Scriptures from his

4:6

Athletic Training in Paul's Greek World

In our day, when some athletes are millionaires and some school teachers are paupers, the complaint of Isocrates (around 400 BC) could be printed in an op-ed: "I am amazed that so many cities deem those who excel in athletic contests to be worthy of greater rewards than those who, by painstaking thought and endeavor, discover something useful, and that they do not see at a glance that while the faculties of strength and speed naturally perish with the body, yet the arts and sciences abide for eternity, giving benefit to those who cultivate them."[a] Ephesus was the venue for great sporting events, the *Artemesia* and the *Ephesia*, where the victors, among other rewards, might be given legal immunity. Elsewhere Paul uses athletic imagery positively for the contest of the Christian life.

a. *To the Rulers of Mytilene* 5; see also *Panegyricus* 1–2.

youth, he means using the Old Testament in the service of his Christian faith (2 Tim 3:15). Hence, "words of faith" here stands for the basic formulations of the Christian faith, whether in the Old Testament, as understood in the light of Christ and his words, or in the apostolic preaching, both oral and written. The word of God is food, as Jesus reminded Satan (Deut 8:3; Matt 4:4) and the apostles reminded their disciples (1 Cor 3:2; 1 Pet 2:2). And the one who feeds others with this food must first feed himself. Paul is supposing Timothy does so, but he wants to reinforce his disciple's daily spiritual formation in **the sound teaching you have followed.**

We have not finished with Paul's insistence on right teaching, for the theme will reappear in this and the other Pastorals. Obviously in Paul's mind there is a crisis of false teachings that needs to be met (1 Tim 4:7). The nature of them here seems to be the same as in 1:4—myths, fables, fairy tales, not so much direct attacks on the faith as mixtures of the faith with speculations or fantasies that corrupt it (the old New Age!).

4:7   Paul's letters to his delegates frequently follow the template of letters well known in the rhetorical schools of his day. The letter of Pseudo-Isocrates to Demonicus is an example: "**Train yourself** [same Greek expression] in self-imposed tasks, that you may be able to endure those which others impose upon you."[1] Paul uses the metaphor of an athlete's training, employed widely in the Greek world for training in discipline or virtue and even given a religious sense in the

1. *To Demonicus* 21.

Fig. 5. The footrace track at Delphi. Paul frequently used sporting images in his letters.

Olympic games, which were understood to be presided over by the gods. The apostle thus challenges Timothy to become an athlete of Christ, training himself **for devotion**. In the Pastorals this term (*eusebeia*) means more than prayer. It stands for the entire comportment of the Christian who lives in this world while belonging to the next, bearing witness to the holiness attainable even now in this world because of Jesus Christ. This requires what today we would call formation. The training imagery suggests a repetitive devotion to the kind of practices that will make a person fit for the *agōn*, the competition of the arena. That would surely mean prayer, study of the Scriptures in the light of Jesus ("the words of the faith"; 4:6), and practice of the virtues Paul has recommended. No mention is made of asceticism, perhaps because of the false asceticism urged by the opponents or perhaps because Timothy is already in delicate health (5:23).

Writers in the Greek world both hailed physical exercise and sports and despised them by contrast with intellectual pursuits. Paul does not condemn **physical training**; he shows its limited value compared to the life of Christian devotion, for which Jesus himself promised rewards both in this life and in the life to come (Matt 19:29; Mark 10:30; Luke 18:30). Building on the blessings promised to the righteous in the Old Testament, Jesus proclaimed the Beatitudes, each of which has a promise attached (Matt 5:3–12; Luke 6:20–23). **4:8**

This saying is trustworthy and deserves full acceptance apparently refers to the statement immediately preceding. It confirms the gospel promise of **4:9–10**

happiness both in this life and in the next, a promise that is not dimmed even in the midst of the severest suffering (Rom 5:3; 2 Cor 1:3–11; 6:9–10). **For this**, meaning "with this goal in mind," that is, the rewards of godliness in this life but especially in the next, **we** (Paul associates Timothy with himself) **toil and struggle.** The Greek verbs continue the athletic metaphor, evoking their exhausting labors for the sake of the gospel (compare 2 Cor 11:23–28). The Christian life, and all the more so the ministry, is a life of toil inspired by love (1 Thess 1:3) and by **hope** in **the living God.**

The Bible uses the designation "living God" at least twenty-nine times, contrasting sharply with the mute, deaf, lifeless idols of the pagans (Acts 14:15; 1 Thess 1:9). The term is particularly appropriate in a city dedicated to the cult of Artemis, awash with idols. "The living God" is not only the true God, the only God who exists, but also the God who acts in history, the God who *saves.* When Paul says that God **is the savior of all**, does he mean that all will be saved? Hardly, for if so he and Timothy and the other evangelists would not be working so hard to get the good news out. Rather the sense is the same as that expressed in 1 Tim 2:3–4, that God *wishes* all people to be saved and to come to a knowledge of the truth. Those who respond to the good news—**those who believe**—are obviously the ones in whom his saving will is realized.

Reflection and Application (4:6–10)

Nourished by the words of the faith: Once during a retreat at which I was preaching, the group decided to fast at lunch. We would come to the table with our Bibles, share our favorite passage, and tell why we found nourishment in it. We left the table having had a banquet! Catholics, who "train themselves for devotions" like the rosary, need to supplement their diet with daily, prayerful reading of the Scriptures.

Advice to Timothy—Part 2 (4:11–16)

> [11]**Command and teach these things.** [12]**Let no one have contempt for your youth, but set an example for those who believe, in speech, conduct, love, faith, and purity.** [13]**Until I arrive, attend to the reading, exhortation, and teaching.** [14]**Do not neglect the gift you have, which was conferred on you through the prophetic word with the imposition of hands of the presbyterate.** [15]**Be diligent in these matters, be absorbed in them, so that your progress may be evident to everyone.** [16]**Attend to yourself and to your**

teaching; persevere in both tasks, for by doing so you will save both your-self and those who listen to you.

OT: Num 27:18–23; Deut 34:9; 1 Sam 16:12; 17:14
NT: Acts 6:6; 13:2–3; 2 Thess 3:7–9; 1 Tim 5:22; 2 Tim 1:6; Titus 2:6–8
Catechism: representing Christ (1552–53), imposition of hands in Holy Orders (1573)
Lectionary: (4:12–16) Mass for the Ordination of Deacons

Timothy is to **command and teach these things.** Conforming to the style   4:11
of the advice-giving letter of elder to younger (like Pseudo-Isocrates to Demonicus), Paul repeats advice given before. It is likely that Timothy needs
the boldness that comes from assurance of his authority. In light of his own
youth, he may well be intimidated by the older men in the community. Some
authorities point to this reference to Timothy's "youth" as an indication that
the letter is pseudonymous, for, if Timothy was in his early twenties when he
joined Paul at Lystra (Acts 16:1), he would be approaching the age of forty at
the time of the writing of this letter. The point at issue, though, seems to be
Timothy's youth in comparison with Paul (already an "old man" according to
Philem 9). Timothy would still be young in comparison to his spiritual father.
In the culture of the day, where elders should be listened to, Paul's age adds
weight to the authority he has as an apostle. Now he offers this weight in support of Timothy, a support he hopes will have its effect when the letter is read
publicly in the Ephesian church.

Obviously, Timothy has no control over what other people think of him,   4:12
and the counsel **let no one have contempt for your youth** is primarily aimed
at Timothy to tell him not to be cowed by what others might say or think. But
inasmuch as the letter will be read publicly, it is also addressed to those who
might discount his authority because of his youth. Ignatius will write to the
Magnesians: "It is not proper for you to take advantage of your bishop's youth,
but rather, looking to the power of God the Father, to show him every mark
of respect."[2]

But although he is not to fear asserting his authority, Timothy should govern
primarily by his example. The Greek word *typos*, translated **example** here, originally meant a mold into which metal was poured. So it is more than something
to be imitated; it is rather something to which something else is to be conformed,
something by which something else is measured. In this sense Timothy should
be the pattern for his flock, someone for them to imitate and even begin to look
like. Paul did not hesitate to tell his readers to imitate him (1 Cor 4:16; 11:1).

---

2. *To the Magnesians* 3.

Now he implicitly does the same for Timothy in relation to those in his charge. Timothy's conduct should be exemplary in his conversations, in the fraternal **love** he shows to all, and in **faith**. The word *pistis* has a wide range of meanings: "faith" as attachment to revealed truth, "trust" in God's promises (Heb 11), "trustworthiness," and "faithfulness" in the discharge of one's duties.

Purity is the NAB's translation of *hagneia*. But just as *pistis* can also mean "fidelity," so *hagneia* can also mean "integrity." The combination of the two Greek words meaning "fidelity and integrity" was frequent in imperial times as words of praise for judges and civic-minded citizens. In the promiscuous Roman world, Timothy should be a model of chastity, but as a leader he should also exemplify fidelity and integrity. Are the demands of leadership in the Church and in our world any different today?

4:13   While awaiting Paul's arrival, Timothy is to attend to three pastoral duties, the definite article before each of them indicating that they are well-established activities. **Reading** here means public reading, proclamation of the word. Ancient Greek manuscripts were difficult to read because they were often not well written, and for economy's sake words were not spaced separately but run together and punctuation was unknown. An important component of education, for those who could afford it, was to learn the technique not only of deciphering the words but also of declaiming the reading in a way that was pleasing to the audience. This demanded serious preparation and practice. Even private reading was done out loud. In Israel that is what "meditating" on the law (Ps 1:2) meant—mouthing it: "Keep this book of the law on your lips. Recite it by day and by night" (Josh 1:8). The Christian liturgy was the successor to that of the synagogue, where reading and explaining the law and the prophets was the heart of worship. The tradition goes back at least to Ezra, who "read plainly from the book of the law of God, interpreting it so that all could understand what was read" (Neh 8:8). Thus when Jesus came to a sabbath service in his hometown, he was given a copy of the prophet Isaiah to read, and then he commented on it (Luke 4:16–21).

It is to this important duty that Paul calls Timothy's attention. He is to read the Old Testament and, by this time perhaps, any available apostolic letter that contained "the words of the faith" (1 Tim 4:6) and comment upon it for the community. Or he is to appoint competent lectors to do it, as we know happened in the second century.[3] Saint John Chrysostom's homilies, in which he follows the scriptural text line by line, would be a good example of this kind of reading. In our day, reading the Scriptures for the worshiping community

3. Hippolytus, *Apostolic Tradition* 12.

is a ministry that happily many are taking seriously enough to be trained for it and to prepare the text carefully before proclaiming it.

But Timothy is to do more than read and explain. He should "exhort," that is, appeal to the heart, a role Paul describes in 1 Cor 14:3 as the particular gift of the prophet, though it is the charge of the bishop as well (Titus 1:9). When Paul and his companions arrived at the synagogue in Antioch of Pisidia, after the reading of the law and the prophets, they were asked, "If one of you has a word of exhortation for the people, please speak" (Acts 13:15). This would basically correspond to what we would call a good, Scripture-based homily or sermon today. Its purpose is to appeal to the heart and conscience in such a way as to build up faith, hope, and love (Rom 15:4).

Finally, Paul lists **teaching**, which here in the Pastorals means the teaching of sound doctrine. The growth and stability of the Christian community cannot be assured merely by exhortation. If teaching without exhortation may fill the head without warming the heart, exhortation without teaching will eventually evaporate. The faithful need a clear understanding of their faith, and it is the role of the teacher to provide it. In Eph 4:11 the roles of teacher and pastor, though distinguished, are closely paired, suggesting that the pastor also assures that teaching is done, either by himself or others. Whereas the prophet exhorts (1 Cor 14:3), the teacher instructs. Religious instruction and sound theology today, as then, are indispensable components of a Church that is alive.

Paul reminds Timothy, however, that the duties he has just described are not   4:14
mere functions of an assignment. There is a power available to Timothy that comes from God, and it is a special **gift**. The Greek word for gift is *charisma*. It is often a technical term in Pauline literature for a gift of the Holy Spirit enabling one to perform a function for the benefit of the whole Church. It is not the same as natural talent, though it may perfect one's natural talents. The gifts of praise (like tongues) and prophecy (hearing and speaking a "now" word from the Lord) and healing and various gifts of service are all charisms (1 Cor 12–14), but so are the more settled functions of teaching and pastoring (Eph 4:11). The context in our present text suggests that a charism is an abiding inward gift that can lie dormant or be neglected and needs to be fanned into flame (2 Tim 1:6).

When and how did Timothy receive this gift? On the one hand, through prophecy, that is, **the prophetic word.** The immediate meaning that comes to mind is an oracle by someone in the community, whether a recognized prophet or another person spontaneously moved by the Holy Spirit—perhaps a presbyter or even Paul! It was thus that Paul and Barnabas were designated for their mission in Acts 13:2–3. Prophecy continued in the early communities well into the fourth century, and, though always subject to discernment, it was highly respected. Some scholars suggest that "prophecy" here means a consecrating prayer. But that is not the ordinary meaning of prophecy elsewhere in Paul. The prophecy designating Timothy would, of course, be discerned and confirmed by Paul and the elders, but they recognized the designation as divinely inspired.

The prophecy was accompanied by **the imposition of hands**, a rite found already in the Old Testament, where Moses lays his hands on Joshua to convey authority as his successor (Num 27:18–23; Deut 34:9). Jesus' frequent way of healing the sick was by laying his hands on them.[4] The early Church continued the practice as a way of communicating the Holy Spirit (Acts 8:17; 9:17; 19:6) and establishing in office (6:6). Some scholars see a contradiction between this text, which speaks of **the imposition of hands of the presbyterate**, and 2 Tim 1:6, where Paul says that Timothy was ordained by "the imposition of my hands." But there is no need to see one as excluding the other. Even today, when priests are ordained, the bishop lays on his hands, and this is sufficient to assure the ordination; but the attending priests do also, indicating the collegial character of the sacrament and the welcoming of the newcomer to the college of the presbyterate. It is possible to translate "of the presbyterate" as "*for* the presbyterate," understanding the office to which Timothy was installed rather than the persons who installed him. However, it seems more likely, given the frequent reference to the group of presbyters, especially at Ephesus (Acts 20:17), that Paul is referring to a share that the local leaders had in the rite.

4:15–16   Paul now restates in a positive and more forceful way what he has been saying so far. A shepherd can easily be distracted by secondary matters, to the neglect of his own spiritual life and his care for others. The apostles learned this quite early and decided to leave the service of tables to others and to "devote ourselves to prayer and to the ministry of the word" (Acts 6:1–4). "Prayer" here assumes personal prayer but it probably refers to leading the prayer of the community. In that case, the temptation to neglect what is primary would still hold, as when a community's leaders get so absorbed in social work that they neglect the care and attention due the worship of the community. This concentration on the essential will enable Timothy to make great strides that will be evident not only to himself but to everyone else as well. Concluding this section, Paul reminds Timothy to take care of himself spiritually—**attend to yourself**—but in the same breath he urges him once more to attend to the **teaching** ministry.

4. Mark 5:23; 6:5; 7:33; Luke 4:40; 13:13.

For the ordained overseer of churches, these two aspects are not opposed. In living out this vocation he will **save both** himself and others.

Reflection and Application (4:11–16)

Before advising Timothy about his specific pastoral duties, Paul points to virtues in which his disciple and delegate should excel. It is all too easy for ministers to give more attention to their work than to their own personal growth in holiness. But ministry is quite different from a task to be performed—and certainly quite different from a secular job, where the priority is performance with little regard to the worker's life of virtue. The minister is trying to communicate a way of life, and his method must be that of Jesus, who first lived the word and *then* taught it (Matt 5:19). Although Paul is speaking of the responsibilities of ordained ministers here, the principle is equally applicable to lay Christians, who should view their vocation in the world as a ministry. Both by their example and their work they can proclaim the gospel according to their particular circumstances.

Ministers who find themselves in charge of those older than themselves may experience exactly what Timothy seems to have experienced. The "grace of state," that is, the grace that accompanies the office to which God has called them, will enable them, like Timothy, to be firm and gentle, respectful of age but not cowed by it. (Paul will return to this thought in 1 Tim 5:1.)

Reading, exhortation, and teaching—these are the three primary ministries on which Paul insists that Timothy focus his efforts. The bishop and the priest

Holding Fast to Scripture   LIVING TRADITION

Vatican Council II declared:

> Therefore, all the clergy must hold fast to the Sacred Scriptures through diligent sacred reading and careful study, especially the priests of Christ and others, such as deacons and catechists who are legitimately active in the ministry of the word. . . . The sacred synod also earnestly and especially urges all the Christian faithful, especially Religious, to learn by frequent reading of the divine Scriptures the "excellent knowledge of Jesus Christ" (Phil 3.8). "For ignorance of the Scriptures is ignorance of Christ." . . . And let them remember that prayer should accompany the reading of Sacred Scripture, so that God and man may talk together; for "we speak to Him when we pray; we hear Him when we read the divine saying." (*Dei Verbum* 25)

consider it a priority to read, exhort, and teach from the Scriptures, which supposes that they nourish themselves on the word of God continually. Today this speaks to seminarians who are preparing for ministry but also to the laity about the importance of knowing their faith both for their own spiritual growth and also to "be ready to give an explanation to anyone who asks you for a reason for your hope" (1 Pet 3:15).

Rules for Different Groups

1 Timothy 5

Anyone engaged in Church ministry knows that the needs of Church members and even of other ministers differ according to their age, status, and particular vocation. That is why we have youth groups, young adult groups, retreats for men, and retreats for women. That is also why it is important for a minister to be sensitive to the particular needs of these different groups. So it was not enough for Paul to give Timothy directives about his teaching and his personal conduct. The apostle now turns to his delegate's relationship with various members of the community, according to their age, gender, and office.

Duties toward Members of Various Ages (5:1–2)

¹Do not rebuke an older man, but appeal to him as a father. Treat younger men as brothers, ²older women as mothers, and younger women as sisters with complete purity.

OT: Lev 19:32
NT: Mark 3:31–35; Rom 12:10
Catechism: extension of fourth commandment (2212), chaste friendship (2347)

Paul offers Timothy advice on how to relate to persons of various ages and both genders in the community. If the Church is the family or household of God, it obviously includes persons of different ages and both genders. Children are not mentioned, probably because they are under the direct responsibility of their parents for both their upbringing and their religious education. Both the Hellenistic world and Jewish tradition strongly inculcated respect for elders: "It is the duty of a young man to show deference to his elders and to cling to the best and most approved of them, so as to receive the benefit of their counsel and influence. Let everyone among us revere in deed and word whoever is older."[1] "Stand up in the presence of the aged, and show respect for the old; thus shall you fear your God" (Lev 19:32). "Insult no man when he is old" (Sir 8:6). When it is necessary to correct an **older man**, and Paul certainly foresees the possibility, Timothy should **not rebuke** him as a military officer or boss might bawl out a subordinate. Rather Timothy should exhort, that is, **appeal to him** not only with admonition but with encouragement as well (the nuance of *parakaleō*).

While not relinquishing his ultimate authority, Timothy should approach the men of his own age and younger on the basis of equality, as **brothers**, with the affection appropriate to those who share the same life and call (literally "with the affection of brothers," according to Rom 12:10).

5:2   Timothy should treat the **older women** with the kindness and respect he would show his own mother (in Rom 16:13 Paul speaks of Rufus's mother as his own). He should especially relate to the **younger women** with the loving respect one would observe with one's **sisters**. Not only is Timothy's virtue at stake but also the reputation of the Church. Paul is a realist here. The Christian community provides a closeness and equality not available in other environments and, for that reason, a challenge to greater vigilance regarding the observance of boundaries and **purity** of heart (Matt 5:27–30). The context for the mention of all these considerations regarding relationships here, however, is the duty of correction that Timothy as Church leader must occasionally exercise—hardly a pleasant duty, but one that requires a great deal of practical wisdom.

Reflection and Application (5:1–2)

I experienced the reality of the situation Paul describes in 1 Tim 5:1 when I was appointed superior of a community with members much older than myself. Occasionally I did have to confront such persons for both their own sake and the sake of the community. It was a delicate challenge. Confrontation need not be rebuke, and mine was not. But I was also amazed at how the elderly religious respected me, if for no other reason than that I was the superior, the one appointed to be in charge of the community.

1. Cicero, *De Officiis* 1.34.122.

Priests and religious have a particular position of trust. The faithful, both men and women, often share with them intimate matters, whether inside or outside the confessional. Such a depth of sharing can at times also lead to temptation if the priest or religious is not solidly grounded in their vocation and prayer and does not exercise prudent common sense in how they conduct themselves in these relationships. The same challenge can easily face lay ministers who serve with members of the opposite sex.

Widows (5:3–16)

³Honor widows who are truly widows. ⁴But if a widow has children or grandchildren, let these first learn to perform their religious duty to their own family and to make recompense to their parents, for this is pleasing to God. ⁵The real widow, who is all alone, has set her hope on God and continues in supplications and prayers night and day. ⁶But the one who is self-indulgent is dead while she lives. ⁷Command this, so that they may be irreproachable. ⁸And whoever does not provide for relatives and especially family members has denied the faith and is worse than an unbeliever.

⁹Let a widow be enrolled if she is not less than sixty years old, married only once, ¹⁰with a reputation for good works, namely, that she has raised children, practiced hospitality, washed the feet of the holy ones, helped those in distress, involved herself in every good work. ¹¹But exclude younger widows, for when their sensuality estranges them from Christ, they want to marry ¹²and will incur condemnation for breaking their first pledge. ¹³And furthermore, they learn to be idlers, going about from house to house, and not only idlers but gossips and busybodies as well, talking about things that ought not to be mentioned. ¹⁴So I would like younger widows to marry, have children, and manage a home, so as to give the adversary no pretext for maligning us. ¹⁵For some have already turned away to follow Satan. ¹⁶If any woman believer has widowed relatives, she must assist them; the church is not to be burdened, so that it will be able to help those who are truly widows.

OT: Jdt 8:4–5
NT: Luke 2:36–38; John 13:14; Titus 2:6–8; James 1:27
Catechism: widowhood as consecrated (922), as an order (1537), as a form of chastity (2349), as a sacramental (1672)
Lectionary: Common of Holy Men and Women for Widows

We touch here one of the main themes that runs through both the Old   5:3
and the New Covenants. The Old Testament repeatedly hails the Lord as the

champion of widows and orphans: "The LORD, your God, . . . executes justice for the orphan and the widow" (Deut 10:17–18). He is the "father of the fatherless, defender of widows" (Ps 68:6). Jesus' compassion for widows is highlighted by the synoptic Gospels. Whereas, during a visit to the temple, the disciples notice only the rich, Jesus points out the poor widow whose generosity surpasses the others (Mark 12:41–44). When Jesus sees a dead man being carried for burial, "the only son of his mother, and she was a widow," he is moved with compassion to raise and restore the man to his mother (Luke 7:11–15). And John relates Jesus' confiding his own mother, presumably widowed, to the beloved disciple (John 19:25–27).

It is estimated that forty percent of the women between forty and fifty in the ancient world were **widows**.[2] The Christian community would not be immune to the causes of those statistics, and the large number of widows would present a significant pastoral concern.

The question here, however, is how to translate the Greek verb *timaō*, which many translators, like our NAB, render **honor**. Certainly this translation is possible. But the sense of giving financial support is also expressed by this Greek word and fits the context better here. The word is used in this sense in Sir 38:1: "Hold the physician in honor." The commandment to "honor your father and your mother" bore with it the obligation of financial support in their need, as Jesus argues with his opponents in Mark 7:9–13. And in 1 Tim 5:17 the statement that elders who serve well are due "double honor" is intended in a financial sense, as is made clear by the maxim quoted in the following verse: "A worker deserves his pay." The meaning "give financial support" in 5:3 throws a meaningful light on the whole passage. In the Jewish synagogue there was a ministry to the needy: the distribution of food to those in immediate need and a kind of "community chest" of funds for those in long-term need. This practice was continued in the early Christian community, if we are to believe the importance attached to it in James 1:27, where it is part of James's definition of "religion that is pure and undefiled," and the picture in Acts 2:41–47 and 4:32–37, where no one was in need because those in the community with resources shared what they had. Widows unsupported by other means would fall into the category of long-term indigents, and the proper handling of their needs occasioned the tension we hear about in Acts 6:1–6, where the Greek-speaking disciples complained that "their widows were being neglected in the daily distribution." Obviously there could be a strain between the needs of the widows and the resources of the community, and Paul is sensitive to that here.

---

2. Winter, *Roman Wives*, 124.

The question Paul is addressing is this: who really needs financial support?   5:4
Those who are "truly widows" would exclude those who have family who could
support them (1 Tim 5:4, 8), those who are young and could remarry (5:11–14),
and those who are living disreputable lives (5:6, 15). It would include those sixty
years old or more, who were married only once (5:9) and devote themselves to
prayer (5:5) and good works (5:10). These are to be enrolled (5:9), that is, put
on the official list for community support.

Some scholars think that an "order of widows," indicated by the enrollment   5:5
in 5:9, was a harbinger of religious life. Indeed, the expectations of prayer and
service to the community is a foreshadowing of later developments. But the
more telling consideration is the very practical one: who deserves the support of
the community and who does not? Paul may very well be reacting to the claims
of some younger women, who would point to their widowhood as reason for
community support, whereas they could have other means of sustenance. And
some of his negative experiences with such unmarried women may lie behind
his pessimistic views of their uncommitted status in 5:13. The preference that
they should marry stands in tension with Paul's positive view of celibacy in
1 Cor 7:25–35, which he does not limit to any age. The **real widow** here, however, corresponds to the role of the celibate in 1 Cor 7:34–35, who is totally
free for the affairs of the Lord. She is **all alone**, having no one but **God** to rely
on, and spends her life in constant prayer. She is like the widowed prophetess
Anna, who "never left the temple, but worshiped night and day with fasting and
prayer" (Luke 2:37). Polycarp in the early second century calls these virtuous,
praying widows "the altar of God."[3] Augustine, citing this verse, sees the widow
at constant prayer as a type of the whole Church: "The whole church is a single
widow"; and he evokes the image of the widow in Luke 18:1–8, who wins the
judge's favorable verdict by her untiring petitions.[4]

The "real widow" is contrasted with those widows who are **self-indulgent**.   5:6
Some commentators take this as descriptive of promiscuity or prostitution into
which destitute women often fall simply because they have no other means of
support. Without a husband, a widow may be more vulnerable to these temptations. But especially in the case of rich widows, "self-indulgence" here may be
merely a description of the kind of indolent luxury that James 5:5 condemns:
"You have lived on earth in luxury and pleasure; you have fattened your hearts for
the day of slaughter." It was the kind of life the rich man lived while Lazarus lay
at his gate (Luke 16:19–31), or the rich who gorged themselves instead of being

3. *To the Philippians* 4.
4. *Ennarations on the Psalms* 131.23.

sickened at the collapse of their country (Amos 6:6). It is this self-preoccupied hedonism, unconcerned about the needy around them and lacking in good works, that makes them **dead** while seeming alive (compare Rev 3:1).

5:7–8   Returning to Timothy, Paul tells him to **command this**, that is, proclaim what Paul has just said, particularly about widows, so that those who are "truly widows" may live up to their calling and those tempted to the life of self-indulgence will not falter. The strong word **command** means that Paul is setting out not a recommendation but a firm policy. It is one of those apostolic decisions that will shape Tradition and ultimately canons that will identify the Church as a visible community. Then, with a claim intended to shock, he insists families must support their own. Whoever does not **has denied the faith and is worse than an unbeliever.** Did Paul mean this literally? Understood correctly, yes. In a world without Social Security, in both Roman and Greek law children were obliged to support their parents. For a Christian to refuse to do so would add scandal to civil disobedience. The believer is not simply one who recites a creed but one who has made a baptismal commitment to the whole of Christian life, an oath of fidelity, as it were, a vow to live the life of love. To refuse such an elemental duty of love as to care for one's own would add a guilt to which the pagan, who never made such a pledge, would be immune.

5:9–10   If the "real widow" is a woman given to prayer (1 Tim 5:5), there are other qualifications that Paul now lists. She is to be at least **sixty years old.** She is also a person of **good works.** Though the practices given here are presented as conditions for her admittance, it is obvious that she would be expected to continue them in the measure her health and strength would permit. But—and this is a pastoral counsel—"younger widows" should not be **enrolled.** What age group would this include? Probably from around the twentieth year to menopause, which, according to Soranus, an early second-century Ephesian gynecologist, occurred between the ages of forty and fifty.[5] But for Paul the widow must be at least sixty in order to be enrolled. This extension may have been motivated, on the one hand, by simply the large number of widows in the community or, on the other, by the greater likelihood that widows of more advanced age would be less likely to regret their commitment. This enrolling would seem to be the equivalent to making a vow of celibacy—the strongest argument for seeing the arrangement to be an "order of widows"—since a later intent to marry would be a violation of a commitment to Christ (5:12). Polycarp in the early second century seems to assume a similar commitment to Christ on the part of wid-

5. Winter, *Roman Wives*, 125.

ows: they have "plighted a fidelity to the Lord."[6] Some suggest that the pledge that they might violate could have been nothing more than their commitment to a life of prayer. However, Paul's harsh accusation of wantonness seems to imply a more serious commitment. Wantonness among younger widows was not unknown in Roman times, and it was among the abuses of family life that Emperor Augustus tried to curb. Paul would consider such promiscuity to be an abandoning of Christ, a going over to Satan, which some in the community have already done (5:14–15).

Paul's encouragement of **younger widows** to marry seems to be in tension with 1 Cor 7:40, where he says that the widow is more blessed if she does not marry. But even there he adds a qualification: "To the unmarried and to widows, I say: It is a good thing for them to remain as they are, as I do, but if they cannot exercise self-control they should marry, for it is better to marry than to be on fire" (7:8–9). Perhaps by the time of writing to Timothy, Paul's pastoral experience and the burden of widows on the resources of the Church led him to suggest that it is generally better for younger widows to marry. Note, however, that this is not something he commands, but rather something he "would like" to be observed (1 Tim 5:14). *5:11–12*

To put it briefly: Paul prefers younger widows to marry, but he directs that only the older ones be consecrated and enrolled. Since the consecrated woman more closely represents the Church as the spouse of Christ, should she fail, the scandal would be all the more grave. A temptation for the younger widows is idleness, gossiping, and **going about from house to house**. These are presumably women of marriageable age who would otherwise be on the community dole. The final verse is surprising in that it mentions only women assistants to widows. Wouldn't men be equally obliged to assist their widowed relatives? It seems that Paul is simply alluding to the fact that normally the ones who would most likely support widows, in time and services if not always with money, would be the women members of their families. An inscription on a tomb in Rome reads, "Erected by her daughter to the noble Regina, her widowed mother, who lived her widowhood for sixty years and was never a burden to the church."[7] *5:13–16*

As we conclude this section, it is remarkable that the early Church not only cared for its widows but gave them a ministry. And this ministry was primarily one of prayer. The Church believed that she was *receiving* from these widows as well as giving. To Paul's description of their ministry here Polycarp will add: "They must pray unceasingly for the community."[8] Although good works

6. *To the Philippians* 4.
7. Cited by Spicq, *Épîtres pastorales*, 1.540.
8. *To the Philippians* 4.

are expected, the primacy is given to prayer. It is a preparation for the great contemplative orders in the Church.

Reflection and Application (5:3–16)

Today, when women can find employment outside the home and government programs care for the retired and the unemployed, the Church, at least in the developed world, no longer needs to formally enroll needy, unsupported widows. However, in every parish today you will find widows, widowers, and elderly persons who have never married given to prayer and to service of the Church. They are not withered branches on the vine but preciously fruitful by their witness, prayer, and service.

Widows were warned against self-indulgence (5:6), but this is a temptation to which all are vulnerable, especially in this age of computer-accessible pornography—even having it thrust on us through television. But we are also glutted with luxury. Anyone who has spent some time in an underdeveloped country will be shocked at the disparity of living standards between that world and ours. Having lived for six years in a country where there were villages without running water, where buses looked like rolling beehives, so packed were they within and cluttered with people without, I experienced culture shock in reverse when I returned to the States, where air-conditioned buses plied the pedestrianless streets with a handful of passengers. The comic strip "Opus" recently featured a young man dying because he went twenty minutes without iBook, iPod, iPod Nano, Shuffle, Blackberry, Game-boy, instant-messaging, or game-playing musical phone: "He's been un-entertained for twenty minutes!"

Two other very important issues for today's families and parishes are raised by this reading. First, adult children have an obligation to care for their elderly parents, and not only in financial ways. In many cases, parents may have sufficient financial resources but need help, assistance, and companionship—and many of them do not receive it. There is a lot of neglect of elderly parents and other elderly relatives. Second, despite government programs and other charitable initiatives, in every parish there are poor, elderly people with unmet physical needs. A truly Christian community seeks out these people and organizes to provide assistance. People need help with their houses and housekeeping, with transportation to stores and doctors and church, with dealing with government bureaucracies, and so on. Paul's words about the responsibility of families and of the whole Christian community to the elderly call for education and initiatives in regard to these issues.

Presbyters (5:17–25)

[17]Presbyters who preside well deserve double honor, especially those who toil in preaching and teaching. [18]For the scripture says, "You shall not muzzle an ox when it is threshing," and, "A worker deserves his pay." [19]Do not accept an accusation against a presbyter unless it is supported by two or three witnesses. [20]Reprimand publicly those who do sin, so that the rest also will be afraid. [21]I charge you before God and Christ Jesus and the elect angels to keep these rules without prejudice, doing nothing out of favoritism. [22]Do not lay hands too readily on anyone, and do not share in another's sins. Keep yourself pure. [23]Stop drinking only water, but have a little wine for the sake of your stomach and your frequent illnesses.

[24]Some people's sins are public, preceding them to judgment; but other people are followed by their sins. [25]Similarly, good works are also public; and even those that are not cannot remain hidden.

OT: Deut 19:15; 25:4
NT: Acts 20:17, 28, 33–35; 1 Cor 9:6–18; 2 Cor 13:1; 1 Thess 5:12–13; 1 Pet 5:1–4
Catechism: presbyters today (1567), material needs of the Church (2043), reputation (2477)

This section does not deal with the virtues required of presbyters. That was **5:17** dealt with in 1 Tim 3, where "bishop" or "overseer" seemed to be an equivalent of "presbyter." Here it is a question of the duties of the Church and especially of Timothy *toward* the **presbyters**. The word **honor** (Greek *timē*) can also have the meaning "wage, stipend, salary." Both meanings seem to rule here. Are the presbyters occupied full time at their ministry? We can't be sure, but it is obvious they are not mere volunteers. The early Church realized that these ministries were important enough to endow them with monetary support and to encourage excellence by rewarding with additional stipend—**double**—those who do their service **well** (the Greek word *kalōs* also has the connotation "beautifully"). This would be especially true of those who preach and teach. We can see from this that not all the presbyters did so. Some apparently functioned more like members of a board of trustees, whereas others were more directly engaged in the spiritual formation of the community.

Paul finds sanction for the support of the presbyters first in a text from Deut **5:18** 25:4 in the Greek Bible. Oxen were used in biblical times, and are still used today in some underdeveloped countries, in the threshing of grain. The farmer would harvest by hand the sheaves of grain and then lay them out on a flat, preferably stone, threshing floor. He would then harness an ox to drag a sled over the stalks, thus crushing out the grain. Afterward, in the evening breeze, the harvester would use a winnowing fork and throw the remains into the air. The grain, being heavier, would fall directly to the ground, while the wind would carry off the chaff. The Bible prescribed that the beast dragging the sled should not be muzzled, that is, it should be allowed to eat of the stalks during its labor. Already in 1 Cor 9:9 Paul applied this principle to those who preach the gospel. They have a right to be supported by their ministry. This prescription shows how advanced the Ephesian community is, for when Paul began his ministry in a new city he regularly worked to support himself, allowing others to support him only after a strong basis of trust had been established.

The second citation, **a worker deserves his pay**, is coordinated with the first and thus appears also to be a reference to Scripture. No Old Testament text says this precisely, but the underlying principle is given in Deut 24:14–15 and James 5:4. The text corresponds exactly, though, to Luke 10:7 (see also Matt 10:10). This, then, would be the first witness in the New Testament quoting a word of Jesus as **scripture**. If this letter is as late as some scholars think, it could well be that the writer has in front of him the very text of Luke. More likely, though, this was a well-known saying of Jesus resolving an issue faced from the earliest hour: should those who labor for the gospel receive compensation for their labors?

5:19   First Timothy 5:19 is another indication of a rather developed church. That Timothy should not act on **an accusation against a presbyter** without confirmation of **two or three witnesses** might be just common sense and the application of Jewish principles of law (Deut 19:15), mentioned five times in the New Testament (see also Matt 18:16; John 8:17; 2 Cor 13:1; Heb 10:28). But the statement may also suggest that such accusations have indeed been made. Christians living in the Greek world might be prompted by the widespread example of frivolous accusations. Ceslas Spicq cites a Greek inscription concerning Alexandria where, "the city having become almost uninhabitable because of the number of accusers and each household being prey to the menace," the Roman prefect Tiberius Julius Alexander was obliged to suppress any unfounded denunciation and require the accusers to supply solid proof of their case.[9] Persons in authority are especially vulnerable, since their concern for the common good sometimes requires refusal of a subordinate's unreasonable demands, and this could lead to retaliatory accusations. On the other hand, abuse of authority is the worst kind, and the Church needs a procedure to deal with it.

5:20   **Those who do sin** refers obviously to a moral fault. Other errors or shortcomings in administrative duties should be corrected privately. But where the

---

9. Spicq, *Épîtres pastorales*, 1.544.

community is vulnerable to scandal, the correction should be made **publicly**. It is not clear whether this means before all the presbyters or before all the Church. In any case, just as it is important to disregard unsupported accusations, it is equally important to react energetically to moral lapses in the leaders, lest other leaders and the faithful dare to do the same.

I charge you before God and Christ Jesus and the elect angels is exception-   5:21
ally solemn, as if Paul were putting Timothy under oath. The scenario is the final judgment: God, Christ, and the righteous angels all have a role, biblically, in the final judgment.[10] The great temptation of one in authority is to be influenced to **favoritism** by friendship or less worthy motives—a vice of judges condemned over and over again in the Scriptures. Timothy and all in pastoral authority need to carry out their leadership roles without favoritism or partiality, for they too will be judged by the heavenly magistrates.

What kind of rite does Paul mean in cautioning Timothy not to **lay hands**   5:22
too readily on anyone or to **share in another's sins**? Some scholars, giving at-tention to the last half of the verse, suggest that the laying on of hands was not ordination to office but reconciliation of heretics or sinners. Thus, doing this hastily, without assurance of real repentance, would be to share in their sins. It is true that Tertullian witnesses to this practice in North Africa toward the end of the second century, but everywhere else in the Pastorals the laying on of hands has to do with ordination. Hence that is the meaning to be retained here. The sense is quite like that of 1 Tim 3:6, 10: bishops and deacons must be of proven character before they are installed. The need for leadership in a young community can easily impel one to appoint persons with little track record of virtue. But to do so is to risk being responsible for their later abuse of the office and even for their personal sins. Haste can be a sin of imprudence with rotten fruits later in the ministry of those chosen. Pseudo-Isocrates, in his letter to Demonicus, which has so many parallels to the Pastorals, writes: "When you are placed in authority, do not employ any unworthy person in your administration; for people will blame you for any mistakes which he may make."[11] Obviously, one can never have absolute certainty of the future probity and success of a candidate, for even among the Twelve one turned traitor, another denied his Master, and all fled. But the point here is to exercise the maximum of prudence in the selection of those to be ordained.

The counsel to **have a little wine for the sake of your stomach and your fre-**   5:23
quent illnesses seems logically out of place but not surprising in this somewhat

---

10. God in Heb 12:23; Christ in John 5:22, 27; 2 Cor 5:10; the angels in Dan 7:10.
11. *To Demonicus* 37.

disjointed letter. On the other hand, Paul may have intended a corrective to a possible misinterpretation of "keep yourself pure" immediately preceding. Timothy might take it in an ascetic sense, like the Nazirites or the Rechabites who abstained from wine, symbol of the settled life (Num 6; Jer 35:5–6). But Paul knows Timothy's delicate health, and he accepts the universal opinion of the age that wine has multiple medicinal benefits. The good Samaritan used it with oil on the wounded man on the roadside (Luke 10:34).

5:24–25   After this parenthesis, Paul returns to the theme of sins discussed in 1 Tim 5:22. If Timothy has to deal with candidates whose **sins are public**, these sins have already preceded them, and Timothy then knows something of their character. Nothing is said here about candidates who have repented of their public sins, but we can at least say that a previous scandalous life should be a red flag, urging great caution, if not rejection of the candidate. Others come forward with their sins trailing behind them, either because their previous sins come to light only later or because they fall into sin after their ordination. In this case too, careful screening is called for, perhaps even more so because the candidate's weaknesses may not be immediately evident. The same is true, on the positive side, of **good works**. Some are publicly known from the very beginning: it is easier, then, to judge the aptness of the candidate. The good works of others may not have been so public, but a close examination will uncover them. These are general principles, which the context suggests should be applied to the selection of candidates for ordination, either as bishops, priests, or deacons. In part they echo sayings of Jesus that hidden things, good or bad, will sooner or later come to light (Matt 5:14; 10:26).

Reflection and Application (5:17–25)

Paul's counsels read like a checklist for entrance to seminaries even today. But whatever ministry one has—whether bishop, priest, deacon, religious education director, catechist, music minister, extraordinary minister of Holy Communion, or any other Church ministry—one is a public person, representing the Church. One's life should therefore reflect the holiness of the Church. While this does not mean one must be a canonizable saint, it does mean that one should be striving not only to minister but to grow in holiness. Above all, those approved for ministry should not be a source of scandal. In the light of recent crises in the Church, this directive of the apostle is all the more meaningful.

Paul also envisions the possibility that a presbyter might be accused of misconduct. He follows the biblical requirement that an accusation must be

On Admission to the Seminary

LIVING TRADITION

Canon Law stipulates that "the diocesan bishop is to admit to the major seminary only those who are judged capable of dedicating themselves permanently to the sacred ministries in light of their human, moral, spiritual and intellectual characteristics, their physical and psychological health and their proper motivation" (Canon 241). Canon Law also lists a number of physical, moral, or conditional impediments that would bar a man from ordination (Canons 1041–42).

supported by two or three witnesses, since it is possible that an accuser may have a personal vendetta against the accused. Each situation, of course, requires pastoral discernment on the part of Church authority. One may wonder about the discipline that requires the immediate removal of a minister on the basis of a single, unsupported accusation. It seems that this puts the accused under the presumption of being guilty until proven innocent. However, just as a police officer may be placed on administrative leave while his role in a shooting is investigated, so likewise the Church often removes a minister from his post until the charge of misconduct can be resolved. Unfortunately, some bishops failed to follow the rules Paul lays down here and failed to properly discipline priests engaged in sexual misconduct, treating them with favoritism.

Final Directives: Slaves, Truth, Riches

1 Timothy 6

The elderly, the widows, the deacons—we find these groups in the Church today as much as Timothy found them in his. But what about that other category of the faithful in Paul's day: slaves? Was there such a thing as Christian slaves? Or worse yet: Christian masters? This chapter deals first with that issue, then with the false teachers who use their teaching to make money, contrasted with the ideals that Timothy should pursue, then a final recommendation and greeting.

Christians Who Are Slaves (6:1–2a)

[1]Those who are under the yoke of slavery must regard their masters as worthy of full respect, so that the name of God and our teaching may not suffer abuse. [2a]Those whose masters are believers must not take advantage of them because they are brothers but must give better service because those who will profit from their work are believers and are beloved.

OT: Exod 12:43–44; 21:1–11; Deut 16:11–12; 23:16–17
NT: 1 Cor 7:21–24; Gal 3:28; Eph 6:5–9; Col 3:22–25; 4:1; Titus 2:9–10; Philem 15–18
Catechism: slavery (2414)

6:1   To understand this section we need to remove the lenses that color our understanding of slavery according to eighteenth- and nineteenth-century Western norms and put on the lens of first-century Hellenistic and Roman society. Slavery was not limited to any ethnic group; hence race had nothing

Slavery in the Family History

LIVING TRADITION

Slavery was practiced widely well into the nineteenth century and is still widespread in some countries today. It was the great issue of the Civil War in the United States, where many slaveholders were Christians. My great-grandfather on my father's side, a Catholic Irish immigrant, had slaves; my great-grandfather on my mother's side did not, for he didn't believe in slavery, though he fought for the South in the Civil War. I have in my files the notes he made about the slavery he knew. He mentions that a strong, young male slave would bring around twelve hundred dollars on the market, a considerable price in those days. Those notes also mention that his father, who did not have slaves, so admired a neighbor's slave named Thomas that he named his son George *Thomas* Coleman. My parents gave me that middle name too, the name of a slave admired by my great-great-grandfather. I am proud to bear it.

to do with it. Education of slaves was encouraged, and some of them were better educated than their owners. Many slaves had high administrative duties; Erastus, the "city treasurer" mentioned in Rom 16:23, was very likely legally a slave yet was the most distinguished member of the Corinthian community. Slaves could own property, even other slaves. They were not prohibited public assembly. Nor were they generally in the state of slavery forever, for they could expect to be emancipated by the age of thirty or forty. When the slaves of a Roman citizen were emancipated, they were ordinarily given Roman citizenship. Tradition has it that Pope Callistus had at one time been a slave. But the slave was not his own master, and many of them lived and worked in brutal conditions in mines, agriculture, ships, and households.

The New Testament neither explicitly approves nor condemns the institution of slavery, but it proclaims the equality of all, slave and free, in Christ (Gal 3:28). That was something new. It is unrealistic to imagine that the seedling Church, trying to adjust within its own ranks to this newness, would lead a social campaign to eliminate slavery from an empire in which even the slaves who rebelled in Rome (between 140 and 170 BC) were not trying to abolish the institution as such but only, as prisoners of war, to escape and if possible to enslave their owners. Instead, the new community of love focused upon virtuous behavior on the part of both master (Col 4:1) and slave (3:22–25). Paul's concern for Onesimus in the letter to Philemon reflects his own attitude toward the master-slave relationship. Paul does not openly ask Philemon to emancipate Onesimus, although that avenue is laid open as a possibility, but to receive him

The Lot of Slaves

BIBLICAL BACKGROUND

So how did one come to be a slave? Capture in war often peopled the victor's land with many slaves. When the Greek-speaking king of Syria Antiochus III lost a war with Rome in 188 BC, slaves were brought to the capital of the empire as prisoners, among them many Jews. Vespasian took six thousand prisoners in the Jewish war and sent them as slaves to Nero for work digging a canal across the Corinthian isthmus. Other persons became slaves simply by being kidnapped and sold. Still others fell into unpayable debt and sold themselves into slavery, usually according to a contract for a certain number of years. Some did this simply because their lives of poverty were so miserable they preferred to belong to someone's household, even as a slave. Children who were abandoned and exposed by their parents, if found alive, were sometimes adopted as slaves. At times parents sold their children, especially their daughters, into slavery. Finally, there were those born into slavery, that is, of parents who were slaves. Slavery was so important a factor in the society and economy of the first-century Mediterranean world that scholars estimate that one third of the populace of the major cities were slaves. In short, slavery was largely an economic arrangement.[a]

    The slave was his master's property (a "body"), and the owner was free to do with him or her what he wished with impunity. Sexual abuse, even death, was within the unchallenged power of the master. Obviously the manner of treating slaves differed greatly from owner to owner. When the head of a household became Christian, the whole household frequently followed suit, including the slaves,[b] but there were cases where the slave was Christian and his owner was not. First Timothy 6:2a supposes both possibilities. If some masters were known for cruelty, slaves were also known for lying, so much so that laws required their testimony in court to be verified by torture.

a. See Muhammad A. Dandamayev and S. Scott Bartchy, "Slavery," in *The Anchor Bible Dictionary*, ed. David Noel Freedman et al. (New York: Doubleday, 1992), 6:58–73.
b. Acts 16:15, 31–34; 18:8; 1 Cor 1:16; 16:15.

---

back "no longer as a slave but more than a slave, a brother" (Philem 16). By the end of the first century, Clement of Rome points to the heroic love shown by many Christians who sold themselves into slavery so that the money they gained might be used to feed the hungry![1]

    Here in 1 Timothy, only the slaves are discussed, not the masters. Their status is a **yoke**, a traditional symbol of servitude, indicating Paul's awareness that this

1. *1 Clement* 55.

condition is not what most people would prefer. It is possible that Paul is referring to presbyters who are slaves but who should not, because of their position in the Church, despise their **masters**. From what we have just seen about the social status of slaves, such an advancement would not be unusual in the Hellenistic world; Pliny refers to two women deacons who were slaves.[2] More likely, however, Paul is simply referring to all slaves in the Christian community. They are not merely to give their masters "servile" obedience but more than that, **full respect**, because they deserve it—a strange thing for Paul to say in light of what he knows of occasional abusive masters. Paul does not specify why the masters deserve respect, though we may assume it is the principle of authority, which he upholds elsewhere, even if it abused those under it (Rom 13:1). But we can assume that, on the part of the slave, the foundation for respect would not be the virtue of their masters but the slaves' consecration to Christ, who, though Lord and Master, became a slave and gave his life as a ransom for all (Mark 10:45; Col 3:24).

In light of the specific situation in the community of Ephesus, Paul points to two other motives. (1) The honor of **the name of God**: Paul's Jewish heritage emerges here, for the honor of the Lord's name was at stake in the Israelites' relation with the Gentiles (Ezek 36:17–20). And even more so does the New Testament insist on the message that Christian behavior sends to outsiders, for edification or for scandal (Matt 5:16; 1 Tim 3:7; Titus 2:5; 1 Pet 4:4). The way the slave behaves either honors or dishonors the name of God. (2) Christian **teaching**: the masters who know nothing of the Christian faith would come to know it first by the behavior of their Christian slaves, for praise or blame. The reputation would then fall back on the Christian formation the slave received, hence on the gospel.

Where the masters are Christian **believers**, the relationship becomes more delicate, because in the Lord and at the Eucharistic table master and slave are equals—they are both slaves of Christ! And that makes them **brothers**. But this situation could easily lead the Christian slave to presume, in the household or work setting, to override the conventional boundaries. Instead of breaking the bond with his master, the *agapē* that both enjoy should draw them closer together (**believers** and **beloved** evoke both faith and charity), and the slave should express this by an even greater devotedness. In virtue of this new relationship, what the slave gives and the master receives is no longer payment but gift. The NAB's **those who will profit** ("those who benefit" in RSV, NIV, and NRSV) hardly does justice to the Greek expression, which means the receiving of an unmerited favor. It was used in the Hellenistic world at times for the emperor's

6:2a

2. *Letters* 96.

bestowal of a magnanimous gift upon his subjects. Understood this way, it is the slave who is the benefactor, endowing his master with his service as gift. In the Lord, therefore, there is an equality by which the slave is "no longer . . . a slave but . . . a brother, beloved" (Philem 16). Thus, serving lovingly and without coercion, the slave typifies better than the master that service of charity that Paul enjoins (Gal 5:13) and Jesus exemplifies (Mark 10:45; John 13:1–16).

Reflection and Application (6:1–2a)

Unfortunately in the history of Christianity, masters were not always bene-factors of their slaves, as Paul himself was well aware (Col 4:1). Often passages like these were appealed to in order to maintain a system that in the secular order did not reflect the equality and brotherhood called for in the Christian community. But the point applicable today to all civic and social relationships, especially the employer-employee relationship, is this: the bond of justice, the covenant by which persons are bound with rights and duties, is crowned with another kind of bond—that of love, a love born of Jesus Christ, who showed that love by becoming a servant, by washing the feet of his disciples. Around the Eucharistic table in the earliest Christian communities all were equal, all were brothers and sisters, no matter what their social rank or economic ties. And that community of love could not help but spill over into the world outside, not to be blind to justice but to enable and ennoble it with love.

The Church's Teaching on Slavery

LIVING TRADITION

In our passage Paul discusses only the attitude and behavior of slaves. He balances this in Col 4:1 by saying, "Masters, treat your slaves justly and fairly, realizing that you too have a Master in heaven." The teaching of the Church today is very clear. The Catechism states (2414): "The seventh commandment forbids acts or enterprises that for any reason—selfish or ideological, commercial, or totalitarian—lead to the *enslavement of human beings*, to their being bought, sold and exchanged like merchandise, in disregard for their personal dignity. It is a sin against the dignity of persons and their fundamental rights to reduce them by violence to their productive value or to a source of profit. St. Paul directed a Christian master to treat his Christian slave 'no longer as a slave but more than a slave, as a beloved brother, . . . both in the flesh and in the Lord' [Philem 16]" (emphasis original).

There is something of a parallel here with Jesus' counsel to his disciples: "Should anyone press you into service for one mile, go with him for two miles" (Matt 5:41). Roman soldiers in Palestine were permitted to requisition the native population for service. Thus a soldier could nab a Jew and force him to carry his gear for a mile. If the disciple of Jesus volunteered to carry it an extra mile, the soldier might very well ask what motivated such a generous offer, and this shift of the relationship from compulsion to charity could give the disciple a chance to speak to the soldier about Jesus, who carried our burdens to the cross.

False Teaching and True Wealth (6:2b–10)

> [2b]Teach and urge these things. [3]Whoever teaches something different and does not agree with the sound words of our Lord Jesus Christ and the religious teaching [4]is conceited, understanding nothing, and has a morbid disposition for arguments and verbal disputes. From these come envy, rivalry, insults, evil suspicions, [5]and mutual friction among people with corrupted minds, who are deprived of the truth, supposing religion to be a means of gain. [6]Indeed, religion with contentment is a great gain. [7]For we brought nothing into the world, just as we shall not be able to take anything out of it. [8]If we have food and clothing, we shall be content with that. [9]Those who want to be rich are falling into temptation and into a trap and into many foolish and harmful desires, which plunge them into ruin and destruction. [10]For the love of money is the root of all evils, and some people in their desire for it have strayed from the faith and have pierced themselves with many pains.

OT: Job 1:21; Ps 49:14–21; Eccles 5:12–16
NT: Matt 6:19–21, 24–34; 7:15–20; 10:9–10; Mark 10:17–27; 11:15–19; James 5:1–6
Catechism: incredulity and heresy (2089), immoderate love of riches (2445)
Lectionary: (6:6–11, 17–19) Mass for a Country or City and for Those Who Serve in Public Office; Mass after the Harvest

For the third time in this letter Paul comes back to the false teachers. His first words may be simply the kind of repetition characteristic of dictation. Normally they would refer to the directives just given, though they may also point to what follows. **Whoever teaches something different** can be identified by not clinging to the **words of our Lord Jesus Christ**. This supposes that Paul, Timothy, and the faithful of Ephesus have at their disposal oral and probably written sayings of Jesus. Some of these may be embedded in stories about Jesus that circulated before being incorporated into our Gospels. That Paul knew of

6:2b–3

such sayings is clear from his much earlier letter to the Corinthians, where he distinguishes between his teaching and that which comes directly from Jesus (1 Cor 7:10–12). If the author is later than Paul, he may have had an early form of one of the synoptic Gospels at hand. In any case we can see that the words of Jesus were considered the authoritative foundation for resolving any issue. The "reading" to which Paul referred in 1 Tim 4:13 would certainly have included these words. The teaching of the apostles builds on these words with "teaching that leads to godliness," which the NAB simplifies as **the religious teaching**.

6:4–5   The first negative mark of the false teacher, **conceited**, suggests that he is deluded or blinded by the smoke of his own importance. He **understand[s] nothing** and **has a morbid disposition for arguments and verbal disputes**. This inane thirst for speculation leads to a number of vices, the first of which is **envy**. Sterile competition betrays a desire simply to win an argument, to put down the opponent, to stand in solitary splendor over one's defeated adversaries. Worse yet are personal attacks, verbal abuse, name calling, slanderous claims, and suspicions of the most serious kind. A further effect is the **mutual friction** that contaminates minds. Saint John Chrysostom's commentary is often cited here: like sheep with a skin disease contaminating the rest of the flock by rubbing against them, these people corrupt others by fostering conflicts.[3] The metaphors of health and sickness continue here. These unfortunate people are unable to react positively to the truth. In 2 Thess 2:10 Paul attributes the refusal of some to believe in the gospel to their refusal of a prior grace—the grace of *loving* the truth. If one does not have a basic orientation toward the light, seeking it with all one's being, the light will appear as a threat to one's self-made world.

In the text here, Paul seems to be targeting people who use **religion** as a business, for financial gain. T. S. Eliot remarked, "Those who serve the greater cause may make the cause serve them" (*Murder in the Cathedral*, part 1). Paul himself, of course, took up a collection in his churches for the poor in Jerusalem, and he often received financial help from his faithful, especially when he was in prison (Phil 4:10–14). But it is another thing to use religion simply to make money.

6:6–8   Real religion does bring **great gain**, but it demands of those who profess it a simplicity of lifestyle. The gain it brings is the promise of eternal life, but even in this life the assurance that God will supply one's needs (Matt 6:24–34; Mark 10:29–30). On the part of its practitioners, religion's real benefit demands inner freedom regarding material wealth, being content with the necessities of life. The Greek word *autarkeia* (**contentment**) was a common philosophical term

3. *Homilies on 1 Timothy* 6:5.

for independence from material goods. Paul agrees with Job and the Wisdom tradition: "Naked I came forth from my mother's womb, / and naked shall I go back again" (Job 1:21). All that one has gained one must ultimately forfeit, hence the absurdity of making wealth the goal of one's life. What one needs for life is very little: food and clothing. Jesus told his disciples to pray just for the bread they need today (Luke 11:3) and not to "worry about your life, what you will eat [or drink], or about your body, what you will wear" (Matt 6:25), "for life is more than food and the body more than clothing" (Luke 12:23). Jesus was echoing the teaching of Prov 30:8 ("Give me neither poverty nor riches") and Sir 26:4 ("Be he rich or poor, his heart is content"). The Bible repeatedly warns against the danger of riches: "The lover of gold will not be free from sin, / for he who pursues wealth is led astray by it."[4]

First Timothy 6:9 specifies the problem as *wanting* **to be rich**, that interior, insatiable cupidity for gain: "The struggle for wealth blinds the eyes" (Sir 27:1). Those who love wealth have already fallen into temptation, but it is a temptation that brings other temptations with it (a wordplay is perhaps intended in the Greek terms *peirasmos* [**temptation**] in 1 Tim 6:9 and *porismos* ["gain"] in 6:5). Thus the lover of wealth is trapped into a maze of other desires that are both foolish and harmful. **Foolish** echoes Jesus' story about the avaricious rich man: "You fool, this night your life will be demanded of you" (Luke 12:20). **Harmful** suggests that greed brings with it other sins or at least painful, hurtful consequences. As a matter of fact, these desires act like a storm or overloading that sinks a ship (the technical meaning of the verb **plunge**; see Luke 5:7). What is lost may not always be one's wealth, but, more gravely, one's person, one's eternal salvation: "What profit would there be for one to gain the whole world and forfeit his life?" (Matt 16:26). To complete the sinking image, the lover of wealth must decide to abandon ship or he will go down with it. In an alternative image, Sirach warns that those who buy and sell must earnestly hold fast to the fear of the Lord or else "suddenly your house will be thrown down" (27:3).

The love of money may not be the only root of evil, but it is the most common and evident one. And some (Paul here is talking about Christians!) have been led not only to vice but even to an abandoning of the faith. One thinks of Judas or Ananias and Sapphira (Acts 5:1–11). Paul himself will experience the pain caused by Demas who, "enamored of the present world," deserted him (2 Tim 4:10). The specific persons Paul apparently has in mind are the false teachers who have not openly rebelled against the faith but, yielding to cupidity, little by little strayed from the fold and are promoting a pseudoreligion for

6:9

6:10

---

4. Sir 31:5; see also Prov 15:27; Matt 6:24; Mark 4:19; Luke 12:13–15; James 5:1.

profit. Their experience will be that of the lovers of wealth in general: not only final shipwreck but even now the self-inflicted pains that St. Thomas Aquinas describes thus: "They have pierced themselves with many pains, even in the present, because they experience anxiety in acquiring, fear in possessing, sorrow in losing."[5]

Reflection and Application (6:2b–10)

In San Antonio, Texas, for many years Raul Jimenez, a restaurant owner, fed thousands of people for free every Thanksgiving day. When the Archbishop said, "Raul, at this rate you will go bankrupt," he replied, "Archbishop, I have never seen a hearse pulling a U-Haul!" No, but thousands attended his funeral.

Paul Coaches Timothy for the Battle (6:11–16)

[11]**But you, man of God, avoid all this. Instead, pursue righteousness, devotion, faith, love, patience, and gentleness. [12]Compete well for the faith. Lay hold of eternal life, to which you were called when you made the noble confession in the presence of many witnesses. [13]I charge [you] before God, who gives life to all things, and before Christ Jesus, who gave testimony under Pontius Pilate for the noble confession, [14]to keep the commandment without stain or reproach until the appearance of our Lord Jesus Christ [15]that the blessed and only ruler will make manifest at the proper time, the King of kings and Lord of lords, [16]who alone has immortality, who dwells in unapproachable light, and whom no human being has seen or can see. To him be honor and eternal power. Amen.**

OT: Exod 33:20; Deut 10:17; 2 Macc 13:4
NT: John 1:18; 1 Cor 9:24–27; Gal 5:22–23; Eph 6:10–13; 2 Tim 4:1, 7–8; Rev 17:14
Catechism: spiritual battle (2015), perseverance (2016)

6:11   Moving toward the conclusion of his letter, Paul becomes more insistent and solemn in his personal advice to Timothy, as he addresses him with great solemnity. **Man of God** is a title that evokes at once both the high office he holds and the demands of it. Used only here and in 2 Tim 3:17, "man of God" (RSV, NIV, NRSV; "someone dedicated to God," NJB) is an Old Testament title reserved for Moses, David, and the prophets. As the man of God, Moses receives

5. Cited by Spicq, *Épîtres pastorales*, 1.565.

the revelation of the Lord (Josh 14:6), legislates in God's name (Ezra 3:2), and blesses the people (Deut 33:1). David is called man of God in the context of giving laws concerning worship (2 Chron 8:14; Neh 12:24). But it is in reference to the prophets that the title "man of God" appears most frequently (Judg 13:8; 1 Sam 2:27; 9:6; etc.). It was the role of the prophet to communicate the Lord's fresh word to his people and also to communicate the people's need to the Lord by interceding for them (Jer 15:11). Hence "man of God" connotes a prophetic authority, which means being a channel of God's will for his people and of the people's needs to God.

From this and what follows we can glimpse something of the situation Timothy is in. Confronted with difficulties, especially the pseudoteachers, he may be tempted to become discouraged and indecisive, and Paul wants to reaffirm his divine call and hearten him to act courageously upon it. He is not only to flee the greed of the false teachers; he is to **pursue**, "compete," and "lay hold"—three commands ticked off like a coach giving a disheartened player a pep talk and sending him or her back on the field. **Righteousness** refers to right relationships with God and with the people Timothy is pastoring. **Devotion** is the frequent *eusebeia* of the Pastorals, that quality that refers not only to his personal piety but to his regulation of the worship of the communities as well (1 Tim 2:2).

We might expect to see attached to **faith** and **love** the third member of the traditional trio, hope. Instead we find **patience**. However, the Greek word *hypomonē*, often also translated "endurance," is so closely related to hope that it can almost stand for it. Paul speaks of the "endurance in hope" (1 Thess 1:3); "by endurance . . . we might have hope" (Rom 15:4). It is as if hope proves itself through endurance. Hope in Paul's writings does not mean the kind of wishful thinking the word has come to mean in our language, as when we say, "I hope it doesn't rain on our picnic." It is rather divine assurance that fires indomitable perseverance. **Gentleness** is the virtue that makes the pastor accessible, as it did in Jesus: "Come to me, all you who labor and are burdened. . . . Learn from me, for I am meek and humble of heart" (Matt 11:28–29, where "meek" reflects the same Greek word rendered "gentleness" in 1 Tim 6:11). But it is also the virtue that Paul recommends when it is necessary to correct others (2 Cor 10:1; Gal 6:1), a task those in leadership positions are frequently required to do.

In 4:7 Paul told Timothy to *train* himself for godliness. Here he must go into the arena and *fight* for it. Combat imagery would appeal to the Hellenistic mind, shaped as it was by love of competitive sports, so it is not surprising that Paul would use it frequently (1 Cor 9:25; Col 1:29; 1 Tim 4:10; 2 Tim 4:7). In Eph 6:10–17 Paul develops a long metaphor detailing the weapons to be

    6:12

used in spiritual combat. In Christian tradition there are many images for the growth of the Christian life: a journey, ascending a mountain, following Jesus, purification, illumination, a deepening union. The combat image is less popular today, perhaps because it suggests violence. Yet Jesus said, "The kingdom of heaven suffers violence, and the violent are taking it by force" (Matt 11:12); and he demands of his followers a certain violence to self if one is to experience the new life of grace (Mark 8:34–38). Still, the fight is "beautiful." NAB's **compete well for the faith** loses something of the power of the Greek, which literally says, "Fight the beautiful fight of the faith." The combat of the faith is very different from the kind of disruptive quarreling that Paul described in 1 Tim 6:4–5. Seeking the truth in love (Eph 4:15), its aim is ultimately unity in love. But there are times when the price is costly, when hard decisions have to be made, when one's personal preferences must be sacrificed, when evil must be confronted, when one's fears must be overcome. It is much harder to work for truth and unity, for human and spiritual solidarity, than it is to respond with violence.

The third command Paul gives is to **lay hold of eternal life**. Since Timothy has done so in his previous commitment to Christ, the sense here could be "don't lose your grip on the eternal life you have already embraced" or "grasp it even more firmly." On the other hand, Paul himself in Phil 3:12–13 says he has not yet laid hold of final union with Christ in the resurrection but presses on toward the goal. He would thus be encouraging Timothy to do the same. The **noble**, or beautiful, **confession** of faith **in the presence of many witnesses** may have been at the occasion of his ordination at Paul's hands (2 Tim 1:6), but more likely it refers to his profession of faith at baptism. Initiation into the faith in the early Church was not a private thing, even less so was it secretive. Other Christians stood by, supporting the convert and praying for his or her perseverance in the sacred and permanent engagement undertaken.

6:13   Having mentioned witnesses, Paul's thought moves to **charge** Timothy in the sight of two other witnesses. Two witnesses were required to sustain any accusation (Deut 19:15; Matt 18:16), but here it is less a matter of accusation than of solemn adjuration, the kind of oath one would take today in assuming a public office. And the witnesses are not the human witnesses who originally surrounded Timothy. The two witnesses are God and Jesus Christ. **God** is not only "the living and true God" to whom the convert turns (1 Thess 1:9), but the God **who gives life to all**, the God without whom nothing else would exist. As for **Christ Jesus**, in the context of public **testimony** (our English word "martyr" comes from the Greek word used here) Paul could have evoked Jesus' resurrection or his second coming, which would have been more than enough warrant. Instead he points to the **noble confession** that Jesus gave **under Pontius Pilate**. This could refer to what Jesus said before Pilate about his kingship (Matt 27:11; John 18:37) or to his bearing witness to the truth (18:37). But it can also mean the heroic death that was the outcome of that testimony, just as later martyrs would be pronouncing their own death sentence by their public confession (see the letter of Pliny the Younger cited in the sidebar at 1 Tim 3:11). Indeed, Jesus referred to his death as a baptism (Mark 10:38–39), and early Christians, in the shadow of the Roman sword, considered their baptism as a solemn oath to be ready to die for Christ. We hardly think of baptism that way today, but that is what it meant then, and it would mean the same today in countries where to become a Christian is to invite death. Paul could not have thought of a graver way to speak his mind to Timothy. The oath that Timothy took at his baptism and that Paul now enjoins once more is witnessed not only by the life-giving God but by "the faithful and true witness" (Rev 3:14), Jesus, the risen Lord who bears the marks of his own bloody testimony, the act by which he loved his own unto the end (John 13:1; Gal 2:20; Rev 1:5). Hence it is less the fear of judgment weighing over Timothy as it is the awesome gift of infinite love.

That is why Timothy must hold the **commandment** tightly. What com- | **6:14**
mandment? If this were a letter of John the Evangelist, we would expect it to be the commandment of love (John 14:15, 21; 15:12). Although Paul himself said that the whole law is fulfilled by love (Gal 5:14), the baptismal context seems to suggest more. The commandment certainly includes the directives Paul has given in the letter, particularly about right teaching, but could hardly be limited to that, since the solemnity of the context indicates divine, not merely Pauline, sanction. That is why most scholars say that the command simply means the entire Christian gospel: "All that I have commanded you" (Matt 28:20). It is this that Timothy must guard **without stain or reproach**, two synonyms that amount to a superlative: "absolutely pure" or "perfectly spotless." It is the kind of purity that James says is the authentic religion (James 1:27), the kind of purity that is the mark of the bride of Christ in her final glory (Eph 5:27).

This view of final glory appears in the last phrase of the verse, as the goal of all Timothy's striving: **the appearance of our Lord Jesus Christ**. Whoever wrote this letter (and the other Pastorals as well; see 2 Tim 4:8 and Titus 2:13) clearly believed in the second coming of Christ as the climax of the Christian life. That coming is described here as an epiphany, the kind of glorious manifestation that the Hellenistic world associated with the magnanimous arrival of the emperor to a city. Paul elsewhere calls it the parousia (1 Thess 2:19; 3:13; 4:15; etc.).

6:15   The thought of Christ's coming leads Paul into a crescendo, a hymn he may have known from an early liturgy or one he may have composed on the spur of the moment. The second coming will happen **at the proper time**—perhaps a caution to those impatient for its arrival or attempting to guess what has not been revealed (Acts 1:6–7). **Ruler** is a late Old Testament title for God (Sir 46:5 LXX; translated "Sovereign" in 2 Macc 12:15). But our text does not specify whether the ruler is God or Christ. In the Roman Empire **blessed**, or "happy," was a frequent attribute of imperial power. For that reason there is special interest here in the expression **only ruler**. "You would have no power over me," Jesus said to Pilate, "if it had not been given to you from above" (John 19:11). Whereas in Rom 13:1–7 Paul says that human authority has been established by God, for a Church menaced with persecution by the Roman authorities, it would be bold indeed to say that God or Christ is the *only* ruler. The Greek for **King of kings and Lord of lords** here is not the same as in Rev 17:14 and 19:16. It reads literally "King of those reigning and Lord of those exercising sovereignty." The present tense indicates those who are at the present time exercising power. In the Roman world this was a dangerous confession to make. While the Church must pray for kings and all in authority, there are times when one must obey God rather than men (Acts 5:29, 32).

6:16   The contrast with reigning potentates continues. In affirming that God **alone has immortality** Paul is not thinking of the angels here or the glorified body of Christians (1 Cor 15:53–54) but of the pretenses of emperors to what God alone possesses. Despite their humanness, emperors like Tiberius and Caligula were held to be immortal. Already in the Old Testament, **light** is one of the things most associated with divinity. God creates light and in that light creates everything else (Gen 1:3). Light dwells with him (Dan 2:22). He robes himself with light (Ps 104:2). He *is* light (1 John 1:5) and the Father of lights (James 1:17). This light makes him **unapproachable** to the human eye, like a mountain that cannot be scaled: "no man sees me and still lives" (Exod 33:20); "none can see him, however wise their hearts" (Job 37:24); "no one has ever seen God" (John 1:18). The New Testament holds out the assurance that the faithful in the future life will enjoy the light of God (Rev 22:5) because they will see him face to face; but in this life even they see darkly and imperfectly (1 Cor 13:12). This is quite a contrast to the mortal emperors frequently shown with rays of light shining from their heads. The finale acclaims the one to whom all **honor and eternal power** belong.

Reflection and Application (6:11–16)

Paul frequently concludes a topic with a doxology, a prayer of praise. This habit comes from his Jewish heritage, but it also shows us how Paul lives constantly in an attitude of praise. "I will bless the LORD at all times; / praise shall be always in my mouth" (Ps 34:2). Often in the doxology he looks to the final consummation of the divine plan, as he does here. Earthly powers are not to be feared, no matter what vaunted claims they may make. God alone and his Christ are the rulers of heaven and earth. Good theology, too, should lead to doxology, as my Dominican professors manifested by ending their lectures with a prayer of thanksgiving and praise.

Treasures to Come and a Final Word (6:17–21)

> [17]Tell the rich in the present age not to be proud and not to rely on so uncertain a thing as wealth but rather on God, who richly provides us with all things for our enjoyment. [18]Tell them to do good, to be rich in good works, to be generous, ready to share, [19]thus accumulating as treasure a good foundation for the future, so as to win the life that is true life.
> [20]O Timothy, guard what has been entrusted to you. Avoid profane babbling and the absurdities of so-called knowledge. [21]By professing it, some people have deviated from the faith.
> Grace be with all of you.

OT: Deut 30:19
NT: Matt 6:19–21; Luke 12:16–21; 16:19–31; 2 Thess 2:15; 3:6; 2 Tim 1:12–14; Titus 1:9
Catechism: apostolic Tradition (83), deposit of faith (84), magisterium (85–87)

If you were in Paul's shoes and wanted to leave a parting word, what would   6:17
it be? Would it be a summary of everything you have said in the letter? Would it be to add a lesser point that you had forgotten to mention? Or would it be capsule advice that Timothy should carry with him throughout his life? This is the way Paul wraps up his letter to his "dear child" Timothy and to the church that will also hear this letter read.

After the previous doxology this segment looks like a postscript. Scholars who like consistency propose either that it is an interpolation or that it should go somewhere else in the letter, for example, after the treatment of the love of riches in 6:10. But doxologies in the middle of a letter are not foreign to Paul (Rom 9:5; 11:36; Gal 1:5; Eph 3:20–21). Moreover, this somewhat disjointed letter may reveal the quirks of dictation. Perhaps, as Ceslas Spicq suggests, Paul on rereading his letter up to this point felt he needed to say something more positive about the use of wealth to complement his negative statements in 1 Tim 6:10.[6] He, after all, frequently received gifts in money or kind from generous benefactors, some of them wealthy. It is probable that by the time this letter was written there was a considerable number of wealthy Christians in Ephesus. He calls them **rich in the present age**, since he is going to contrast them with those who are acquiring wealth for the age to come. Those who are rich in the present world are easily tempted to be haughty, to look down on the poor, even to treat them as inferior. To avoid this snobbery they need to learn to have the mind of the lowly (Eph 4:2), whom God exalts (Luke 1:51–53). Besides the temptation **to be proud,** they tend to **rely on** their riches—**so uncertain a thing**—**rather** than **on God,** like the man who says to himself, "'You have so many good things stored up for many years, rest, eat, drink, be merry!' But God said to him, 'You fool, this night your life will be demanded of you; and the things you have prepared, to whom will they belong?'" (Luke 12:19–20). Learn from him who is richest of all, and see what he does with his wealth—he shares it magnanimously to make others happy. As the poor look to human benefactors to supply their needs, we look to God, who supplies **us with all things for our enjoyment.** This more positive view of earthly benefits corrects the false asceticism of those teachers denounced in 1 Tim 4:3–5. Hilaire Belloc is noted for his poem: "Wherever the Catholic sun doth shine, / There's always laughter and good red wine. / At least I've always found it so. / *Benedicamus Domino!*"

6:18   Those more blessed with earthly goods ordinarily would have more resources to help others and thus **to be rich in good works,** to serve the Church and those in need. Paul plays on the word "rich," using it four times in these two verses, moving from material wealth to spiritual. Material wealth is amassed by getting, spiritual wealth by giving. The Greek word *koinōnikos* (**ready to share**) has several levels of meaning. It can mean social awareness, but more often in community contexts it means sharing goods in common, as Josephus tells us the Essenes did[7] and as Acts 4:32 tells us the early Jerusalem community did. That seems to be the meaning here: realize that you are part of a larger body, and, since people are more important than things or money, use your wealth to create community.

6:19   The previous verse is a summary of one of the major themes of Luke. The one who amasses material wealth has an uncertain future despite his efforts

6. Ibid., 1.575.
7. *Jewish War* 2.122.

The Deposit of the Faith

LIVING TRADITION

The expression Paul uses in 1 Tim 6:19, translated in the NAB as "what has been entrusted," is but a single noun in the Greek. It is the scriptural basis for what the Church has called the *depositum fidei* ("the deposit of the faith"). Already Irenaeus (AD 140–202) wrote: "We guard with care the faith that we received from the Church, for without ceasing, under the action of God's Spirit, this deposit of great price, as if in an excellent vessel, is constantly being renewed and causes the very vessel that contains it to be renewed."[a] The Second Vatican Council also spoke of this deposit as a combination of Scripture and Tradition: "Sacred tradition and Sacred Scripture form one sacred deposit of the word of God, committed to the Church. Holding fast to this deposit the entire holy people united with their shepherds remain always steadfast in the teaching of the Apostles, in the common life, in the breaking of the bread and in prayers (see Acts 2:42, Greek text), so that holding to, practicing and professing the heritage of the faith, it becomes on the part of the bishops and faithful a single common effort" (*Dei Verbum* 10).

a. *Against Heresies* 3.24.1.

(Luke 12:33). But whoever uses material wealth properly by generously sharing it will amass spiritual wealth. As wise stewards invest money to make more and thus provide a solid base of financial security **for the future** (see Luke 19:11–27), so the spiritually wise will dispense their wealth and accumulate a secure future in eternal life (16:9). Invest now in your retirement fund—the real retirement fund!

O Timothy, Paul exclaims, with unusual affection and urgency. What Timothy has received from Paul is a sacred trust. The word "deposit," given in some translations for **what has been entrusted to you**, was used for entrusting money or words or secrets or even a person to a third party (Lev 5:21, 23; Tob 10:13). In any case, the stress is on the trustworthiness of the receiver. For that reason, deposits were often consecrated by placing them in a temple, which served as a bank. According to the books of Maccabees, the temple of Jerusalem served as such a bank (2 Macc 3:10–11; 4 Macc 4:3–7), and so did the temple of Artemis in Ephesus, where Timothy lived. Like such a deposit, what Timothy has received is a sacred trust. It comprises the whole gospel message, which Paul has described in various ways throughout the letter. Paul's delegate is not to add or subtract, and, in the context of the major concern of this letter, he is to keep the message in its purity against the **babbling** of the false teachers. The

6:20

word *bebēlous* suggests the nonsense syllables babies use before learning words or simply endless and mindless talking, such as the Cynic Zeno complained about concerning one of his disciples, whose chatter led the master to tell him: "Your father must have been drunk when he begat you."[8]

6:21   "The absurdities" may be the teachings that deny the truths of the faith or simply the methods of discourse employed by these so-called rhetoricians, who delight in arguing (the Greek word is *antitheses*) but do not arrive at real "knowledge." The false *gnōsis* ("knowledge") may be an early form of gnosticism, but more likely it is the kind of titillation with "knowledge [that] inflates with pride," in contrast to divine "love [that] builds up" (1 Cor 8:1). Some who began as Christians in Ephesus ended up committing themselves to this heresy (**professing it**). They have, like lost sheep, strayed from the fold and **from the faith** it professes.

The final greeting is given in the plural—**all of you**—indicating that, while the letter is addressed to Timothy, Paul anticipates that it will be read publicly. This was not an uncommon practice in the Hellenistic world, when a prince or superior would write directives to his delegate. A public reading would assure two things: (1) that the delegate be held to fulfill the directives not only by the sender but also by the public who hears them; and (2) that everyone know that the delegate has authority from the sender to implement the directives.

Reflection and Application (6:17–21)

In God's eyes, wealth is meant to create community. A recent study done at the University of British Columbia and Harvard concluded that people who give generously of what they have to others are happier than those who do not. Is this surprising? Jesus said, "It is more blessed to give than to receive" (Acts 20:35). Anecdotal evidence confirms that those who tithe, whether to the Church or to the needy, enjoy a greater happiness in this life—and Jesus and Paul agree that it is also an investment in the happiness to come.

---

8. *Diogenes Laertius* 7.18.

The Second Letter to Timothy

Whether this letter was written by the historical Paul or by a later disciple, its author wants us to hear the authoritative message of the apostle and experience what he is experiencing at this eleventh hour of his life. He is in prison in Rome (see sidebar "Life of a Roman Prisoner," p. 162), between a first hearing and a final trial, with little or no hope of gaining his freedom or saving his life. He has "completed the race." And although the letter contains a number of practical directives and a hope for Timothy's arrival before winter (4:21), it is in other ways Paul's last will and testament, his farewell message, given to his closest, beloved disciple. It is somewhat like Paul's farewell address to the presbyters of the church of Ephesus in Acts 20:17–35, except that now the end appears to be imminent.

Timothy's Gifts and Paul's Lot

2 Timothy 1

If you were in prison and facing execution, how would you begin a letter to your closest friend? During my last visit to a dying fellow Brother in my community, we shared memories of our times together, full of gratitude even in the midst of the sadness at imminent parting. So here we find a mixture of shared memories and pain, particularly Paul's feeling of abandonment.

Address and Greeting (1:1–2)

> ¹Paul, an apostle of Christ Jesus by the will of God for the promise of life in Christ Jesus, ²to Timothy, my dear child: grace, mercy, and peace from God the Father and Christ Jesus our Lord.

NT: Acts 16:1–3; Rom 1:1; Phil 2:19–24; 1 Tim 1:2
Lectionary: (1:1–8) Memorial of Saints Timothy and Titus

1:1   The address is typical of Paul's addresses elsewhere and virtually the same as the address in 1 Timothy. The apostle is an ambassador of Christ not by his own choice but **by the will of God** (1 Cor 1:1; 2 Cor 1:1; Eph 1:1; Col 1:1) or the "command of God" (1 Tim 1:1), which has made him a slave of God (Titus 1:1) or of Christ (Phil 1:1). God called Paul to proclaim that in Christ the life promised by the prophets has been fulfilled (Rom 1:2) and that the **promise of** eternal **life** is now available to anyone who has faith in **Christ Jesus**. All the promises made by God in the Old Testament have found their fulfillment, their "yes," in him (2 Cor 1:20) and in the Holy Spirit, who was promised in the Old Testament and given by Jesus himself (Luke 24:49; Acts 1:8; Gal 3:14).

It is difficult for non-Jews to appreciate how central to Paul and to the Jewish Christians was the realization that God's promises were fulfilled. The Jews, unlike the Gentiles, knew they were God's people, to whom the Lord had sworn in a covenant that he would be their savior. That was a promise, God's promise; and now it has been fulfilled. That is basically what Paul means when he says that the gospel reveals the *justice* of God (Rom 1:16–17; NAB: "righteousness")—that is, not the justice he metes out to sinners but his justice to his own sworn word to save his people. God's justice, then, is the fulfillment of his promise. Here he describes the promise simply as "life," a shorter version of "the word of life" in Phil 2:16, where, ironically enough, he speaks of running the race, whose end he contemplates in this letter (2 Tim 4:7). Elsewhere this life is described as eternal (1 Tim 1:16; 6:12; Titus 3:7; John 3:15–16).

Why does Paul choose to introduce his letter by saying that he was called by God to proclaim the promise of life rather than describing his vocation in some other way? The reason is not hard to find. Facing his own imminent death, Paul chooses to reaffirm his faith that Jesus gives life, not only here but in the "far better" lot of union with Christ after death (Phil 1:23). It is remarkable that Paul speaks of Jesus three times in this brief greeting, an indication of his conviction that only through the mediation of Christ (1 Cor 1:4) and in union with him (Gal 2:20) can one truly live. It is this conviction that will inspire everything in this letter, including Paul's attitude toward his impending death.

As in 1 Tim 1:2, Paul addresses his delegate not as son but as "child," indeed as *agapētos teknon* (**dear** or beloved **child**). Though Timothy apparently was not converted by Paul (Acts 16:1), he became his first permanent collaborator, of whom Paul was able to say to the Philippians, "I have no one comparable to him for genuine interest in whatever concerns you. . . . As a child with a father he served along with me in the cause of the gospel" (Phil 2:20, 22). The metaphor here, like the others of spiritual parenting in Paul, is meant to convey the tender love that Paul feels for Timothy. As the shadow of the Roman sword reminds Paul of what really counts for eternal life—love (2 Tim 1:1; 1 Cor 13:12–13)—he tells Timothy he is deeply loved.

In the Old Testament, "beloved son" can carry the meaning "only son" or "firstborn" (Gen 22:2, 12, 16), with the right of succeeding the father and receiving the inheritance. Although Paul uses "child" instead of "son," the idea of succession can hardly be far from his mind, since Timothy will carry on Paul's work after his death and is already doing so now in Ephesus. As my

1:2

family gathered around my father's deathbed, we heard him whisper, as best he could, to my brother, the eldest son: "Take care of them." That, in short, will be Paul's message to Timothy, as it was Jesus' message to Peter: "Feed my sheep" (John 21:17).

The triple blessing that Paul wishes for Timothy—**grace, mercy, and peace**—is exactly the same as in 1 Tim 1:2 (see the commentary on this verse).

Reflection and Application (1:1–2)

That Paul chooses to call Timothy his "beloved" or "dear" child, instead of "true child" as he did in 1 Timothy and Titus, suggests something of the emotion he feels in this, his last will and testament. Many times in ministering to the dying, I have found them desperately eager for reconciliation in their families, even for embracing all with love. Paul must feel the need for that embrace with Timothy. In fact, he will ask him to come as soon as possible (4:9).

Thanksgiving (1:3–5)

³I am grateful to God, whom I worship with a clear conscience as my ancestors did, as I remember you constantly in my prayers, night and day. ⁴I yearn to see you again, recalling your tears, so that I may be filled with joy, ⁵as I recall your sincere faith that first lived in your grandmother Lois and in your mother Eunice and that I am confident lives also in you.

NT: Acts 20:37; Rom 9:1–5; 11:29; Eph 6:4, 18; Phil 3:4–5
Catechism: the Jewish people (839–40), domestic church (1655–56), parents as educators (2221–26)

1:3   Paul follows the typical format of letters of his day, and of his own letters, with a thanksgiving, which in this case is filled with memories of his past relationship with Timothy and the faith that has made him a "true child" of Paul (1 Tim 1:2). The **worship** Paul renders to God means a life of prayer and devotion (as in Rom 1:9). Adding **with a clear conscience** may well be an allusion to the injustice done him by his arrest and imprisonment. If he is in prison, it is because he was faithful to his conscience and to his proclamation of the lordship of Jesus. Was he arrested because he was considered to be a troublemaker among the Jews, or was it because hailing Jesus as King of kings and Lord of lords was a threat to Nero? At any rate he associates himself with the "cloud of witnesses"—**my ancestors**—that have gone on before him (Heb

12:1). Paul can only be referring here to his Jewish forebears, who clung to the faith even under persecution and martyrdom. Thanks to them, Paul is blessed to know the fulfillment of what they could only discern dimly, the fulfillment of the promise in Jesus Christ.

The ancient Gentile world considered the preservation of the traditions of one's ancestors to be not only a noble thing but also something associated with worship of the gods. Though the Israelites did not worship their ancestors, their worship of the true God was intimately connected with the revelation to their ancestors, as the Lord revealed himself to Moses: "I am the God of your father . . . the God of Abraham, the God of Isaac, the God of Jacob" (Exod 3:6). The Bible does not relate tales of the gods but stories of human beings to whom God reveals himself. The handing down of the faith from generation to generation forms a distant background for the importance of sacred Tradition as we find it in the Pastorals. Our text also underlines the heritage that Christians owe to the Jews, through whom salvation comes (John 4:22). Though the rapidity of change in our modern world has tended to focus attention more on what lies ahead than on the past, in the Christian community veneration of the great spiritual heroes of the past, the saints, keeps the sacredness of the past before the Church's eyes and urges fidelity to sacred Tradition in the midst of the turning world.

For Paul, to think of someone is to pray for that person (Phil 1:3). That Paul prays for Timothy **night and day** is another way of saying "unceasingly" or "constantly" (1 Thess 1:2–3; 2:13; see 5:17), fulfilling the Lord's admonition about being in a perpetual state of prayer (Luke 18:1; 21:36). One can imagine what night was like in a Roman prison, but Paul uses many of those dark hours for intercessory prayer (as he and Silas did at Philippi; Acts 16:25), particularly for his "child" who has replaced him in the care of the Ephesian community.

Fig. 6. Nero, the brutal emperor under whom Paul was martyred.

In his confinement and concern for Timothy, Paul tells of his ardent desire to **see** his disciple once **again**. He remembers the **tears** that welled up in Timothy's eyes when Paul was taken from him by the emperor's police. This parting scene must have been the one most fixed in the apostle's memory. Perhaps Paul himself is experiencing a tearful moment as he recalls Timothy's

1:4

Todd Bolen/BiblePlaces.com

139

tears. But it is balanced by the **joy** he anticipates when he will see Timothy again. The NAB's "as I recall," translating an unusual Greek construction that literally says "receiving a remembrance," suggests that Paul may have received some report or token from Timothy, perhaps a letter or a visitor, that has brought these memories to mind.

1:5   It is Timothy's **sincere faith** above all that Paul recalls, which also means an appreciation of his disciple's faithfulness as well. Timothy received this faith not from Paul but from his "grandma" (the Greek word *mammē* is the familiar form of **grandmother**) and his **mother**. Is Paul referring to their pre-Christian Jewish faith, in which Timothy was raised or simply to their becoming Christian before Timothy? Because Paul speaks of the faith that **lived** in these women rather than their forming Timothy from his youth (if their Jewish influence on him has been so strong, why was he not circumcised as a child? [see Acts 16:3]), it seems more likely that they became Christians shortly before him. But if they had taught Timothy the Jewish Scriptures from his infancy (2 Tim 3:15), then their decision to embrace the gospel of Christ would have had a great influence upon his own.

Reflection and Application (1:3–5)

This text goes a long way in underlining the importance of the family in the formation of its members in the faith. César Chávez, a devout Catholic who grew up from poverty to a middle-class, well-salaried administrative job, then abandoned it in 1964 to live like the oppressed farm workers and organize them, was, like Timothy, formed in the faith by his grandmother

Parents Form Children in the Faith

LIVING TRADITION

The example of Timothy's mother and grandmother evokes this statement in the Catechism: "Through the grace of the sacrament of marriage, parents receive the responsibility and privilege of *evangelizing their children*. Parents should initiate their children at an early age into the mysteries of the faith of which they are the 'first heralds' for their children. They should associate them from their tenderest years with the life of the Church. A wholesome family life can foster interior dispositions that are a genuine preparation for a living faith and remain a support for it throughout one's life" (2225, emphasis original; see also 2226).

and mother.[1] In certain cultures, especially the Hispanic, the grandmother generally is held in an honor little short of cult, and her influence on the family is profound. In the middle of the night I received a call from one of my Hispanic students who had just learned of the death of his grandmother. He was almost hysterical. When his other grandmother died later the same semester, he was devastated.

Spirit and Gift (1:6–8)

> [6] **For this reason, I remind you to stir into flame the gift of God that you have through the imposition of my hands. [7] For God did not give us a spirit of cowardice but rather of power and love and self-control. [8] So do not be ashamed of your testimony to our Lord, nor of me, a prisoner for his sake; but bear your share of hardship for the gospel with the strength that comes from God.**

OT: 1 Kings 18:38–39; 1 Macc 13:7; Sir 34:13–14; 48:1–3
NT: Luke 3:16; 9:26; Acts 1:8; Rom 1:16; 8:15; 1 Tim 4:14
Catechism: graces and charisms (2003–4, 799–800), Holy Spirit as fire (696, 1127)
Lectionary: (1:6–14) Mass for the Ordination of a Bishop

At first reading the larger section we find ourselves in here seems to be a **1:6** mixture of exhortation, doctrine, and personal testimony, but there is in fact a unity, which is marked by the reference to the Spirit at the beginning (1:7) and end (1:14).

What is the connection, intended to be strong (**for this reason**), between this section and the preceding? Paul has affirmed Timothy in his sincere faith, but he is concerned that discouragement over the difficulties of Timothy's office may keep him from exerting his leadership with full energy and therefore that he may not adequately meet the challenge to his faith that these difficulties present. Jesus, when asked by his disciples to increase their faith, told them that the little faith they had, though it be as small as a mustard seed, could move mountains, if they would just use it (Luke 17:6). It is not a question of Timothy's acquiring something he does not already have, but rather of activating what he already has. His situation is not as bad as that of the church of Sardis, told by the seer of Revelation to "strengthen what is left" (Rev 3:2), but one can sometimes fail to act simply for not realizing the power available. It is something like

---

1. See Jacques E. Levy, *César Chávez: Autobiography of La Causa* (New York: Norton, 1975).

Later Importance of 2 Tim 1:6 for the Church

LIVING TRADITION

St. Augustine and the medieval theologians developed the notion of the actualization or "awakening" of an earlier grace received, as can happen at a later time to those baptized in infancy.[a] This verse was cited by the Council of Trent in support of the sacramental character of orders (session 23, chapter 3).

a. See K. McDonnell and G. T. Montague, *Christian Initiation and Baptism in the Holy Spirit* (Collegeville, MN: Liturgical Press, 1994), 94–95.

the instance of a woman I knew who did not know that the car her husband recently purchased had a police overtake gear, until, being harassed at night on an isolated highway, she floored the accelerator and in seconds was out of sight of the harasser.

The same Greek verb used here for **stir into flame** appears in the ancient Greek version of Gen 45:27 to describe how Jacob's spirit "revived" when he learned that his son Joseph was still alive and in 1 Macc 13:7 to describe how the spirit of the discouraged people was "rekindled" by the stirring speech of Simon. The basic image is that of coals that have been covered with ashes and need to be stirred and fanned into flame. Saint John Chrysostom comments: "It takes much zeal to stir up the gift of God. . . . It is in our power to kindle or extinguish this grace. . . . For by sloth and carelessness it is quenched, and by watchfulness and diligence it is kept alive."[2]

Unlike other gifts of the Holy Spirit that are imparted directly to the baptized and are to be sought for the building of the Church (1 Cor 12; 14), the charism of leadership was mediated to Timothy by Paul's **imposition of . . . hands**, hence, ordination. In the Old Testament the spiritual gifting for leadership is sometimes given directly (Num 11:24–30), at other times through anointing or the laying on of hands (Deut 34:9; 1 Sam 16:13). God's provision of these two means—directly by the Spirit or mediated by the laying on of hands—provides, on the one hand, the assurance that the community will be animated by the movements of the Spirit and, on the other, that order, which is the work of the Spirit as well, will be preserved by the visible designation of authority. And this charism will have a permanence that the other charisms may not have. (On the participation of other elders in the ordination of Timothy, see 1 Tim 4:14.)

2. *Homilies on 2 Timothy* 1.

The **spirit** given here implies, of course, the Holy Spirit, explicitly named in 1:14. But the immediate sense is the Spirit's charism for ministry, the bestowal of an interior power ordered to an external mission, such as was prophesied of the messiah in Isa 11:2 or of the eschatological prophet in 61:1.   **1:7**

> The spirit of the Lord GOD is upon me,
>> because the LORD has anointed me;
> He has sent me to bring glad tidings to the lowly,
>> to heal the brokenhearted. (Isa 61:1)

Fear and timidity, or **cowardice**, have no place in one endowed with this spirit. Already in the Old Testament, the "fear of the Lord" removes human fear: "The spirit of those who fear the Lord will be fully alive . . . He who fears the Lord will never be afraid" (Sir 34:13–14, my translation; see also Ps 27:1). That is because the spirit is one **of power**. This is almost a redundancy, since the word "spirit" implies power and can be used as a synonym for it (Luke 1:35; Acts 1:8; 1 Cor 2:4). It is the power by which Jesus worked miracles (Acts 10:38), a power given to the disciples at Pentecost (1:8) and to Paul himself (Rom 15:19) and manifested in the founding of his new communities (Gal 3:5; 1 Thess 1:5). But it is also a power available for witnessing (Acts 1:8), preaching with boldness, and enduring hardship; this is the charism that Paul wants Timothy to stir up.

But the most characteristic effect of the Holy Spirit is **love** (Rom 5:5), and it is this divine love that inspires hope and consequently endurance (5:2–5). The power given to the minister, then, proceeds from love, leads to love, and is tempered by love. Or better, it is the very power of love itself. On the one hand, it is different from the blustering kind of authoritarianism that governs by fear. On the other hand, it is not soft or subject to manipulation or weathervane subservience. In a leader it can be the most compelling power of all. When I saw the face of Pope John Paul II as my hand touched his in an audience in 1984, the words "gentle granite" leapt to my mind. That image would fit the aspect of love that Paul is depicting here. It is especially love for Christ that impels the minister (2 Cor 5:14), the love the shepherd should have first of all for the Good Shepherd (John 21:15–17) and then for his flock (10:15; 2 Cor 11:11). Of course this love is simply a response to Christ's love, for it is "not that we have loved God, but that he loved us" (1 John 4:10), of which Paul is keenly aware: "[He] loved me and [gave] himself up for me" (Gal 2:20).

The third element of this triad is **self-control** (*sōphronsynē*). A series of Greek words cluster around the notion of self-control, prudence, wisdom, decency. Paul expects all Christians to exert self-control over their passions (Gal 5:23).

Sōphronsynē suggests strict ascetic control. Is this advice what Timothy needs? He is already ascetic, so that Paul has to recommend that he take a little wine for his stomach's sake (1 Tim 5:23). Paul also condemns the false asceticism of those who forbid marriage and abstinence from certain foods (4:3). What is extreme is not necessarily what is holiest. When we look at the overall teaching of the Pastorals, we find an ethic of balance and moderation. Food is good and is to be taken with thanksgiving (4:4–5). The Christian should avoid excess in wine (3:3, 8; Titus 1:7; 2:3), but moderate use is recommended (1 Tim 5:23). Youthful passions are to be shunned (2 Tim 2:22), but young women should marry (1 Tim 5:14). Riches are dangerous, and one should be content with sufficient food and clothing (6:7–10). But a certain amount of ownership of property in the congregation is taken for granted (6:17–19).

So here in 2 Tim 1:7 it would seem that the word translated "self-control" would be better rendered "prudence," in the sense of balance, levelheadedness, not going to one extreme or another, the kind of virtue especially needed of leaders, indeed of bishops (1 Tim 3:2–3; Titus 1:8). The pastor needs to model the kind of balance he expects of his flock. He needs to be measured in his judgment, listening well but not remaining voiceless when error and sin need to be condemned. Symbol and leader of unity, he needs the kind of spirit that will promote reconciliation and the practice of truth in love (Eph 4:15). In Titus 2:4 the verb form *sōphronizō*, related to our noun translated "self-control," means "to teach, to form others." Thus the word is related to the bishop's responsibility to teach (1 Tim 4:11; 6:2b; 2 Tim 2:24). Mature and formed himself, he will be able to teach and form others.

When we look at the triad "power, love, self-control" as a whole, it is remarkable that the most important, love, occupies the center. It is like the fuselage of a plane, which rides on two wings that balance each other. The gift of the

The Shame and Power of the Cross

LIVING TRADITION

St. John Chrysostom preaches: "In themselves death and imprisonment and chains cause shame and reproach. But when . . . the mystery is viewed aright, they will appear full of dignity and a matter for boasting. For it was that death on the cross that saved the world when it was perishing. That death connected earth with heaven; that death destroyed the power of the devil and made men angels and sons of God; that death raised our nature to the kingly throne."[a]

a. *Homilies on 2 Timothy* 1:8.

Spirit is one of power, but it is also the spirit of order, and it is both because it is the spirit of love.

Honor was an important value in the Gentile and Jewish worlds of Paul's **1:8** day,[3] and so it is not surprising that the categories of honor and shame should enter his discussion. He is not ashamed of the gospel (Rom 1:16), and he trusts that in fidelity to his mission he will not be put to shame (2 Cor 10:8; Phil 1:20). So too Timothy, activating the grace of his office, should not be ashamed either of his **testimony to our Lord** or of the imprisonment of Paul. By rendering the Greek with the preposition *to* the NAB translators limit somewhat the scope of Timothy's testimony: it is testimony *to* Jesus, *to* his identity and saving acts; but the Greek is more literally "the testimony *of* our Lord." This is a dense expression, probably meant to include the witness that Jesus himself gave before Pilate and unto the cross, the proclamation of that fact by Timothy, and Timothy's own witnessing to it by his life and leadership, which could possibly entail his own imprisonment and martyrdom. To preach the cross to both pagan and Jew is to proclaim the weakness and the foolishness of God in the face of people who overvalue signs of power and the wisdom of eloquence (1 Cor 1:18–25). To believe in the cross and to preach the cross is to share in its shame—and its power!

But there is a more immediate challenge for Timothy, and that is not to be ashamed that his hero and mentor, Paul, has been arrested and treated as a criminal (2 Tim 2:9). It is not a mere question of persecution by some members of the Jewish community. The case has become one of the empire, and that could sound mortal peril for anyone associated with the apostle. Some of Paul's disciples have withdrawn for that reason. Renewal in the Holy Spirit will keep Timothy from doing so or even from muffling his proclamation of the gospel. Paul literally says, "Do not be ashamed of the testimony of our Lord or of me, his prisoner." Thus Paul is not a prisoner of Nero; he is a **prisoner** of Christ! In a single stroke Paul asserts his assurance that his journey to the dungeon has been his Master's way of bringing him into a deeper communion and conformity with himself (Phil 3:10).

The notion of communion is prolonged now in a word Paul coins: "cosuffer." The Greek word *kakopatheō* means "to suffer evil," and to it Paul prefixes *syn-* ("co-, with"), as he does elsewhere with Greek verbs (Rom 8:17; Phil 1:27), so that the meaning is "to suffer evil along with," which the NAB translates

---

3. Many recent socioscientific studies of the ancient Mediterranean world highlight honor and shame as important categories for understanding the New Testament. See, e.g., Jerome H. Neyrey, ed., *The Social World of Luke-Acts* (Peabody, MA: Hendrickson, 1991), 25–66.

as **bear your share of hardship**. Thus Paul emphasizes the communion he invites Timothy to experience with Paul and Christ **for** the sake of **the gospel**. Suffering was part of the deal when Jesus called Paul to be his minister (Acts 9:16), and now that vocation has reached its climax. If Paul is now filling up in his body what is lacking to the sufferings of Christ for the Church (Col 1:24), it is possible for Timothy to share in that grace. The author of the letter to the Hebrews literally says, "Think of those in chains as yourselves being in chains with them, and those who are ill treated as dwelling yourselves in the body" (Heb 13:3). This verse is a great challenge to every Christian today to be united with the suffering and persecuted Church, which during the twentieth century had more martyrs than in all the previous centuries put together and continues to suffer today in many countries in Africa and Asia. Like Timothy, that means being in communion with the "chained" and also enduring whatever sufferings the gospel testimony may entail in one's own surroundings.

To do so one is not left to one's own limited resources. The Christian's energy source is God himself: **with the strength that comes from God**. If one must use the charisms of service "with the strength that God supplies" (1 Pet 4:11), that strength is all the more needed when one is called to scorn the shame of bearing the cross (Heb 12:2).

Reflection and Application (1:6–8)

When we get a new credit card, the first thing we are told to do is to activate it by calling a certain number. Receiving the Holy Spirit in the sacraments of baptism and confirmation also demands an activation on our part, like the "stirring into flame" that Paul urges Timothy to do with the grace of his ordination. We do that through prayer, retreats, Life in the Spirit Seminars, and many other ways to "train for devotion" (see 1 Tim 4:6–10).

I Know Him in Whom I Have Believed (1:9–12)

> [9]He saved us and called us to a holy life, not according to our works but according to his own design and the grace bestowed on us in Christ Jesus before time began, [10]but now made manifest through the appearance of our savior Christ Jesus, who destroyed death and brought life and immortality to light through the gospel, [11]for which I was appointed preacher and apostle and teacher. [12]On this account I am suffering these things; but

I am not ashamed, for I know him in whom I have believed and am confident that he is able to guard what has been entrusted to me until that day.

OT: Ps 31:6
NT: Rom 1:16; 6:9; 1 Cor 15:54–56; 2 Cor 11:23–29; 1 Tim 2:7; Heb 2:14–15
Catechism: predestination (600, 2012), Jesus conquered death (1019), evil and suffering (309–14)
Lectionary: (1:8b–10) Second Sunday in Lent (A)

Where does one look to find divine strength? In 2 Tim 1:9 Paul finds it in   1:9
what God has already done in Christ. This verse and the two following have a
rhythmic, hymnlike quality, to such an extent that many scholars feel Paul borrowed a known liturgical hymn used perhaps for baptism or ordination. In any
case, the passage perfectly fits the development of Paul's thought at this point in
the letter. "Savior" is the title given to God six times and to Christ four times in
the Pastorals. Here the specific past saving act of God—**he saved us**—is evoked,
obviously the sending of his Son, whose death on the cross and resurrection
brought that salvation to the human race. But the close connection of **called**
with the saving act suggests that for the recipients the two are in reality one:
God saves us in calling us to embrace the gospel (Gal 1:6) and baptism (Titus
3:5), to be united with his Son (1 Cor 1:9), and to enter the kingdom and share
eternal life (1 Thess 2:12; 1 Tim 6:12).

It seems redundant to say, as the Greek literally does, "he called us with a
holy calling." This is similar to Rom 1:7 (also 1 Cor 1:2), where Paul addresses
his readers as "beloved of God . . . called to be holy," which can also mean "holy
because called." So here the idea could be that the call is holy because it comes
from God, or the call is to holiness of life, as the NAB would have it: **called us
to a holy life**. But perhaps the expression (*klēsei hagia*) is meant to evoke the
"holy assembly" (*klētē hagia*), the term used for the people called out of Egypt
to be the assembly of God in the desert (Exod 12:16; Lev 23:2). Perhaps all of
these meanings floated around in the author's mind. In any case, whatever is
holy is so because it belongs to God.

Paul, whose struggle with his fellow Jews was long and bitter over "works"
and "grace," could hardly pass up the opportunity of repeating that it was not
our works that merited salvation, for God planned from all eternity to grace
us with his mercy in Christ Jesus. Second Timothy 1:9–10 sounds very much
like Eph 1:1–10. Calling and choosing us was not a second thought on God's
part. He always had it in his heart. That **grace** was **bestowed on us in Christ
Jesus**, for it is only in union with him that we receive it: the only begotten was
"full of grace. . . . From his fullness we have all received, grace in place of grace"
(John 1:14–16).

1:10   God has now revealed the secret of his heart **through the appearance of our savior Christ Jesus**. The role of "savior," used of God in the preceding verse, is applied here to Christ. Paul frequently coordinates the agency of God with that of Christ. While this does not of itself prove the equality of Christ with God (human figures are called saviors in the Old Testament; Judg 3:9, 15; Neh 9:27), it dovetails nicely with more explicit Trinitarian texts elsewhere. Paul's choice of the words **manifest, appearance,** and **brought . . . to light** contrasts with the plan "before time began," which for ages God kept secret. Instead of using a more traditional phrase like "God sent his Son," Paul wants to emphasize that what was hidden from eternity is now revealed. Paul elsewhere calls God's plan the "mystery" (1 Cor 2:7; 15:51; Eph 1:9; 3:9; etc.). Unlike the secret rites of the mystery religions, the mystery that was once concealed in God's mind is now revealed and is in the process of reaching the whole world, like the morning sun that touches the mountaintop and will eventually reach the deepest valley. Paul uses the term *epiphaneia* ("epiphany") for this **appearance,** thus taking the term earlier used for Christ's glorious manifestation at the end of time ("manifestation" in 2 Thess 2:8; "appearance" in 1 Tim 6:14) and applying it to the incarnation or to the whole of Christ's life, death, and resurrection. This is "realized †eschatology," that is, the transfer of an end-time expectation to the present. The Greek word *epiphaneia* was frequently used for a visible manifestation of a hidden divinity. It was at Ephesus precisely that the city council in AD 48 acclaimed Julius Caesar as "the God made *manifest . . .* and common *saviour* of human life."[4] The Ephesian Christians would therefore have been thoroughly familiar with this language when it was applied to Christ. It was a daring thing to apply such imperial titles to Christ, as the Romans would take seriously any threat to their emperor.

The effects of this epiphany of **our savior Christ Jesus** in time are twofold. The negative effect is to rob death of its power: he **destroyed death**. It is possible to give the Greek verb the strong sense "to destroy or annihilate" (2 Thess 2:8), but the root meaning of the word has the nuance "to render inoperable or disable." Like a disabled tank, death is still there, but it has no power, thanks to Christ's victory. It is permanently "out of service." This is an important shade of meaning, for Christians do not live in the illusion that physical death does not exist. It is real. But because of Jesus it no longer poses the threat it once did. Since death has no more power over Jesus (Rom 6:9), when Christians die "with him" (2 Tim 2:11), or "for the Lord" (Rom 14:8), they experience death

---

4. A. Deissmann, *Light from the Ancient East*, trans. L. R. M. Strachan (repr. Grand Rapids: Baker Academic, 1965), 344 (emphasis original).

in a radically different way than they would have as unbelievers. They are no longer slaves to the paralysis that the certainty of death brings. Paul even personalizes death in this passage (as his use of the definite article in "*the* death" indicates), suggesting that Christ has had a personal encounter with the enemy, the devil (whose work is death; John 8:44). As the letter to the Hebrews puts it, Christ came "that through death he might destroy the one who has the power of death, that is, the devil, and free those who through fear of death had been subject to slavery all their life" (Heb 2:14–15).

The positive effect of Christ's ministry was to give life, and Paul describes it in the mode of revelation: **brought life and immortality to light**. He sees the risen Christ, light of the world (John 8:12), radiating the light of the resurrection through the darkness that could not restrain it (1:5) and showing that God has destined humankind not only for immortality but for incorruptibility, the quality of the risen body (1 Cor 15:42–54). "He will change our lowly body to conform with his glorified body" (Phil 3:21). "Life and immortality" could be translated "an incorruptible life." This illumination is not, therefore, enlightenment in a merely intellectual or spiritual sense, and certainly not in a Buddhist or New Age sense, which is impersonal and wholly subjective. It is rather the gift of incorruptible spiritual and bodily life, the resurrection, for which the gospel presents the guarantee. Paul's faith and hope enable him to experience something of that light even if he is in the darkness of a Roman prison. That light contacts the human race **through the gospel**, the proclamation of the good news, which Paul sees continuing despite his being in chains (2 Tim 2:9).

And that brings us back to Paul. To spread that light, to proclaim that gospel, Paul was chosen and appointed by Christ to be **preacher and apostle and teacher**. The word for preacher is *kēryx*, meaning originally "herald" (discussed in 1 Tim 2:7). The gospel is a living message; it cannot be communicated unless someone—an apostle—is sent to do it (Rom 10:14–15). But it also requires more than the initial proclamation; teaching must follow, in order to strengthen and guide the new life begun. Paul is qualified and commissioned to fulfill all three roles. His letters contain written examples of his proclamation, his directives as apostle, and his teaching.   1:11

On this account, which is the same expression used in 2 Tim 1:6, **I am suffering these things**. Paul means that there is no other reason for his sufferings than his commitment to Christ and his mission. His example should be an encouragement to Timothy, whom he has urged similarly to bear hardship willingly for the sake of the gospel (1:8). The phrase "these things" covers all Paul's sufferings during his ministry but particularly those of his present confinement.   1:12

Imprisonment generally brings shame to anyone, whether guilty or innocent, but not so for Paul: **I am not ashamed**. He has a reason for glorying in his chains as others would not: he knows the one for whose sake he is bearing them; it is the one **in whom I have believed**. "Have believed" is in the perfect tense in Greek, indicating a permanent and uninterrupted state since his first act of faith. The object of his belief here is not a creed but a person—the omission of whose name has a powerful rhetorical effect on the reader, who also knows the one in whom he or she has believed. "Believe" here has the sense of trust and security as well as commitment.

What specific outcome does Paul expect with such certitude? That Christ will **guard what has been entrusted to me**. "What has been entrusted" is a single noun in the Greek. It refers to some entrusted object, something given in trust. Some commentators, ancient and modern, take this trust to mean the life that God has given to Paul, as well as the eternal life to which he looks forward, a trust that Paul in turn entrusts to the Lord, like Jesus at the cross saying, "Into your hands I commend my spirit" (Luke 23:46), quoting Ps 31:6, which is used even today as the Jewish night prayer *Adon Olam* and in the Church's divine office for night prayer. There is much in the context that favors this understanding. But elsewhere in the Pastorals the word *parathēkē* ("what has been entrusted") means the revelation that Christ entrusted to Paul, and this is the sense in which he will use it two verses later (2 Tim 1:14). The better understanding, then, is that Paul is so in love with Christ and the responsibility that Christ gave him to proclaim the good news, that he is not thinking of his own personal fate at death but rather of the fate of the "deposit," the trust he has been given, that is, the gospel message or the faithful Christians it has engendered. On the verge of having to let go of this entrustment, he is certain that Christ will provide the means for its continuance **until that day**, that is, until he comes.

Reflection and Application (1:9–12)

Christ has destroyed—or disabled—death. Not every Christian death is necessarily peaceful, particularly if it happens suddenly or as a result of violence. But how often Christians who have been living their faith show an amazing serenity as they surrender their spirit to the Lord in death. I remember Margaret, a devout and socially active friend with whom I prayed in her last moments. There was a seraphic smile on her face, as if she were already seeing God.

"I know in whom I have put my trust." While trekking with my novices through the steep Himalayan foothills in Nepal, I once put my trust in a slippery rock as I tried to cross a waterfall. It was a treacherous rock, and I found myself flying headfirst down the waterfall toward an unknown but likely fatal destiny. But one of my novices quickly put his foot out into the water and found a firm and reliable rock that enabled him to reach out and catch me. There are reliable and unreliable things to stand on, and there are reliable and unreliable persons as well. I had experienced both. Paul is thoroughly convinced of the reliability of the one he has leaned on since meeting him on the road to Damascus.

Guarding the Trust (1:13–14)

[13]Take as your norm the sound words that you heard from me, in the faith and love that are in Christ Jesus. [14]Guard this rich trust with the help of the holy Spirit that dwells within us.

OT: Deut 6:6–9; 11:22–25
NT: Rom 5:5; 1 Cor 6:9; Gal 1:8; 1 Tim 6:20
Catechism: Tradition (81), faith and love (1814–16, 1822–29), guarding with help of the Spirit (86), sense of the faithful (91)
Lectionary: (1:13–14; 2:1–3) Common of Pastors and of Doctors of the Church

If there was any doubt about the meaning of "what has been entrusted to me" in 1:12, it is removed by this passage, which clearly speaks of Paul's teaching as the trust, now confided to Timothy. Timothy must follow the **norm** (*hypotypōsis*) set by the teaching of Paul, his very words. The Greek word is sometimes used for the architect's plan for a building, the pattern for a cloak, the outline of a speech, the first sketch of a painting. On the one hand, Paul's words set the direction for Timothy's teachings, but, on the other, he is not expected simply to mouth the phrases of his mentor. He is to fill them out, using his judgment as to how these words apply to situations unforeseen by Paul. This is a magnificent image for a dynamic tradition. The same dynamic is at work in Jesus' teaching in the Gospels. Jesus did not tell his disciples to parrot his words without concern for changing circumstances. His disciples were to convey his message as a seed meant to grow and bear fruit in whatever soil it was planted (Mark 4:14–20), bringing greater understanding and development. As Vatican Council II put it, *traditio proficit, crescit perceptio*: "The tradition . . . develops. . . . There is a growth in the understanding" (*Dei Verbum* 8).

Still, the emphasis is on holding tightly to the tradition, as do Mary and all others who hear the word of God and *hold on* to it (Luke 8:21). Holding means first of all clinging to it in **faith**, for, however much the Tradition will

1:13

151

respond to the deepest longing of the human heart, it is not a merely human wisdom, and only faith will give the insight necessary to perceive what the Tradition means when new questions arise. To cling to the Tradition in faith is also to do so in **love** both for God and especially for neighbor, for there are no disputes more bitter than those fought on religious grounds. Thus even our battles for the truth should be undertaken in love (Eph 4:15). In the book of Revelation, Jesus praises the church at Ephesus for its fidelity in the midst of doctrinal turmoil but chides it for losing its love in the process (Rev 2:1–6). It is faith and love together that assure continued union with Christ Jesus.

1:14   Paul calls this trust **rich** or "beautiful" (*kalos*). "Rich" catches the nuance of endless wealth available in the tradition, while "beautiful" suggests something that can be the source of endless contemplation. Timothy has resources beyond his own strength for guarding this trust. If he was encouraged earlier to fan into flame the gift of the Holy Spirit that he received at his ordination (2 Tim 1:6–7), he should know that the **holy Spirit**, first guardian of the Tradition (John 16:12–15), **dwells** in him as it does in Paul. It is not clear whether the expression **within us** refers here to all Christians who have received the Holy Spirit (Acts 2:38) or to the specific apostolic charism given to Paul and Timothy to fulfill their office. In any case, the light and strength of the Holy Spirit are available upon request in prayer (Luke 11:13).

Reflection and Application (1:13–14)

This section, along with the preceding, provides a precious foundation for the Catholic Church's understanding of Tradition. Whereas the preceding deals with the deposit of the faith as such, this section allows for development in the Tradition. The Second Vatican Council expressed it this way:

> This tradition, which comes from the Apostles, develops in the Church with the help of the Holy Spirit. For there is a growth in the understanding of the realities and the words which have been handed down. This happens through the contemplation and study made by believers, who treasure these things in their hearts (see Luke 2:19, 51) through a penetrating understanding of the spiritual realities which they experience, and through the preaching of those who have received through episcopal succession the sure gift of truth. For as the centuries succeed one another, the Church constantly moves forward toward the fullness of divine truth until the words of God reach their complete fulfillment in her. (*Dei Verbum* 8)

It is not only the clergy but laypeople who are bearers of the Tradition. Even as the parent teaches the child the sign of the cross, he or she is guarding and handing on the Tradition. Although it is important to know and understand what God has revealed, this Tradition is not preserved by mere study. One cannot understand the things that have been given us by God without the Holy Spirit:

> "What eye has not seen, and ear has not heard,
>   and what has not entered the human heart,
>   what God has prepared for those who love him,"
> this God has revealed to us through the Spirit. (1 Cor 2:9–10)

Defections and Loyalty (1:15–18)

[15]You know that everyone in Asia deserted me, including Phygelus and Hermogenes. [16]May the Lord grant mercy to the family of Onesiphorus because he often gave me new heart and was not ashamed of my chains. [17]But when he came to Rome, he promptly searched for me and found me. [18]May the Lord grant him to find mercy from the Lord on that day. And you know very well the services he rendered in Ephesus.

OT: Gen 37:23–24; Ps 22:2; 38:12; 142:5; Isa 53:3
NT: Matt 27:46; Rom 15:32; Eph 6:20; 2 Tim 4:19; Heb 11:36
Catechism: fidelity to promises (2101), solidarity (1939), charity and friendship (1829)

This little section contains so many personal traits that even many scholars who hold that Paul did not write the Pastorals think this section is from his pen. Timothy in Ephesus knows what happened when Paul was arrested. Many of his disciples and friends turned their back on him, not because of a disagreement over his teaching, but simply to avoid being identified with someone seized by the imperial police. **Everyone** is hyperbole, for obviously Timothy and Onesiphorus and presumably others remained faithful. The exaggeration, though, reveals Paul's emotional state at being **deserted**, like Jesus asking his closest disciples, "Do you also want to leave?" (John 6:67). It is not clear who precisely is meant by **everyone in Asia**. Did the defection happen in Asia when Paul was arrested? Did he appeal for the intervention of friends there who let him down? Is he referring to Asian Christians settled in Rome, who should have come to help him (St. John Chrysostom's view)? If Paul's case had surfaced as a dispute among Jews, there would have been little to fear even from

1:15

the Roman authorities. Proconsul Gallio in Corinth had actually dismissed a dispute for that reason (Acts 18:14–16). Jews had been granted a great deal of autonomy since the time of Julius Caesar because of their support of him against the Parthians.

But civic disturbance was another matter. Claudius had expelled the Jews from Rome in AD 49 (Acts 18:2). Roman historian Suetonius says this was because of a civic disturbance of a certain "Chrestus," a probable misspelling of Christ.[5] Nero, however, persecuted Christians precisely because they were Christians. That Paul alone was arrested and not any of his disciples, however, would seem to indicate that his ministry or his position as the leader of a movement opposed to the worship of the gods or of the emperor would have been sufficient to accuse him of a capital offense. His disciples could fear being guilty by association, and this could explain their defection.

Phygelus and Hermogenes are not mentioned elsewhere in the New Testament, and we know nothing further about them. Paul's mentioning them may be intended to alert Timothy to their harmful influence, like that of Alexander (2 Tim 4:14–15). On the other hand, there is not a word of blame for them, and certainly not even hope that God would repay them for what they have done. Has Paul learned from the Master to pray for the disciples who abandon him (Luke 22:32)?

1:16–18   But, as has often happened in the case of martyrs, there are those heroes who risk their necks to stand by their Christian brothers and sisters who are on death row for the faith. **Onesiphorus** was one of these. That Paul asks the Lord to bless his family and household suggests that he may be dead (martyred too?). Onesiphorus must have been an outstanding member of the Ephesian community, perhaps even a deacon, for Timothy knows him well. Arriving in **Rome**, this disciple hastened to find Paul. The Greek suggests he had to do some searching among the Christians in the city, which he did quickly and diligently, until he found Paul. Then, in a beautiful play on words, the apostle prays that he who **found** Paul will **find** mercy before the Lord on that day. Was Paul already aware of the teaching of Jesus that found its way into Matt 25:31–46, where entrance into the kingdom is given to those who hear the words, "I was . . . in prison and you visited me" (25:35–36). If Onesiphorus is dead (see also on 2 Tim 4:19), this prayer of Paul's would be New Testament evidence of prayer for the deceased (as in 2 Macc 12:42–46).

5. *Claudius* 25.4.

Reflection and Application (1:15–18)

Short of betrayal, perhaps the greatest human suffering is that of being abandoned by one's friends when we are in a desperate situation. By the same token, those who remain faithful to us are all the more deeply cherished. If a friend of ours were arrested and jailed, would we visit them, or would we shun them out of fear of looking bad?

Counsels to Timothy

2 Timothy 2

In the midst of sufferings, where does one find strength not only to survive but somehow to let the sufferings bring one closer to God? Paul will now look at this issue both for himself and for Timothy (2:1–13). Then, from 2:14 to the end of the chapter, Paul advises Timothy and his readers to avoid futile disputes and especially to reject the teaching that the resurrection has already taken place.

Source and Fruits of Fidelity (2:1–7)

¹So you, my child, be strong in the grace that is in Christ Jesus. ²And what you heard from me through many witnesses entrust to faithful people who will have the ability to teach others as well. ³Bear your share of hardship along with me like a good soldier of Christ Jesus. ⁴To satisfy the one who recruited him, a soldier does not become entangled in the business affairs of life. ⁵Similarly, an athlete cannot receive the winner's crown except by competing according to the rules. ⁶The hardworking farmer ought to have the first share of the crop. ⁷Reflect on what I am saying, for the Lord will give you understanding in everything.

OT: Prov 4:9
NT: Luke 16:13; 1 Cor 9:24–27; 15:3–9; Phil 2:25; 2 Tim 4:7–8; James 5:7
Catechism: spiritual battle (2015), tradition (81)

2:1   Addressing Timothy once more with fatherly affection, Paul challenges him to join the procession of faithful transmitters of the Tradition that have gone before him, beginning with his grandmother and ending with Onesiphorus. This means, first of all, to realize that he has strength available that is supernatural, the **grace** that comes through the mediation of **Christ Jesus**, to whom Timothy is united in faith. This is advice that Paul could give to any Christian.[1] But the burden of leadership and pastoring is especially heavy, and those who think they can handle it with their own strength are foolish indeed, for they are trying to do supernatural work with natural means.

Virtually all that Timothy has learned has come to him from Paul in the course of their long ministry together. But what does **through many witnesses** mean? Commentators explain it in various ways. It is not likely that "witnesses" are the various modes by which Paul has transmitted his teaching to Timothy—conversations, Scripture sharing, letters, preaching, or living example—since the term usually applies to persons. On the other hand, the early Church considered the Scriptures (which would certainly include words of the Lord) to be witnesses and repeatedly invoked them to confirm teaching. But if the reference is to persons, as seems more likely, it could mean the faithful Christians who handed on the faith along with Paul, and even before him, or, finally, those who witnessed Timothy's profession of faith (1 Tim 6:12). Whatever the specific reference, the point is that what Timothy heard from Paul was not something private, whispered into his ear. Nor was it an occult mystery. It did not originate with Paul, nor was it his property. It was the public faith of the community. And as others had "handed it on" (the meaning of "tradition") to Timothy, he must do the same. The sacred deposit is a gift that is given to be given.

The Greek imperative *parathou* (**entrust**), which echoes the *parathēkē* ("trust") of which Paul spoke in 2 Tim 1:14, means that the handing on should be done with the kind of care that such a precious treasure deserves. This means, first of all, careful discernment of those to whom the trust will be confided. Among members of the community two qualities are required. They must be trustworthy and competent, **faithful people who will have the ability to teach others**. The word translated **faithful people** is sometimes translated "trustworthy men." It is not, however, the male gender-specific *androis* but the generic *anthrōpois*, which can apply to both men and women, as it probably does here, reflecting Paul's own formation of both men and women disciples.

The metaphors of the three professions—**soldier**, "athlete," and "farmer"— were used in the literature of the times for lives that demand self-sacrifice and hard labor. The soldier here is not a temporary recruit but the committed

2:2

2:3–4

---

1. A woman whose husband walked out on her, leaving her with six children, told me, "Without the grace of God, I could never have survived this."

Serving in Christ's Army

LIVING TRADITION

Saint Ignatius of Antioch, who died during the reign of Emperor Trajan (98–117), wrote a letter to his disciple Polycarp that resembles very much the advice giving we find in the Pastorals (thus fitting the form of the *mandata principis* letters of the day). Perhaps in dependence on Paul, Ignatius uses the same image that Paul uses here in 2 Tim 2:4, that of the soldier: "Please him in whose army you serve and from whom you receive your wages. Let none of you turn deserter. Let your baptism be your shield, faith your helmet, love your spear, endurance your armor."[a]

a. *To Polycarp* 6.2.

---

professional, not the officer but the man in the ranks, who usually had the toughest job. Obviously, soldiers are often **recruited** in time of war. For soldiers who are urgently mobilized to meet the enemy, it is particularly inappropriate to become entangled in business affairs. Like Jesus' first recruits, the one enlisted by the Lord to become a fisher of men must leave everything (Luke 5:11). More and more today, pastors are leaving the monetary affairs even of their own flock in the hands of competent laypersons, so that they may do for their people what only priests can do—administer the sacraments (Acts 6:2–4). But for Paul the motive is not so pragmatic. It is rather to foster a personal relationship. It may be romantic to think of soldiers giving up civil life to please their recruiter, though soldiers did take an oath (*sacramentum*) to the emperor, and some in addition took an oath of personal fidelity to their commanding officer; but Paul is clearly thinking of Timothy's total dedication to Christ. It is this personal relationship more than mere utility that should inspire Timothy's disengagement from temporal affairs. Considering the growth of the church in Ephesus, Timothy is probably not doing any kind of secular work, as Paul did at times (Acts 18:2–3), but is supported by the community.

2:5   Paul takes it for granted that the athlete's life is strenuous, so he moves on to an additional trait that the metaphor provides: **competing according to the rules**, which itself could demand rigors.

The **rules** according to which Timothy is to compete are the commands of Christ. "The whole law is fulfilled in one statement, namely, 'You shall love your neighbor as yourself'" (Gal 5:14). "Bear one another's burdens, and so you will fulfill the law of Christ" (6:2). In a pastor this will require a great

An Athlete's Discipline

At Olympia men had to practice under supervision and observe a strict diet for one whole month before the games. Epictetus applies this to life: "Show me proof, whether you have striven lawfully"—using exactly the same expression used in our text—"eaten what is prescribed, taken exercise, obeyed your trainer."[a] Athletes who violated the rules were usually fined and sometimes beaten. Pausanias tells of "bronze statues of Zeus . . . made from money paid in penalties by athletes fined for dishonoring the games,"[b] and the bases of sixteen of these statues have been discovered. Epictetus addresses a young man who wishes to compete in the Olympics, telling him to count the cost:

> You have to submit to discipline, follow a strict diet, give up sweets, train under obedience, at a fixed hour, in heat or cold; you must not drink cold water, nor wine just whenever you feel like it; you must submit to your trainer precisely as you would to a physician. Then when it is time for the contest, you have to "dig in" next to your opponent. You will sometimes dislocate your wrist, sprain your ankle, swallow quantities of sand, take a scourging [penalty for a foul]; yes, and then sometimes get defeated along with all that. After considering all this, go into the games, if you still wish to.[c]

a. *Discourses* 3.10.8.
b. *Guide to Greece* 5.21.2–4.
c. *Discourses* 3.15.2–5.

deal of patience and perseverance, both with his flock and in relation to those outside, who may even persecute him. "Let us . . . persevere in running the race" (Heb 12:1).

This patience applies well to the **hardworking farmer** who works the soil. He should **have the first share of the crop**. The emphasis here is not on the reward that is due (Deut 20:6; Prov 27:18) but on the toil it takes to earn it, which will be Timothy's lot. Nevertheless, the **crop**, or "fruit," is not only eternal life (John 4:36) and the fruitfulness of the ministry (15:2, 5, 16) but the financial support of the community, which Paul already affirmed as legitimate in 1 Cor 9:7–11. On this last point Paul is prudently brief. **Reflect on what I am saying, for the Lord will give you understanding in everything**. Paul leaves to Timothy the application of his teaching, for he trusts that in prayer the Lord will give to his disciple the understanding and the wisdom to apply Paul's teaching to the local circumstances that Timothy alone knows well.

2:6–7

Reflection and Application (2:1–7)

This text amply justifies the period of serious theological and ministerial preparation required for ministry, especially for the priesthood and for those who teach theology or catechesis. One bishop has invited all lay pastoral ministers in his diocese to get a master's degree in theology at his expense, and this program has now been in process for a number of years. But as one learns also by doing, Paul's example of mentoring Timothy also suggests the important role pastoral ministers have in mentoring others in ministry, thus preparing a succession of "faithful people who will have the ability to teach others."

When someone I am counseling is facing a difficult decision, I have found it best not to talk a great deal about the problem, especially if the path to be chosen is clear, but rather to invite the person to prayer, which ordinarily brings light and strength to do the right thing. One very successful method of prayer in spiritual counseling is allowing Jesus to come into the person's situation and then asking the person what he or she hears Jesus saying about it. While not always applicable, this allows the counselor to limit his role to that of discerning

The Office Is Sacred, Not Secular; It Deserves Support

LIVING TRADITION

Paul's directives that the consecrated minister should not get involved in worldly affairs and that he deserves support from the community find contemporary applications in Canon Law:

> Clerics are to refrain from all those things that are unbecoming to their state. Clerics are to avoid those things that, although not unbecoming, are alien to their state. (Canon 285)
> Clerics are forbidden personally or through others to conduct business or trade either for their own benefit or that of others without the permission of legitimate ecclesiastical authority. (Canon 286)
> Most especially, clerics are always to foster that peace and harmony based on justice which is to be observed among all persons. Clerics are not to have an active role in political parties and in the direction of labor unions unless the need to protect the rights of the Church or to promote the common good requires it in the judgment of the competent ecclesiastical authority. (Canon 287)
> When clerics dedicate themselves to the ecclesiastical ministry they deserve a remuneration which is consistent with their condition in accord with the nature of their responsibilities and with the conditions of time and place; this remuneration should enable them to provide for the needs of their own life and for the equitable payment of those whose services they need. (Canon 281)

what the person senses in his or her mind and heart and allows the person to be motivated more by the voice of the Lord than by the voice of the counselor.

In Chains, I Serve (2:8–10)

[8]**Remember Jesus Christ, raised from the dead, a descendant of David: such is my gospel,** [9]**for which I am suffering, even to the point of chains, like a criminal. But the word of God is not chained.** [10]**Therefore, I bear with everything for the sake of those who are chosen, so that they too may obtain the salvation that is in Christ Jesus, together with eternal glory.**

OT: 2 Sam 7:11–16; Ps 89:4–5; Isa 11:1; Jer 23:5
NT: Acts 13:22–23; Rom 1:3–4; Phil 1:12–14; Col 1:24
Catechism: lineage of David (437)
Lectionary: (2:8–13) Mass for the Dead; (2:8–13; 3:10–12) Common of Martyrs

It may seem strange that Paul would tell Timothy to **remember Jesus Christ.**   **2:8** But remembering here, as so often in the Bible, is not merely a calling to mind. It is the fixing of one's attention, an activation of faith in the mystery. In the midst of pastoral problems it is possible to forget the very person who has inspired such a revolutionary faith in the first place. Whereas elsewhere in the Pastorals Paul habitually speaks of "Christ Jesus," here he reverses the order of names and places "Jesus" first, thus highlighting the humanity of the savior. He then quotes what is probably an early creedal formula that was the heart of the earliest *kērygma*: **Jesus Christ, raised from the dead, a descendant of David** (see also Rom 1:3–4). Descent from David was important to prove the Christian claim that Jesus was the Messiah, fulfilling the prophecies of Nathan (2 Sam 7:12; Isa 11:1; Jer 23:5). The resurrection was his solemn enthronement at God's right hand, fulfilling beyond expectations the messianic promises of the Old Testament: "The Lord said to my Lord, / 'Sit at my right hand'" (Acts 2:34). **Such is my gospel** means: "This is the gospel I preach, and this is the gospel you must attend to."

For which can also be translated "for whom," that is, for Christ. The word   **2:9** **criminal,** used elsewhere in the New Testament only for the men crucified with Jesus (Luke 23:32, 33, 39), may very well hold the clue to the cause of Paul's arrest, for it was under Nero that the profession of the Christian faith was declared a crime.[2] It would not be necessary, then, to think of Paul being the reason for

---

2. Tacitus, *Annals* 15.44; Suetonius, *Nero* 16.

Life of a Roman Prisoner

BIBLICAL
BACKGROUND

Luke describes Paul's first Roman imprisonment as a kind of "house arrest," with the opportunity to proclaim the gospel "without hindrance" (Acts 28:31). But the tone of our present letter makes the case appear more sinister now. We are not sure of the exact conditions of Paul's confinement. The general conditions in Roman prisons were abominable. If the dungeon of the Mamertine Prison, near the Forum, is any indication, the prisoners were kept in the lower of two chambers made of blocks cut from tufa, the local porous rock. This 30-foot-diameter room could be reached only by a hole in its ceiling that opened on a smaller room for the guards. But if Paul was able to receive visitors and write letters, even if by dictation, then it is likely that he was in a less confined situation, more likely military custody (*custodia militaris*). In any case he was bound with chains, perhaps even chained to a Roman soldier. By this time Paul had learned well to identify with the Master, whose preaching and healing career brought him bound to those who condemned him.

a civil disturbance. It was sufficient for him to be known as a Christian and, what is more, as a leader in the Christian community. The preacher of the word may be restrained by **chains**, but not the word of God! The "gospel" message is practically personified here, echoing in still another way the incredible power of God's word: it is like fire, a hammer shattering rock (Jer 23:29), a two-edged sword (Heb 4:12), fertile seed (Mark 4:14, 20). History has shown the gospel's incredible ability to survive persecution and the fate of its preachers. "For just as it is impossible to bind a sunbeam or to shut it up within the house, so neither can the preaching of the word be bound."[3]

2:10   And it is the suffering of persecution, specifically imprisonment, that Paul now sees as his ministry to the word: **I bear with everything for the sake of those who are chosen**! This is not the first time, of course, that the apostle has had to confront the mystery of his call to itinerant preaching being stifled by finding himself in a criminal's chains ("far more imprisonments" in 2 Cor 11:23). Philippi (Acts 16:16–24), Ephesus (probably the site of his prison letter to the Philippians; see Phil 1:7), Jerusalem (Acts 21:33), Caesarea (23:31–26:32), and Rome itself in an earlier imprisonment had given him plenty of occasion to meditate on the mystery. Paul spent nearly half his ministry in jail! And mystery indeed it is. And yet, like Jesus, he knew that when death was at work in

3. John Chrysostom, *Homilies on the Statues* 16.12.

him, life was at work in his people (2 Cor 4:12), that he was filling up what was lacking in the afflictions of Christ for his body, the Church (Col 1:24). **Those who are chosen** means those who have already answered the call of God's grace and embraced the faith, as well as those yet to come. Paul bears his chains with the assurance **that they too** (i.e., with Paul) may enjoy **salvation . . . in Christ Jesus**—a salvation that climaxes in **eternal glory.**

Reflection and Application (2:8–10)

There are two ways a Christian, and especially a Christian minister, can promote the gospel and the kingdom: by work and by suffering. And who is to say that work is more effective than suffering, if suffering is one's call and is borne in union with Christ? It is part of the mystery that Jesus redeemed the world ultimately not by preaching, teaching, and healing, but by suffering unto death. To the flesh, promoting the gospel by suffering seems nonsense, a waste, a diminishment, a defeat. To the Spirit, it is God's secret weapon. But it takes faith to use it.

On the campus where I work there is a retirement and nursing facility, where my Marianist brothers endure in faith the physical and emotional suffering that signals their imminent death. On that same campus I spend my daily energies teaching, preaching, counseling students, and giving the sacraments. Who, ultimately, is promoting the kingdom better? God's way of judging is not our way.

I once met a retired Jesuit at a retreat house. I had earlier noticed that he limped, the result of a stroke. He had had a very prestigious career, even serving on the General Administration of the order. When I had the occasion to sit next to him at table, I asked, with the naïveté of a busy young priest, "And what do you do now, Father?" His firm, unabashed reply astounded and confounded me: "I say my prayers, and I wait."

Heart of the Letter (2:11–13)

----

¹¹**This saying is trustworthy:**
  If we have died with him
    we shall also live with him;
¹²**if we persevere**
    we shall also reign with him.
  But if we deny him
    he will deny us.

>^{13}**If we are unfaithful**
>   **he remains faithful,**
>   **for he cannot deny himself.**

OT: Num 23:19; Deut 7:9; Isa 49:7
NT: Matt 10:33; Rom 3:3–4; 6:5; 8:17; 1 Cor 1:9; 1 Tim 1:15
Catechism: final perseverance (2016)

2:11   Repeating a catchphrase of the Pastorals (1 Tim 1:15; 3:1; 4:9; Titus 3:8), his equivalent of Jesus' "amen, amen, I say to you," Paul points to the following (rather than the preceding) **saying** as support of what he has just said. The link is in the theme of suffering that leads to glory, a view of faith that continues to sustain Paul as he not only suffers but faces imminent death himself. Although Paul, no slouch at rhetoric himself, could have composed these poetic lines (the opening line is virtually equivalent to Rom 6:8: "If . . . we have died with Christ, . . . we shall also live with him"), the majority of scholars think that he is quoting an early liturgical hymn, perhaps used as a baptismal commitment song. Even to quote a well-known hymn is a powerful rhetorical technique, for the reader or listener easily identifies with what is familiar. But why would Paul think of quoting this hymn at this point? No doubt for its opening words, as he faces his own death.

     Have died with—another instance of "with" verbs so treasured by Paul—appears in 2 Cor 7:3 to express intimate identification in love: "You are in our hearts, that we may die together and live together."

     In the early Church, menaced more often than not by persecution, to receive baptism was to be consecrated and committed to die for Christ should events demand it. In fact, the very sacrament was considered by Paul to be a death with Christ: "If we have grown into union with him through a death like his, we shall also be united with him in the resurrection. . . . If, then, we have died with Christ, we believe that we shall also live with him" (Rom 6:5, 8). The difference from the other examples of "dying with" is, of course, that those who die with Christ and for him are assured of life eternal with him.

2:12   If for the Christian, dying with Christ is past (the baptismal understanding of this death is obvious from the past tense: "we have died") and the resurrection is future, what is the present life? To **persevere** or "endure." It is the characteristic of love to endure all things (1 Cor 13:7). The virtue of endurance (*hypomonē*) appears in the noun form fifteen times in the Pauline letters and here in the verb form. The Church soon found out that those who receive the word do not always persevere. A momentary spiritual thrill may quickly fade, like the seed that falls by the wayside or onto rocks or into weeds. Only the persevering

Dying With

In India until recently, wives would sometimes throw themselves on the funeral pyres of their husbands or ask to be fixed there so that they might die with them (the practice known as *suttee*). In the Mediterranean world, soldiers at times vowed to fight with their leader and to die with him. Greek geographer Strabo, who lived shortly before Paul's time, tells of an Ethiopian practice whereby, if the king were maimed, "his closest associates would suffer the same thing, and they even die with him."[a] And Plutarch tells of a custom among the Iberians (had Paul learned of this in Spain?): "For those stationed about their leader to die with him if he fell, and the Barbarians in those parts call this a 'consecration.' . . . Sertorius was attended by many thousands of men who had thus consecrated themselves to death."[b] The disciples of Jesus were similarly devoted to him. Thomas suggested going with Jesus to Jerusalem to die with him (John 11:16), and Peter insisted that even if he had to die with Jesus, he would not deny him, and the others said the same (Mark 14:31). Unfortunately, the outcome of these aspirations were not consistent with their words.

a. *Geography* 17.2.3.
b. *Sertorius* 14.4 (Loeb Classical Library translation).

bear fruit for eternal life (Luke 8:15). It is this virtue, born of supernatural hope (1 Thess 1:3), that enables Christians, like Paul, to bear contradictions, trials, and weaknesses (1 Cor 4:9–13; 2 Cor 6:4), because they do so in union with Christ (1:5; Col 1:24) and in the assurance of the divine promise: **we shall . . . reign with him**.

But Paul is aware that defection and desertion are possible: **but if we deny him**. In fact, he has experienced both recently, as the two letters to Timothy attest. He is not thinking in particular, however, of the judgment that may fall on his betrayers (2 Tim 4:14); rather he is thinking of the unspeakable disaster that would befall any disciple who would deny the Lord: **he will deny us**. It is the same warning expressed in Matt 10:33: "Whoever denies me before others, I will deny before my heavenly Father." Given the contrast here with perseverance, the meaning is probably not so much a malicious denial as a sin of cowardice, the kind of weakness Peter showed in denying his Lord. Though the early Church hesitated for some time about reconciling those who repented of their denial of Christ during persecution, at length she came to the conclusion that she could do no less than her Master had done for Peter: to forgive and reconcile. The denial by the Lord here, then, must fall only on those who

Dying with Christ

Dying with Christ need not be martyrdom. Any Christian who dies in union with Jesus enjoys the same promise of life (1 Thess 4:14). Yet the martyrs embody this mystery in a supreme way. One of the best documented accounts of the early martyrs is that of Perpetua and Felicity and their companions. Felicity gave birth to a child in prison shortly before her martyrdom. It was a painful childbirth, one month premature. A jailer, hearing her groan, asked her what she expected to do in the worse ordeal she would soon face with the beasts. She replied: "My sufferings here are my own; there another will be with me, suffering for me and I for him."[a]

a. Clearly our natural sufferings, like childbirth, can be a sharing in the passion of Christ. But Felicity here is recalling the extraordinary help of Christ and the Holy Spirit when faced with the extraordinary call of martyrdom. See Matt 10:16–20.

persist in their obstinacy and never repent. It is a terrible thing to hear from the Lord, "Amen, I say to you, I do not know you" (Matt 25:12).

2:13   Moreover, lest divine justice be conceived in vindictive terms, Paul hastens to add (if it was not already in the hymn) that human infidelity does not elicit divine infidelity. Perfect parallelism with 2:12 would demand "if we are unfaithful, he will be unfaithful," but the break of the parallelism serves to highlight the difference between the two statements. If we are commanded to love our enemies (Matt 5:44), it is because God loves his (5:45). The poetic passage is sealed, then, on a highly positive note: God's covenant fidelity. "God is **faithful**," affirmed already in the Old Testament (Deut 7:9; Isa 49:7), is one of the most frequently repeated phrases of Paul (1 Cor 1:9; 10:13; 1 Thess 5:24; 2 Thess 3:3). This fidelity to his sworn promise was the theme of Paul's letter to the Romans, for the "righteousness of God" that is revealed in the gospel is simply the proclamation that in Jesus God has fulfilled all that he had promised (Rom 1:16–17). For God to be unfaithful would be to deny his very self. Saint Athanasius comments: "Now the so-called gods of the Greeks, unworthy of the name, are faithful neither in their essence nor in their promises. They do not abide everywhere. The local deities come to naught in the course of time and undergo a natural dissolution. But the God of all . . . is ever the same and unchanging, deceiving neither in his essence nor in his promise."[4]

4. *Against the Arians* 2.10.

Reflection and Application (2:11–13)

In his letter to the Roman Christians, Paul had spoken of dying and rising with Christ in baptism. But here, in the shadow of the Roman sword, it is the real death of martyrdom he is facing, the ultimate dying with Christ. Yet his faith in the promise of resurrection is as firm as ever. Lesser challenges to fidelity face us daily. Our faithfulness to the cross, like Paul's, is less our own than it is a sharing in the very fidelity of God.

Against Fruitless Disputes (2:14–19)

> [14]Remind people of these things and charge them before God to stop disputing about words. This serves no useful purpose since it harms those who listen. [15]Be eager to present yourself as acceptable to God, a workman who causes no disgrace, imparting the word of truth without deviation. [16]Avoid profane, idle talk, for such people will become more and more godless, [17]and their teaching will spread like gangrene. Among them are Hymenaeus and Philetus, [18]who have deviated from the truth by saying that [the] resurrection has already taken place and are upsetting the faith of some. [19]Nevertheless, God's solid foundation stands, bearing this inscription, "The Lord knows those who are his"; and, "Let everyone who calls upon the name of the Lord avoid evil."

OT: Num 16:5, 26; Isa 26:13; 28:16; 52:11
NT: Rom 12:1; 1 Cor 15:12–19; 1 Thess 4:14; 1 Tim 1:3–7, 19–20; 4:6–7; 5:13
Catechism: resurrection present and future (655, 658)

Having placed the ministry within the sweep of salvation history, Paul now turns again to the practical order. In this loosely organized section, the author alternates between instructions to be given to the faithful and personal advice to Timothy, making it likely that the letter is being dictated between successive interruptions.   **2:14**

One of the most important tasks of the pastor is to **remind** his **people** (in season and out of season; 2 Tim 4:2) of the great truths of salvation—**these things**. In Ephesus, these things are apparently being neglected in favor of uselessly **disputing about words**. These three English words are one word in Greek, meaning literally "making war with words." Used only here in the Bible, it can mean either speculative discussions that harm rather than build up the faith or a method of arguing in the hopes of winning through mere eloquence or rhetoric, of putting down the opponent with cleverness rather than substance. If one has the truth, rhetoric can be a help to persuasion—as every preacher should know. But rhetoric without substance is a smokescreen and a waste of time (think of political sound bites). Undiscerning listeners can be spiritually ruined. Paul had faced this situation early in his ministry, when he contrasted the "word of wisdom," the gospel of the crucified, with the "wisdom of words," the inflated rhetoric that was mesmerizing the Corinthians (1 Cor 1–3). "The teacher should not serve the words but the words the teacher."[5]

2:15   The weapon Paul recommends first to Timothy is his personal example. The unsuspecting may for a while be seduced by the rhetoric of words, but they will find in Timothy the authentic gospel embodied and real. It is significant that Timothy is told to **present** himself **as acceptable to God** rather than before others, for it is fidelity to God that must come first, no matter what others may think. Timothy, in the employ of God, is a **workman** (*ergatēs*, used for the presbyters in 1 Tim 5:18) whose competence and uprightness must be such that he need never be blamed. His primary job is to dispense **the word of truth**, the gospel. This word is put in his hands to handle rightly. The rare Greek word translated **without deviation** is used of the farmer who keeps the plow in a straight furrow or a mason who fits the stones exactly according to the architect's blueprint. It appears in Prov 3:6 and 11:5 with the sense of cutting a path, perhaps through a dense forest, directly to the destination, as opposed to a wandering, circuitous route. Saint John Chrysostom applies it to using the sword of the Spirit "to cut off whatever is superfluous and foreign to your preaching."[6] The word conveys both the sense of orthodoxy in what is communicated and the proper expression of it. That is why seminarians and deacons are taught both theology and the art of preaching. The word of God deserves the best service of human words.

2:16–17   In contrast once more, those who engage in worldly and empty talk **will become more and more godless**. In Matthew's Gospel Jesus says that one must give an account not only of one's evil words but even of one's careless words (Matt 12:36). When one's words are not governed by God's wisdom, they can easily degenerate into unhealthy talk, criticism, and gossip, to say nothing of deviation from the truth of the gospel. If an early form of gnosticism is at issue here (see 2 Tim 2:18), the reference may be to the libertinism that its proponents were justifying. Is it any surprise that the sterility of late Scholastic theology in the fourteenth and fifteenth centuries was accompanied by serious moral

5. Augustine, *On Christian Doctrine* 4.28.61.
6. *Homilies on 2 Timothy* 2:15.

corruption? **Gangrene** was known in the ancient world for its drive to feed on, and hence spread to, healthy cells and organs. So too, the influence of these false teachers tends to infect others, and therein lies its particular danger. Paul is not talking mere theory here. Two persons whom he knows are proponents of the kind of teaching he is talking about. **Philetus** is not mentioned elsewhere in the New Testament, but we met **Hymenaeus** already in 1 Tim 1:20 as someone whom Paul had excommunicated. Apparently he has continued his harmful influence, probably in Ephesus itself.

These men **have deviated from the truth** by teaching **that [the] resurrection   2:18 has already taken place**. What did they mean by that? It depends largely on how the original Greek text reads. But there is a problem here. Some reputable manuscripts have the definite article, *the* resurrection, while other manuscripts lack it, meaning simply that "resurrection" or "a resurrection" has taken place. To indicate the uncertainty of the text, the NAB places "the" in square brackets. Paul could hardly be condemning these teachers for proposing that *Christ's* resurrection has already happened or that a spiritual resurrection has already taken place through baptism, for all that is Paul's own teaching.[7] More likely they are denying the future bodily resurrection in favor of a totally realized eschatology, namely, that the only resurrection is the spiritual resurrection that has already happened to the baptized. This would fit well with the Greek tendency to so privilege the spiritual side of man as to despise his material side and thus consider bodily resurrection an absurdity (Acts 17:32). Paul had already countered a form of this in 1 Cor 15, where some Christians were denying the resurrection of the faithful, although apparently they were willing to admit the resurrection of Jesus, for Paul argues from Jesus' resurrection to the resurrection of those who believe in him. Our passage possibly contains in the teaching of Hymenaeus and Philetus an early seed of †gnostic teaching, which in one form or another so spiritualized the goal of human life that there was no need for resurrection of the body. Tertullian says that this is the teaching of the Valentinian gnostics,[8] and Irenaeus says the gnostics claim that the resurrection has happened in their acquisition of truth.[9] In any case, the teaching of Hymenaeus and Philetus is destroying the faith of some members of the community in Ephesus.

Despite these errors, **God's solid foundation stands** firm. The Greek word   2:19 *themelios* is used in secular literature and in the Septuagint in the literal sense

---

7. See Rom 6:4–11; 1 Cor 15:1–4; Eph 2:6; Col 2:12; 3:1.
8. *Prescription against Heretics* 33; *Resurrection of the Flesh* 19.
9. *Against Heresies* 2.48.2.

for the foundations of cities or houses and in a metaphorical sense for the foundations of mountains, lands, earth, and heaven. The most common use is that of a building's base, laid deep in the earth, an image Paul used earlier in the figurative sense for the Church (1 Tim 3:15; see also 1 Pet 2:5–6). A foundation lays out the shape of the building it will uphold, and in this there is a parallel to the "blueprint" of 2 Tim 1:13. From the notion of a building's foundation developed the modern idea of a foundation in the sense of an institution that is meant to last beyond its founders. That nuance would fit well here, as Paul is thinking of the deposit that will outlast him. Whether this foundation is understood as the Church (as in 1 Tim 3:15) or more broadly as God's saving action for his people, the reason it stands firm is that God himself is its author.

This building bears an **inscription** (*sphragis*), a seal. In the literal sense a *sphragis* could be a stamp upon a brick or tile, a text engraved on a stone, especially a monument, or a wax seal on a document. Like a wedding ring, it could symbolize belonging to someone: "Set me as a seal on your heart, / as a seal on your arm" (Song 8:6). In a religious context, such a seal would mark a consecration, such as the inscription on the gold plate adorning the high priest's miter: "Sacred to the LORD" (Exod 28:36); or the inscription on the cloak and thigh of the Word of God: "King of kings and Lord of lords" (Rev 19:16). A seal was also used to confirm the authenticity of a document. All of these meanings converge here: belonging and consecration (**the Lord knows those who are his**) and authenticity, in the sense that real Christians can be known by their holiness and avoidance of **evil**.

The two quotations in 2 Tim 2:19 allude to the Septuagint version of Num 16. Korah, Dathan, and Abiram had revolted against the leadership of Moses. Since "the Lord knows those who are his" (i.e., Moses is the authentic leader appointed by God in Num 16:5), Moses arranges an adjudication by God before the entire people. Anticipating disaster upon the rebels, Moses warns his people to "keep away from the tents of these wicked men and do not touch anything that is theirs: otherwise you too will be swept away because of all their sins" (16:26). By the allusion to Num 16, Paul is saying that the holy community and its authorized leaders and teachers are the ones consecrated by the Lord, and those who truly belong to this community will separate themselves from the false teachers, who will be judged by God, just as the rebels were in Num 16. In the end, a high moral code is inseparable from true religious faith. Consecration and authenticity are proved by living out one's separation from evil.

Reflection and Application (2:14–19)

In today's sea of New Age alternatives to faith in Jesus Christ, Paul's reminder of "God's solid foundation" is a call to grow in our understanding of the faith through study of Scripture and the teaching of the Church, lest we be seduced by novelty that turns out to be straw. Pope Benedict XVI has repeatedly warned of the subjectivism and relativism of our age. Many today have bought into the idea that it doesn't matter what you believe or whether you believe at all, because who can really be sure of the objective world? It is a modern way of asking Pilate's question, "What is truth?" (John 18:38). Such a view can lead to the disintegration of community, whether in the secular world or in the Church.

Purification for Better Service (2:20–26)

---

²⁰In a large household there are vessels not only of gold and silver but also of wood and clay, some for lofty and others for humble use. ²¹If anyone cleanses himself of these things, he will be a vessel for lofty use, dedicated, beneficial to the master of the house, ready for every good work. ²²So turn from youthful desires and pursue righteousness, faith, love, and peace, along with those who call on the Lord with purity of heart. ²³Avoid foolish and ignorant debates, for you know that they breed quarrels. ²⁴A slave of the Lord should not quarrel, but should be gentle with everyone, able to teach, tolerant, ²⁵correcting opponents with kindness. It may be that God will grant them repentance that leads to knowledge of the truth, ²⁶and that they may return to their senses out of the devil's snare, where they are entrapped by him, for his will.

OT: Prov 15:12, 14; Sir 6:21; 51:23; Isa 42:1–4
NT: Matt 5:8; 12:19–20; Gal 5:22; 1 Tim 1:4–5; 6:11; Titus 3:9
Catechism: purity of heart (2518–19)

After the metaphor of foundation, Paul develops the image of the Church as **household**. In the households of the wealthy there are rich vessels and vessels for ordinary use (literally vessels "for honor . . . for dishonor"). In more frugal Roman times vessels of **gold and silver** were limited to religious uses, but the increasing wealth of the empire led to their appearance in the larger, wealthier households, a practice decried in the reign of Tiberius by two senators, who moved unsuccessfully to outlaw the manufacture of gold vessels for secular

2:20

171

use.[10] At the other end of the spectrum, there were vessels made of fragments of stone or wood "which became vessels for bath water or foot basins or for less noble purposes."[11] Now what application of the comparison is Paul making here? Several possibilities are suggested.

The application may be simply that in the Church some ministers have an apparently more noble task and some have a humbler one—a comparison made in 1 Cor 12:12–26—but without any privileging of one as more necessary than the other. This is the sense of the NAB's **some for lofty and others for humble use**. In this sense, the reader would be challenged to accept the Church with the diversity of ministries and competencies.

However, while the figurative sense of the Greek word *atimia* can be "lowly, insignificant" (which is the meaning the NAB has chosen by translating **humble use**), the literal sense is "without honor, dishonorable." And in this literal sense there are two possibilities. First, in the context of the false teachers, it is possible that "those for honor, those for dishonor" echoes Rom 9:21, where it is part of God's plan that there be in this world, and even at times in the Church, those who cooperate with his plan ("for honor") and those who oppose it ("for dishonor"), the latter contributing to the purification of the elect: "There have to be factions among you in order that . . . those who are approved among you may become known" (1 Cor 11:19). To avoid impairing the holiness of the Church, some Fathers held that Paul here meant the world, with its mixture of bad and good, not the Church. But Cyprian, followed by Augustine, is closer to the truth, when he writes: "Even if weeds appear in the Church, this should not hinder our faith and love. There is no reason to leave the Church just because we see weeds in it. We must work all the harder to become wheat ourselves, so that when the grain is stored in the barns of the Lord, we may reap the fruit of our labor and toil."[12]

2:21   But this interpretation doesn't square well with Paul's desire to eliminate false teaching, if not the false teachers themselves, from the community. So a second literal interpretation takes its cue from Paul's somewhat ambiguous expression in the following verse: **if anyone cleanses himself of these things**. What are "these things"? They would be the vessels of "dishonor" like toilets and drains that are associated with filth, and Paul would be saying that if ministers will rid themselves of all remnants of false teaching, ignorant debates, and even youthful passions mentioned in the next two verses, they can become like gold and silver

10. Tacitus, *Annals* 2.33.
11. Philo, *Contemplative Life* 7.
12. *Letters* 54.3.

vessels, for noble service. Indeed, it seems that the spiritual transformation of the minister is primary in Paul's mind here.

The minister who cleanses himself will then have the following characteristics. (1) **Dedicated**: this is how the NAB translates the Greek passive past participle *hēgiasmenon*, but the term here has the religious sense of being "consecrated," set aside for divine use. It may seem a bit much to say that simply cleansing oneself from bad teaching would be equivalent to consecration. The past participle, which precisely means "having been consecrated," probably indicates that avoiding bad teaching and immoral conduct is demanded by one's prior consecration through baptism and ordination to a holy ministry. (2) **Beneficial** (or "useful") **to the master of the house** (i.e., the Lord): only an uncontaminated vessel can be used by the Lord for his sacred purposes. (3) **Ready for every good work**: whereas "beneficial" looked to one's relationship with the Lord, this quality looks to one's ministry to others. The word suggests that the person is adequately prepared and also willing and eager to undertake whatever needs to be done. This demands a certain flexibility and a willingness to risk taking on tasks that are not familiar. If everyone in the Church stuck to what was easy and familiar, there would be no missionaries—or, for that matter, no significant ministries of any kind. Only risk takers can respond to the developing needs of the Church. **Every good work** would apply not only to ministry within the Church but also to the layperson's consecration to transform the world outside.

Abandoning metaphors, Paul tells Timothy which vices to avoid and which virtues to pursue. **Youthful desires** ("passions" might be more apt here) may sound to the modern reader like the paternalistic counsel of an old man who believes wisdom comes only with the age he has achieved, but the Greek word suggests innovations or undisciplined agitation that takes no account of the common good, the hotheaded intemperance that is perhaps more characteristic of youth but in some persons carries over into adult years (as we say, "a forty-year-old adolescent"). Paul obviously thinks that those who are proposing the new teachings are folk of this kind, whatever their age, and he is painfully aware, from his own earlier experience, how destructive to community such lack of self-discipline can be. Then, in a beautiful alliteration in the Greek (*diōke de dikaiosynēn*) Paul introduces the first virtue, **righteousness** or "justice," a biblical word so rich and used in so many different contexts it is hard to pin it down to a single meaning. While the basic sense is rendering to each person his due, in the Bible it is equivalent to holiness, to that perfection that God himself has and that he expects of his people. In leaders it is often allied with other virtues. **Faith**, for Paul, of course, means

2:22

173

more than trustworthiness. Its object is Christ, and it is the virtue that alone gives entrance to the righteousness of God (Rom 3:22). Timothy's faith should be a rock on which other members of the Church may lean. But the expression of faith is **love**, *agapē* (Gal 5:6)—that selfless, benevolent love—and the fruit of love is **peace** (Gal 5:22). All of these virtues will make the leader an example for the flock and will set him apart from the useless quarrels that are dividing the community.

2:23–24   Repetition is the mother of wisdom! So Paul hammers once more upon the debates that lead to quarrels. A person who engages in **ignorant** disputes is not only uninstructed (Sir 51:23) but undisciplined. In the Wisdom literature of the Old Testament the word refers to one who resists education ("unruly" in Sir 6:21), refuses correction ("senseless" in Prov 15:12), and blabbers foolishly ("fools" in 15:14). Referring here not to ignorant persons but to **ignorant debates**, Paul probably means the same as the dispute about words of 2 Tim 2:14 or the profane, idle talk of 2:16. The leader in the Church is a **slave of the Lord**, having no will but that of the Master. The slave must be like his Lord (Matt 10:25), who himself took the form of a slave, thus setting the pattern for his followers in love and humility (Phil 2:1–7) and challenging those who would be leaders to consider themselves slaves, that is, totally at the service of the community (Mark 10:43–45). Toward those whose methods are dispute and quarreling, it may be difficult to be **gentle**, but even verbal violence is not to be requited with verbal violence. The preferred weapon is simply clear and effective teaching, and this assumes a certain competence: **able to teach**. "Bishops," Cyprian writes, "must not only teach but also learn, because he who grows and advances daily by learning better things, teaches better."[13]

2:25   But patience in the midst of this struggle is also needed. The NAB translates *anexikakon* in 2 Tim 2:24 simply as "tolerant," but the word has the rich meaning "bearing evil without resentment." Second Timothy 2:25 indicates that those who are promoting false teachings are still redeemable, which confirms our preference for understanding the cleansing, or cutting off contact, in 2:21 to refer to the teachings rather than to the teachers of falsehood. The only persons Paul has excommunicated in the Pastorals are Hymenaeus and Alexander (1 Tim 1:20), and Timothy is warned against the latter as a danger to the community (2 Tim 4:14–15). That is why **kindness**, patience, and ongoing instruction are called for. Basil the Great comments: "The superior should not rebuke wrongdoers under the impulse of his own passions. Admonishing

13. *Letters* 74.10.

a brother with indignation and anger does not free the brother from his faults but involves the superior himself in the brother's sins."[14]

Paul does not entertain the illusion that Timothy's strategy will necessarily succeed, for **repentance** and conversion are a grace of God, and pride and stubbornness, like the hard ground of the parable (Mark 4:15), may make the false teachers impenetrable to Timothy's efforts. **Truth** is of course the revealed doctrine. The word **knowledge**, which can also be translated "recognition," here is not the more general *gnōsis* but *epignōsis*, which most often refers to a more exact knowledge of an object of which one is already conscious. That fits the context here well, for the false teachers have some knowledge of the gospel already, and it is their mixture of truth with error that makes it so dangerous. These persons need to have their teaching "purified" or "cleansed" (2 Tim 2:21).

This hoped-for conversion would bring them back **to their senses**. It is as if   2:26 the false teachers have been drunk on the wine of their own misguided ideas and need the clarion call of Joel, "Wake up, you drunkards" (Joel 1:5), or of Paul himself, who literally says, "Sober up! . . . for some [of you] have no knowledge of God" (1 Cor 15:34). Philo contrasts the sinner who persists in his way with the wise person who fails but then "comes to his senses, that is, he repents and recovers as from an illness."[15] If pastoral gentleness is to moderate the approach to the false teachers, it does not mean that their erroneous situation is not serious. They are, in fact, trapped in **the devil's snare** and do not realize the state of stupor they are in (compare Luke 21:34–35). The early Church took more seriously than we generally do today the work of the devil and elaborated a whole program of spiritual warfare to meet it (Eph 6:10–20; James 4:7; 1 Pet 5:8–9). In this case, the work of the pastor is more challenging, since it is not his personal struggle against temptation that is at issue but rather the hold the devil has on another, the entrapment of another's **will**, whose freedom even God respects. But, as always, there is hope: "It may be that God will grant them repentance that leads to knowledge of the truth." Since conversion is a grace, what is implied here is that Timothy and his flock should intercede for the erring.

Reflection and Application (2:20–26)

The application of this text about vessels to Church life today depends on which of the three alternative interpretations one chooses. If we choose the figurative meaning, then we are invited to praise God for the variety of ministries

14. *The Long Rules* Q. 50.R.
15. *Allegorical Interpretation of Genesis* 2.60.

175

in the Church, great or small. If we choose the literal reference for "vessels for dishonor" and take it to refer to dishonorable ministers, the Church certainly has had these. Scandals, even among the clergy, have led some Catholics to jump ship. For those who remain faithful, this departure adds to the pain already felt by the scandal, but they realize that even among the Twelve there was one who denied the Lord and another who betrayed him. The Church is a mix of sinners and saints, and the boundary between good and evil passes through the heart of each one of us: David the devout and David the sinner. The question is: where does the Church, with the word of God, the sacraments, and the Holy Spirit, lead? The Church that makes saints does not encourage sinners in their sin; it challenges and offers them reconciliation. But in the meantime, the process may be messy, and some kind of Church discipline may be called for, though there is always hope for conversion.

But the last, and preferred, interpretation concerns Paul's encouragement to ministers themselves to clean up their act, that is, not only to reject false teaching or any mixture of it but also to grow in purity and in virtue, both in relation to God, because their ministry is a sacred one, and in relation to their neighbor, because they are a vessel used by the Lord.

Part of that vessel's ministry is dealing with opponents. Timothy should deal with them kindly, with the sincere hope that they will be rescued "out of the devil's snare." Surely all of us at one time or another have seen to our dismay someone we loved get caught up in drugs or alcohol or a bad passionate relationship because they would not listen to reason. Well-known psychiatrist Scott Peck tells in his book *People of the Lie*[16] how he was led to believe in the existence of the demonic and the value of exorcism in some cases by a few of his patients' stubborn refusal to admit the truth about themselves. In his therapy he would keep bringing them to the threshold they needed to cross but they would turn away from it. Indeed, he came to believe they were caught in "the devil's snare." But the Church never loses hope, for heaven is peopled with untold numbers of Magdalens and Augustines.

16. M. Scott Peck, *People of the Lie: The Hope for Healing Human Evil* (New York: Simon and Schuster, 1983).

Meeting the Challenges of the Last Days

2 Timothy 3

Persons facing their imminent death often tell those left behind what values they hope the survivors will treasure and live out. Today some people even make a video to leave with family and friends as a permanent memorial. This part of Paul's letter is a bit like that, except that it is a personal confiding to Timothy, like my father on his deathbed telling my oldest brother, "Take care of them." Jesus did the same at the Last Supper and in the commissioning of Peter after the resurrection, and so did Paul to the elders of Ephesus (Acts 20:17–35). This section also warns of difficulties Timothy may have to face.

Worsening of the Last Days (3:1–9)

[1]But understand this: there will be terrifying times in the last days. [2]People will be self-centered and lovers of money, proud, haughty, abusive, disobedient to their parents, ungrateful, irreligious, [3]callous, implacable, slanderous, licentious, brutal, hating what is good, [4]traitors, reckless, conceited, lovers of pleasure rather than lovers of God, [5]as they make a pretense of religion but deny its power. Reject them. [6]For some of these slip into homes and make captives of women weighed down by sins, led by various desires, [7]always trying to learn but never able to reach a knowledge of the truth. [8]Just as Jannes and Jambres opposed Moses, so they also oppose the truth—people of depraved mind, unqualified in the faith. [9]But they will not make further progress, for their foolishness will be plain to all, as it was with those two.

OT: Exod 7:11–13, 22
NT: Matt 7:15; 24:4, 24; Rom 1:29–32; 1 Tim 4:1; 5:13; Rev 9:20–21
Catechism: the Church's ultimate trial (675–77)

3:1   In G. K. Chesterton's *Ballad of the White Horse*, the Virgin Mary appears to King Alfred, giving him a mission to defend Christian England against the invasion of the Danes. She says:

> I tell you naught for your comfort,
> Yea, naught for your desire,
> Save that the sky grows darker yet
> And the sea rises higher.

This is the way Paul begins his farewell address. He brings naught for Timothy's comfort but tells him he is heading into a storm. Jesus did the same in the apocalyptic sections of the synoptic Gospels (Matt 24; Mark 13; Luke 21:5–36). In his Last Supper discourse (John 14–17), Jesus promised his disciples the cross of persecution. But when Paul speaks here of **the last days**, he does not use the apocalyptic language of either the synoptic Gospels or the book of Revelation. No earthquakes, falling stars, or wars. Instead he presents a parade of nineteen vices or, more precisely, nineteen kinds of vice-ridden people (2 Tim 3:2–4). Paul uses the future tense, so we may presume he is speaking of something that has not yet occurred but may very well occur soon, perhaps during the lifetime of Timothy. So his disciple should be prepared. On the other hand, Paul and Timothy have already experienced some of these vices, certainly in the Roman world, even at times within the Christian community (e.g., 1 Cor 5:1–5; 6:12–20; and the case of Alexander and Hymenaeus in 1 Tim 1:20; 2 Tim 4:14–15). So

Was It Then or Is It Now?   LIVING TRADITION

Tertullian's comments about his times (late second century) could easily fit ours: "Evil is ever on the increase, a sign of the final times. Innocent babies are now not even allowed to be born, so corrupted are the moral standards. Nor are children properly trained, so neglected is concern for them. . . . In fact, modesty . . . has in our time become an obsolete subject."[a] And Caesarius of Arles (around AD 500) complains that there is no longer any fear of the general judgment or of hell.[b]

a. *On Purity* 1.1.
b. *Sermon* 71.3.

if these **last days** have not already begun, there has at least been a foretaste of them. In commanding Timothy to "reject them," Paul is clearly expecting that Timothy will encounter persons of this kind, if he has not done so already.

In Gal 5:22 Paul put *agapē*, divine love, at the top of his list of effects of the **3:2** Holy Spirit. In fact, although he lists nine effects, he calls the sum of them "fruit" in the singular, suggesting that they are all contained in love (1 Cor 13; Gal 5:14). In a similar way, here the first on the list of vices is the foundation of the rest: **self-centered**. The person who is self-centered—the Greek means literally "self-loving"—does not, obviously, have an authentic care for self, which is necessary even if we would love our neighbor (Matt 22:39). Rather, self-centeredness sees others only to the extent they are useful to oneself, even if the other is God (2 Tim 3:4). This egoism gives rise to innumerable vices. Paul's list is designed to suggest it is endless.

The first and in some way the most obvious manifestation of self-love is the love **of money**, "the root of all evils" (1 Tim 6:10). It was the vice of the false teachers in Crete (Titus 1:11). Many of the other vices listed here are synonyms or differ from each other only in shade of meaning. The **proud**, biblically speaking, are persons who abuse their power and defy even God, hence, like the tyrant Antiochus Epiphanes, are blasphemers (2 Macc 9:7, 28). **Haughty** suggests looking down on others; **abusive** means injuring the reputation of another and can also refer to blasphemy against God. There has been rebellion against authority at all ages, but the widespread disobedience of children against **their parents**, whom nature instructs them to love, is a sign of the final times, for it is a supreme act of ingratitude, and when this ingratitude is turned against God, it marks people as **irreligious**, that is, not merely indifferent to religion but violently opposed to it. (Is the effort to remove God from public life in our country a symptom of this?)

The list continues with **callous**—those denuded of even natural affection for **3:3** spouse, children, or family, to say nothing of mercy for strangers who ask for help. **Implacable** means those who stubbornly refuse to be reconciled, whether the conflict be as minor as an argument or as major as a war. Being implacable is the opposite of being the kind of peacemaker Jesus called blessed (Matt 5:9). In our day we see much of this in the inflexible attitude of some terrorists who prefer to die in hatred than live in peace. **Slanderous** in the Greek is *diaboloi* (literally "devils"), the plural form of the word used in 2 Tim 2:26 for the devil's trap. In the Greek Old Testament this word was the ordinary translation of "the Satan," the adversary who opposes the work of God, particularly by slandering the just. Those who spread falsehoods about others are doing the devil's work.

Licentious, sometimes translated "undisciplined," means those who cannot, or will not, control their passions. **Brutal** is sometimes translated "cruel," for it means a dehumanizing such that one acts as a beast. "It is because of this kinship with the flesh that those of us who incline toward it become like wolves, faithless and treacherous and hurtful, and others like lions, wild and savage and untamed."[1] **Hating what is good** is literally "not loving the good," and it balances and repeats the "lover of self" that began this series. Love, on the other hand, "does not rejoice over wrongdoing but rejoices with the truth" (1 Cor 13:6).

3:4   One of the most poignant human sufferings is betrayal. Every age of the Church since Judas has had its **traitors**. This has frequently been experienced by the martyrs, many of whom were handed over by supposed friends. But this kind of betrayal will become commonplace in the final times (Matt 24:10). The **reckless** are those who act out of heedless passion, the bull in the china shop. The stubbornly headstrong are destructive of human community and all the more so of community in the Church. Some will be blinded by their own self-conceived ideas (**conceited**), some will be **lovers of pleasure rather than lovers of God.**

3:5   **As they make a pretense of religion** is closely attached to the preceding. As one listens to the list of vice-ridden people, one might say they are godless. But no, the problem is that they *look* godly—which suggests that they have either wormed their way into the Church or, having become Christians, have strayed off into heresy by adulterating the faith. In any case they upset the community. The word "religion" here is the same *eusebeia* that we have often met before. It refers to the true faith. How do they **deny its power**? This could mean that their very conduct contradicts or nullifies the power they pretend to have. It could also mean that their teaching has no power in it, as today some of the New Age movements promote a gnostic self-development theosophy or nature religion that does not require transformation but canonizes self-satisfaction.

It is not clear how we are to understand the command **reject them**. The NAB's translation suggests some form of excommunication. Other translations say "avoid them." Obviously, that might not be possible in one's civil dealings, and it would surely not be possible if they were members of the community. So it seems the NAB's translation is the better one: exclude them from the community. In Matt 18:17 Jesus says of a recalcitrant member, "If he refuses to listen even to the church, then treat him as you would a Gentile or a tax collector." This is a formula for excommunication, that is, for withdrawing from the person the privilege of membership or communion, not out of vindictiveness but simply because he or

---

1. Epictetus, *Discourses* 1.3.7 (Loeb Classical Library translation).

she has behaved in a way that is effectively a withdrawal from the community by flagrant violation of its standards. But there is always hope for repentance and reintegration with the Church, for if we ask how Jesus dealt with Gentiles and tax collectors, he certainly reached out to them as people to be evangelized.

Second Timothy 3:6 gives further insight into the tactics of the false teachers. They do not do their proselytizing in the public arena, the regular gathering of the worshiping community, where they might be challenged by the more mature members or by Timothy himself. Rather they go from house to house—"slipping in"—where they can find **women** in the absence of their husbands. These women are apparently pagans or at most nominal Christians, for they are still **weighed down by sins** and by unruly **desires** and have never come to a **knowledge of the truth**. They are, nevertheless, like the men of Athens, always eager to hear something new (Acts 17:21). Their emotional promiscuity is matched by an intellectual one: they are always dabbling here and there but never letting themselves be confronted by the truth of their own moral mire and the liberating invitation of the authentic gospel. Easy prey for the merchants of falsehood, these women are captivated (literally "made prisoner") by the rhetoric and apparent piety of the teachers (2 Tim 3:5).[2]

3:6–7

The names **Jannes and Jambres** appear nowhere else in the Bible, but a Jewish legend ascribed these names to the magicians who did their tricks before Pharaoh in opposition to Moses (Exod 7:11). They are types of the kind of resistance to the gospel that the false teachers embody. Perhaps, in addition to their doctrinal aberrations, they are inducing these women to superstitious practices. All of this indicates to Paul that their minds are **depraved** and that they are thus **unqualified** to teach anything that pertains to **the faith**.

3:8

Paul's excoriating of these charlatans ends on a positive note. Although their teaching spreads like gangrene (2 Tim 2:17), it is doomed to collapse, because when it is brought into the light, people will see it for what it is. Its bad fruits will attest to its erroneous root. What had been done in the secrecy of homes (3:6) will meet public judgment. This will suffice to stop them in their tracks by exposing the **foolishness** of their program.

3:9

Reflection and Application (3:1–9)

In Philo, the Jewish contemporary of Paul who makes moral allegories of Scripture passages, self-love is an unnatural vice. In fact, self-love is the major

2. Some critics claim that Paul is prejudiced against women in this passage, as in others. But it is clear from this context and throughout the three Pastoral Epistles that he is equally hard on deviant men.

181

vice that ends up opposing even God. And Augustine comments: "Anyone who loves himself by leaving God out of his life doesn't even remain in himself but goes away from himself."[3] While virtue has not been lost in our postmodern world, the image of the virtuous, selfless hero committed to objective truth has in many ways faded into one of the person who is a bundle of impulses inherited or absorbed, excusing himself or herself from any commitment beyond personal subjectivism. The self-centeredness that Paul skewers here has been exposed by more than one social scientist as the plague of today's developed world.

Yet to be fair, it is equally true that we have witnessed in our day outstanding examples of selfless heroism—the firemen at the collapse of the World Trade Center, the soldier who throws himself on an enemy grenade to save his buddies, the 76-year-old Holocaust survivor Liviu Librescu who died trying to keep a gunman from shooting his students at Virginia Tech, the police who daily risk their lives for the defense of others. And what of missionaries, religious and lay, who sacrifice themselves and sometimes lose their lives as well, or the swelling number of college students who volunteer to serve the needy?

So how do we put all this together with Paul's pessimistic view of "the last days"?

In the last analysis his view is not that pessimistic, for he says that the plans of the wicked will one day be exposed for what they are. Error, deceit, and evil itself are their own worst enemies. The Communist empire in the Soviet Union eventually collapsed because it was built on an erroneous conception of humanity. Error and evil may rule for a time and cause untold suffering to many. There is a growing awareness of the evil of abortion in this country, not only because it is the killing of the innocent but because of its lasting effects on women, many of whom have been deceived by a conspiracy of silence on the part of the abortion providers. But truth will out. And for the Christian, Truth is spelled with a capital T because it is Christ (John 14:6). Elsewhere Paul answers the question of evil in his own words: "Where sin increased, grace overflowed all the more" (Rom 5:20). And it continues to do so even in the midst of persecution and the sword, for "in all these things we are winning an overwhelming victory because of him who loved us" (8:37).[4] Putting all of this together, we could say that if the shadows grow darker, it means the sun shines brighter.

3. *Sermon* 330.3.
4. My translation; the NAB reads: "In all these things we conquer overwhelmingly through him who loved us."

Paul's Example and Teaching (3:10–17)

[10]You have followed my teaching, way of life, purpose, faith, patience, love, endurance, [11]persecutions, and sufferings, such as happened to me in Antioch, Iconium, and Lystra, persecutions that I endured. Yet from all these things the Lord delivered me. [12]In fact, all who want to live religiously in Christ Jesus will be persecuted. [13]But wicked people and charlatans will go from bad to worse, deceivers and deceived. [14]But you, remain faithful to what you have learned and believed, because you know from whom you learned it, [15]and that from infancy you have known [the] sacred scriptures, which are capable of giving you wisdom for salvation through faith in Christ Jesus. [16]All scripture is inspired by God and is useful for teaching, for refutation, for correction, and for training in righteousness, [17]so that one who belongs to God may be competent, equipped for every good work.

OT: Prov 1:1–7; Wis 6:10–11; Sir 1:23
NT: Matt 5:11–12; Rom 15:4; 2 Cor 11:23–29; Gal 5:22; 1 Thess 2:13; 2 Pet 1:20–21
Catechism: persecution (769, 1816), inspiration of Scripture (105), read Scripture (131–33)
Lectionary: (3:10–12, 14–15) Admission to Candidacy for Diaconate and Priesthood; (3:14–17) Institution of Readers
Lectionary (Byzantine): (3:10–15) Sunday of the Publican and the Pharisee

In strong contrast to the false teachers, Timothy has been a disciple of Paul   **3:10** from the time of his second missionary journey (Acts 16:1–5). He has **followed** Paul, not only as a companion of his journeys but as a child follows a father. The intensive form of the Greek word for "follow," meaning literally "to walk at one's side," here suggests imitation, understanding, following instructions, as well as firsthand knowledge of the person. The list of nine elements of this "following" contrast with the list of vice-ridden persons in 2 Tim 3:2–5. **Teaching** heads the list, probably to contrast with the noxious influence of the false teachers.

But in ancient times, particularly biblical times, the disciple learned more by imitation than by instruction. That is why living with the master or the rabbi was the best way to learn his **way of life**—his life of prayer, his toil at the ministry, his manner of dealing with setbacks, his way of relating to persons of all kinds, both within and outside the community. This would include his **purpose**, that is, his vision of the mission given him by the Lord and his practical objectives and methods for carrying it out, for example, the policy of going first to the Jews and then to Gentiles or of not invading the arena of other apostles' ministry (Rom 15:20). These objectives were inspired by Paul's **faith** in Jesus Christ, a faith tested repeatedly by trials in which he held firm and "steadfast," which is the sense of the word the NAB renders as **patience**. And Paul carried out his mission with a **love** that, according to his own teaching, *endures* all things (1 Cor 13:7).

3:11   Timothy has learned this way of life from Paul, a way of life tempered by the **persecutions** he suffered, especially in the three cities named in Acts 13:14–14:20, during his first missionary journey. Although Timothy became a companion of Paul at **Lystra** only on his second visit there (16:1–3), Luke may imply that he was among the disciples who gathered around Paul after his stoning there (14:20; 2 Cor 11:25). And it is possible, of course, that Paul was persecuted during his second visit as well. At any rate, the mention of those three cities, rather than others where he suffered persecution, would have resonated with Timothy because they were his home country. **Yet from all these things the Lord delivered me** may be intended to buttress Paul's hope to be rescued once again "from the lion's mouth" (2 Tim 4:17).

3:12   Paul projects his own experience onto a universal screen. Those who take their Christian commitment seriously **will be persecuted**. By the time of the writing of this letter Christians took for granted that persecution would be their lot, for most of them had experienced it, and the words of **Christ Jesus** had rung true. He had promised persecution to his disciples (Mark 4:17; 10:30) and declared blessed those who endure it for righteousness' sake (Matt 5:10) or for his sake (5:11), since authentic discipleship is a prophetic vocation. If Paul warned his communities in his early ministry that they could expect persecution (1 Thess 3:4), he now recalls this from a lifetime of experience marked by the cross.

3:13   In this passage of contrasts, Paul switches from sketching the qualities of authentic discipleship to speaking about **wicked people and charlatans**. Those who degenerate from one degree of evil to another are not only the immoral but those who are fakes, imposters. Paul is implicitly telling Timothy and those who listen to the reading of the letter that they should not be surprised if the chaos they are experiencing gets worse before it gets better. But get better it will, because the wicked are in reality their own enemies. They fall into the pit they have made.[5] They fashion their own punishment (Rom 1:27). If they teach falsehood, they will be the first victims of it. This biblical teaching was a catchword of the Gentile world as well, going back to Hesiod (eighth century BC): "Bad advice is very bad for the giver."[6]

3:14–15   Back to Timothy, continuing the exhortation of 3:10: he is not to be shaken by any novel teaching but to hold firm to the faith and teaching he once learned. The

---

5. Ps 7:15–16; 9:16; 57:7; Prov 26:27; Eccles 10:8; Sir 27:25–27.
6. *Works and Days* 266.

†aorist tense of the verbs **learned and believed** refers to a past moment rather than a progressive growth, hence, the moment of his public profession of faith. Though Timothy's faith, like that of every Christian, was a grace given by God, there were human instruments of the learning. Although Paul certainly formed Timothy more deeply in the faith, filling out his instruction (1 Thess 3:10), it was not from the apostle that he first learned the faith. Already **from infancy** he has known the **sacred scriptures** (literally "the holy letters"). Instead of using the normal term *graphē* for the Scripture, Paul here uses *grammata*, meaning literally "letters of the alphabet." Ceslas Spicq notes that this is a beautiful way of speaking of how a child learns to read—first learning the letters.[7] Of course, by extension, the word means the sacred Scriptures (John 5:47). These were the Jewish Scriptures, which Timothy's mother may have taught him before she became a Christian. These Scriptures become sources of saving wisdom when one accepts them as fulfilled in **Christ Jesus.**

The emphasis in 2 Tim 3:16 is on the usefulness of the Scriptures. What does **all scripture** refer to? Certainly what we would call the Old Testament, those writings that the Jews considered to be **inspired by God** (literally "breathed by God"). But does Paul by this time understand the apostolic writings also to be inspired Scripture? Certainly he thought of the message he preached as inspired by God (1 Thess 2:13), and he considers his letters to have no less divine authority, since they are an elaboration of the gospel. He quotes a word of Jesus in 1 Tim 5:18 as Scripture (see also 6:3). So "scripture" here would seem to cover not only any written words of Jesus but also any apostolic writings that were known at the time. While consigning the message to writing runs the risk of losing something of the freshness and immediacy of oral transmission, the process has the advantage of stabilizing the Tradition, giving the Church solid handles to grasp in times of doctrinal turmoil. And far from limiting the usefulness of the apostolic Tradition, writing favors it, for it makes the Tradition more widely available. Christians have always found Scripture an inexhaustible source of spiritual nourishment, for it is divinely inspired, "not only when it was being written by God breathing through the writers, but also while it is being read, by God breathing through the Scripture, and with Scripture breathing Him."[8]

This particular verse (2 Tim 3:16) lacks a verb, so we must supply one. But where? Many translations render, "All Scripture is inspired by God and is useful." Read this way, the emphasis falls on divine inspiration, providing the major text for the Church's belief in the inspiration of the Bible. But at the time of

3:16

7. Spicq, *Épîtres pastorales*, 2.786.
8. J. A. Bengel (died 1752), cited by Johnson, *First and Second Letters to Timothy*, 39.

Vatican II and the Inspiration of the Scriptures

LIVING TRADITION

A doctrinal elaboration of Paul's words to Timothy is given in *Dei Verbum* of the Second Vatican Council:

> Those divinely revealed realities which are contained and presented in Sacred Scripture have been committed to writing under the inspiration of the Holy Spirit. For holy mother Church, relying on the belief of the Apostles (see John 20:31; 2 Tim 3:16; 2 Pet 1:19–20; 3:15–16), holds that the books of both the Old and New Testaments in their entirety, with all their parts, are sacred and canonical because, written under the inspiration of the Holy Spirit, they have God as their author and have been handed on as such to the Church herself. In composing the sacred books, God chose men and while employed by Him they made use of their powers and abilities so that with Him acting in them and through them, they, as true authors, consigned to writing everything and only those things which He wanted.
>
> Therefore, since everything asserted by the inspired authors or sacred writers must be held to be asserted by the Holy Spirit, it follows that the books of Scripture must be acknowledged as teaching solidly, faithfully and without error that truth which God wanted put into sacred writings for the sake of salvation. Therefore "all Scripture is divinely inspired and has its use for teaching the truth and refuting error, for reformation of manners and discipline in right living, so that the man who belongs to God may be efficient and equipped for good work of every kind" (2 Tim 3:6–7, Greek text). (*Dei Verbum* 11)

Since Paul is speaking mainly about the Old Testament here, it is worth also quoting what Vatican II says about that: "These books, though they also contain some things which are incomplete and temporary, nevertheless show us true divine pedagogy. These same books, then, give expression to a lively sense of God, contain a store of sublime teachings about God, sound wisdom about human life, and a wonderful treasury of prayers, and in them the mystery of our salvation is present in a hidden way. Christians should receive them with reverence" (*Dei Verbum* 15).

Paul's writing, the inspiration of the Law, Prophets, and Writings was taken for granted by all Christians, Jews, and even most of the heretics. Moreover, the context here points toward the usefulness of the Scriptures. Hence an equally legitimate translation is, "All Scripture, inspired by God, is useful." It is not a question of different meanings, only of emphasis.

Jesus had frequently used the Scriptures for **teaching**, not only from memory but, on one occasion at least, by publicly reading from them (Luke 4:16–21). In the apostolic Church, teaching was a charism of the Holy Spirit (Rom 12:7; 1 Cor

12:29). In Eph 4:11 it is closely associated with the office of pastor and obviously was a ministry of the apostle himself (1 Cor 4:17). But teaching should be based on the Scriptures (Acts 8:35; 17:2–3), for they have an unparalleled authority (John 10:35) and a power to instruct, strengthen, and encourage and thus fire hope (Rom 15:4). Their authority makes them an apt instrument for refuting the claims of opponents. Since nonbelievers would not accept the authority of the Scriptures as a basis of argumentation, this **refutation** must envisage the Jewish opponents of the new faith, who met Paul and his companions in nearly every city. For those open to **correction** (Sir 21:6), the Scriptures are also useful to bring them back to the right path. In profane Greek, the word is used for the rebuilding of a city, the restoration of a sanctuary, the correction of an error, and in many places in Philo it is used for moral reform. There is a close parallel in Stoic philosopher Epictetus, who, in discussing the prayerful attitude with which one should approach religious rites, says: "The Mysteries . . . were established by men of ancient times for the purpose of *training* and *reform* of life."[9] The word *epanorthōsis* means **correction**, and its twin, *paideia*, means **training in righteousness**.

We have, then, in this lineup the four practical values of Scripture: (1) teaching, the more general and inclusive term, (2) the authority to dispel opponents, (3) the power to bring about conversion, and (4) the ongoing spiritual formation of the Christian. The history of the Church amply demonstrates how effectively the Scriptures have been used for all four functions.

The last verse in this section builds on the last function mentioned, forma- **3:17** tion, and designates the divinely appointed purpose of Scripture in the life of each Christian, and all the more so of each pastor: not only to train one in righteousness but to make one complete, outfitted for mission. Every Christian and every pastor is endowed with charisms for the building of the Church (Eph 4:7–16), and the Scriptures have a crucial role in enabling disciples to use their charisms effectively. In another metaphor, the word of God is the sword of the Spirit by which the warrior will carry on the spiritual battle (6:17). Here it makes him **equipped for every good work**. No matter what the task of the Christian or the pastor, Scripture is the manual of directions.

Reflection and Application (3:10–17)

Timothy was formed by the Scriptures, of course, but he learned how to be a Christian and a Christian leader from his constant association with his mentor,

9. *Discourses* 3.21.15.

Paul. Today, ministers in the Church are expected to have some theological formation, but they learn how to apply it by hands-on experience with good mentors. Not only are seminarians given a year of internship before ordination, lay ministers also gain their know-how from others in the field. Some of this mentoring is formal, some informal. One of the most influential persons in the life of John Paul II was the layman who mentored him by inviting him to join a Living Rosary group.

It is all too easy to seek to reinforce one's own identity by pasting condemning labels on other individuals or groups, especially if there has been a history of conflict with them. But often this history needs to be revisited, with wrongs acknowledged and a future of reconciliation and cooperation sought. Even so, there are times when evil is so rampant and such power lies in the hands of the tyrant that prophetic witness to the truth, even to the point of shedding one's blood, is the only option, and that has been the vocation of the martyr. This is the kind of situation Paul is talking about here, and it is a challenge to Christians who too easily compromise with the culture around them and become chameleons instead of prophets.

If the Second Vatican Council spends the early chapters of *Dei Verbum* on the inspiration of Scripture, it concludes the document with a chapter entitled "Sacred Scripture in the Life of the Church" (sections 21–26), following Paul's teaching on the usefulness of the written word of God. Since the time of the council, Bible study has become much more widespread in the Catholic Church—something our Protestant brothers and sisters have excelled in for years. The Catholic community is discovering how enriched its sacramental life can become when it is accompanied by an in-depth study of the Scriptures and when homilies are based, as they should be, on the word of God.

Protestant tradition, beginning with Luther, has used the text "all scripture is inspired by God" in connection with its doctrine of *sola scriptura*: Scripture alone is sufficient to interpret itself and to guide the Church and the individual believer. Our text says that Scripture is "useful." It does not say that it is "sufficient," nor is there any biblical text that says Scripture alone is sufficient to interpret Scripture. Hence, *sola scriptura* is a nonbiblical teaching that is used to affirm a nonexistent biblical teaching. Luther's move was in part a reaction to the arid theological debates of his day and an expression of a desire to return to the original sources of revelation. But in the process he negated all postbiblical tradition, such as that of the Fathers, who were responsible for preserving the apostolic Tradition in the face of heresies and schisms. What happened subsequently was that "Scripture alone," as one Protestant theologian said, "became Scripture alone *as understood in our tradition*," as is shown in the abundance of contradictory scriptural interpretations available today. A social scientist may study the phenomenon of this profusion of interpretations as a matter of interest, but the believer must ask the question, "If Jesus is divine, and if he confided his message to be handed on, would he not have provided some kind of assurance that the heritage would be preserved intact from error?" The Catholic response is obviously yes, and that assurance is provided by the teaching authority of the Church.

Final Charge to Timothy and Paul's Faith amid His Loneliness

2 Timothy 4

In days when cassette tapes and video tapes were common, it inevitably seemed that as the tape approached the end of the rewind it sped up. We get that same impression here as Paul is coming not only to the end of his letter but also to the end of his life. The beat picks up with a certain urgency. Paul *charges* Timothy, as if under oath, with the mission of carrying on the apostolic tradition, the precious deposit that Paul himself has faithfully kept. Then he asks Timothy to come as soon as he can, for Paul is feeling something of the loneliness Jesus felt in the garden when he asked his three closest disciples to stay nearby (Matt 26:38).

Timothy's Solemn Charge (4:1–5)

¹I charge you in the presence of God and of Christ Jesus, who will judge the living and the dead, and by his appearing and his kingly power: ²proclaim the word; be persistent whether it is convenient or inconvenient; convince, reprimand, encourage through all patience and teaching. ³For the time will come when people will not tolerate sound doctrine but, following their own desires and insatiable curiosity, will accumulate teachers ⁴and will stop listening to the truth and will be diverted to myths. ⁵But you, be self-possessed in all circumstances; put up with hardship; perform the work of an evangelist; fulfill your ministry.

OT: Josh 1:6–9; Dan 7:9–14
NT: Acts 10:42; 1 Tim 1:3–7; 4:11–16; 5:20; 6:2b–5; 1 Pet 4:4–5
Catechism: final judgment (1038–41), bishops as teachers and rulers (1558), myths (285)
Lectionary: (4:1–5) Common of Pastors and of Doctors of the Church

At this point the letter becomes even more clearly Paul's last will and testa-   4:1
ment. The tone becomes the gravest, the most solemn of Paul's injunctions. In
fact, it is as if Paul puts Timothy under a divine oath. The word **charge** was used
in Greece for rites of succession that would usually be performed in the presence of witnesses. That is precisely the situation here, for Paul is about to pass
on the torch once for all. And here the first witness is **God**; hence it is an oath,
like that of the President of the United States being sworn in with a hand on the
Bible. But at God's side also stands **Christ Jesus, who will judge the living and
the dead** according to their works, when he appears at his second coming to
assume his eternal reign. Why should Paul speak as if putting Timothy under an
oath? The continuance of the apostolic Tradition is at stake. Timothy has already
committed his life to Christ, so the oath here has to do with the responsibilities
of the office given him by the laying on of hands (2 Tim 1:6–7).

The duties are not light. Heading the list is . . . administration? No! The first   4:2
task of the pastor is to **proclaim the word.** "Proclaim" is a better word than
"preach" here, because for Catholics, at least today, preaching means a ten- or
fifteen-minute Sunday homily, whereas the *kēryx* in Greek culture was the herald
of the king who cried out his announcements "on the housetops" (Matt 10:27),
that is, giving the message the widest publicity possible. This would obviously
include preaching to the Christian assembly, and it is important to underline
the primacy of preaching to the congregation among the pastor's duties. But
proclaiming covers the whole process of communicating the gospel within and
beyond the walls of the Church.

One of the principles of Greek rhetoric was to know when to speak and when
not to, but Timothy may have been inclined to appeal to this rule too often as
an excuse for hiding the light of the gospel under the basket of his timidity. At
any rate, Paul urges him to greater boldness, to proclaim the word **whether it
is convenient or inconvenient,** even when there is little or no response or even
opposition. The word is a seed that does not always find receptive soil (Mark
4:14–20). It is the great temptation of the preacher to preach to the choir, that
is, to speak to audiences who have already accepted the challenge of the word,
who will congratulate him on his sermon; or, worse, he may be tempted to trim
the message to the expectations of the audience. Timothy must preach the word
without compromise and incessantly, even at the risk of being unpopular.

Convince may seem a strange command, because it seems to place the responsibility for the other's being convinced on Timothy's shoulders. The command must mean, then, to do all in his power to persuade the erring by refuting their arguments and the sinners by showing them the horror of sin. **Reprimand** has a similar meaning. Again we can sense that Paul is urging Timothy to greater assertiveness in his exercise of authority. If there is danger in authority becoming tyrannical, there is an equal, perhaps even greater, danger when it shirks its responsibility to govern or when, in the case of doctrine or morals, it proves to be a watchdog that never barks. But these commands to assertiveness are balanced by the command to **encourage** (as in 1 Tim 5:1's "appeal"), for there are those in the congregation who need this more than reproof. A basketball coach once told me that bawling out certain players for their mistakes makes them do a better job, whereas the same tactic makes others wilt. The latter need encouragement. It takes discernment and the wisdom of experience to know which remedy to apply.

Through all patience and teaching strangely parallels a virtue with a ministry. But both reveal the manner in which the preceding commands are to be carried out. **Patience**, a fruit of the Holy Spirit (Gal 5:22), is necessary lest the pastor overreact to a situation or give up too easily when results are not immediately apparent. **Teaching**, on the other hand, indicates that in refuting, reprimanding, and exhorting, the reasons for so doing should be given. It is not sufficient to simply say, "Do this because I said so," but, respectful of the other's good will, the pastor will instruct in the process. In this fashion, those under his care will be formed in convictions by which they can act on their own even in the absence of the leader. To the extent that they interiorize the teaching, they can be prepared for leadership themselves.

4:3–4 This spiritual and doctrinal preparation of leaders is all the more important because of the difficult times that lie ahead. **People** will not listen to sound teaching but will run to one teacher after another looking for what will satisfy their vain and **insatiable curiosity**. Had Paul lived today, he might have called them channel surfers of philosophy. Other translations stick to the more literal metaphor Paul uses: these people have "itching ears." Just as scratching an itch often makes it worse, Paul here depicts these passion-driven novelty seekers as always wanting to hear or to teach something new but never being satisfied. Even when they listen to the preachers of the gospel, it is for entertainment rather than transformation, like some of those who listened to the prophet Ezekiel (Ezek 33:32). This compulsion leads them to turn away from the **truth** to **myths**—probably a reference to the problem earlier highlighted in 1 Tim 1:4.

In the midst of the doctrinal chaos of the final times, Timothy is to remain   4:5
self-possessed (literally "sober"). The term does not refer to abstinence from
wine, since Paul recommends that his disciple take some for his stomach's sake
(1 Tim 5:23). Rather it is a term used widely in the rhetoric of the day for not
being carried away by the intoxication of novelties or by terror at the magnitude
of the challenge. It is the latter that may tempt Timothy to give up, particularly
when there is persecution from without and opposition from within the community. He must hang in there with perseverance and patience.

What is **the work of an evangelist?** An evangelist announces *euangelion*,
which in classical Greek meant "good news," such as the announcement of the
birth of a king or, more commonly, the news of victory in war. In the Septuagint
Old Testament it also has the latter meaning (2 Sam 18:22, 25, 27). In a notable
passage, the bearer of good tidings was the messenger who proclaimed the end
of the exile and the return of Israel to its homeland (Isa 40:9). In the New Testament letters the good news is the gospel itself, the proclamation of the saving
death and resurrection of Jesus Christ. The Christian evangelist proclaims this
news, primarily by announcing it to those who have not yet heard it. Philip, who
carries the good news to Samaria (Acts 8:4–8) and introduces the Ethiopian
to the faith (8:26–40), is called an evangelist (21:8). In Eph 4:11 the role is a
charism and an office, distinguished from the roles of apostle, prophet, pastor,
and teacher. Evangelization was part of Paul's calling as an apostle, for he first
evangelized and then founded communities from those he evangelized. Here
evangelization is assumed to be one of the duties of Paul's delegate, Timothy.
It is an apostolic work, a ministry that must be continued. The final **fulfill
your ministry** summarizes emphatically what went before. The reason for the
urgency of these injunctions will be seen in what follows.

Reflection and Application (4:1–5)

I'm sure I have often failed to deliver the tough word the gospel often requires, but I do remember preaching against the death penalty to a conserva-
tive congregation, and it was obvious they were finding the message difficult
to swallow. As I greeted the congregation after Mass that Sunday only one
person thanked me for the homily. There are times when we are called to sow
rather than reap.

One cannot escape the urgency in Paul's commands in this section. While
the immediate reason is Paul's sense of his own imminent death, it raises the
question of urgency in the entire task of evangelization. On the one hand, the

Gospels speak of the word being a seed that will grow of its own accord, even while the sower sleeps (Mark 4:26–27). The emphasis there is upon confidence in the power of the word beyond human efforts. But there is another aspect stressed by the New Testament: the time is short! (1 Cor 7:29), the Lord is coming soon! (Rev 22:20). Today we are more aware than Paul was of the vast numbers of people who have never heard the good news, to say nothing of the millions of nominal Christians who do not know or appreciate or live the gospel in which they were initiated. While holding to our confidence in the power of the word, more pertinent for our times is the cry of Paul: "The love of Christ impels us, once we have come to the conviction that one died for all" (2 Cor 5:14).

Paul's Final Sacrifice Is at Hand (4:6–8)

> [6]For I am already being poured out like a libation, and the time of my departure is at hand. [7]I have competed well; I have finished the race; I have kept the faith. [8]From now on the crown of righteousness awaits me, which the Lord, the just judge, will award to me on that day, and not only to me, but to all who have longed for his appearance.

OT: Deut 34:5–9
NT: Acts 20:24; 1 Cor 9:24–25; Phil 1:1; 2:17; James 1:12; 1 Pet 5:4; Rev 2:10
Catechism: death (1013), new heaven and earth (1042–50)
Lectionary: (4:6–8, 17–18) Solemnity of Saints Peter and Paul

4:6   Although we begin a new section here, it is tightly connected with the preceding one, as the initial **for** indicates. Why is Paul's charge to Timothy so urgent? Because Paul's death is imminent, and his disciple will have to go it on his own from now on. **I** contrasts with "you" of the preceding verse. How does Paul view his death? Not with foreboding or terror but with a realism inspired by faith. He knows that because of his faith in Jesus Christ he is in chains. Now, because of that same faith, he awaits the sword. That is why he can describe his imminent death as **a libation.**

Paul is no doubt thinking of his own blood, which is about to be poured out. He had faced this possibility before, when he wrote to the Philippians, using the same libation language (Phil 2:17), but here, writing to Timothy, he is certain that his death is imminent. Abel's blood that soaked the earth was, in effect, a libation, a sacrifice, for it cried out to God to act (Gen 4:10). Like his Master, Paul sees his death as a sacrifice to God.

194

What Is a Libation?

BIBLICAL BACKGROUND

In ancient sacrificial rites such as we find in the Old Testament, a sacred liquid, sometimes oil (Gen 28:18; 35:14; Mic 6:7), wine (called the "blood of the grape" in Sir 50:15), or water was poured out in sacrifice or consecration. David, hiding from the Philistines, longed for water from his hometown of Bethlehem that was in Philistine hands. Some of his men risked their lives to fetch some of that water, but when they brought it to him, he poured it out on the ground as a sacrifice to the Lord (2 Sam 23:16–17). The idea behind the libation, like that of other sacrifices, is that the liquid is a gift of God and pouring it out is a way of returning at least a portion of it to God. In the Old Testament the animal sacrifices obviously involved the pouring out of blood, which was sometimes also sprinkled upon the altar (Exod 24:6).

He also speaks of death as a **departure**. Actually, the Greek word *analysis* means an untying, a loosening of a rope, as happens when a ship puts out to sea. Already in the secular literature of the day it was used as a euphemism for death. Paul may not have been thinking of its original meaning as he wrote or dictated this word, but he had many times watched the mooring ropes loosened from the dock as he left one shore to seek another. Although he speaks of his death as imminent, he has no assurance of exactly when, for later on he expresses his hope that Timothy will come to him before winter (2 Tim 4:21).

Having confronted the reality that lies ahead, Paul looks to his past. He thinks of it in two metaphors, both derived from athletics and both of which he has used in previous letters. The NAB's **I have competed well** translates the literal "I have fought the good [beautiful] fight." "Fight" (Greek *agōn*) in the Hellenistic world could refer to any contest. It included the combat that took place in a public arena. It could take various forms, particularly boxing but also the brutal gladiatorial spectacles in the Roman arenas. It was quickly applied in the diatribe (a popular literary form in which the author debates with an imaginary opponent) to the moral struggles of life. Thus Plutarch speaks of the encouragement that retired athletes "who have finished the contests of life" give to younger ones as a metaphor for elders who encourage the younger in virtue,[1] which is exactly what Paul is doing here for Timothy. In the literature of Judaism produced around the first century, the suffering of Jewish martyrs under Greek persecution is compared to the contests of athletes, which is all

4:7

---

1. *On the Sign of Socrates* 593e.

the more apt because the suffering and execution of the martyrs often took place in the same arena as the athletic contests: "While being tortured he said: 'O contest befitting holiness, in which so many of us brothers have been summoned to an arena of sufferings for religion, and in which we have not been defeated!'" (4 Macc 11:20 NRSV).

Already early in his ministry Paul spoke of his work for the gospel not simply as a duty but as an *agōn*, a passionate struggle. After his suffering in Philippi, Paul courageously preached the gospel to the Thessalonians "with much struggle" (1 Thess 2:2). And in Col 1:28–29 he says that his goal is to present everyone perfect in Christ Jesus: "For this I labor and struggle, in accord with the exercise of his power working within me." If we ask who is the opponent he has fought, one might think of the angelic powers, "for our struggle is not with flesh and blood but with the principalities, with the powers, with the world rulers of this present darkness, with the evil spirits" (Eph 6:12). In 1 Cor 9:24–27, however, Paul applies the self-discipline required by the *agōn* to himself. We are better off then, not trying to narrow the metaphor unduly but should let it stand for his struggle against all the obstacles in his career, both external and internal ("external conflicts, internal fears"; 2 Cor 7:5). Now he looks back with the grateful joy of the victor who awaits the "crown" (2 Tim 4:8).

The second metaphor is that of the footrace. The word **race** (*dromos*) properly was applied to the course of the stars, then to the track (the horse-race track was called the hippodrome), and then figuratively to the course of one's life (Acts 13:25). Paul had applied the image of the footrace in Phil 3:12–16 to his desire to reach Christ and the goal of his heavenly calling. Now, looking back, he can say, as in Acts 20:24, that he has finished the course Christ laid out for him. The perfect tense of the verb "finish" easily recalls the last words of Jesus on the cross: "It is finished" (John 19:30), meaning "completed, fulfilled, totally achieved." Thus, while implying a final letting go, it is nevertheless, as much as in the preceding figure of the *agōn*, a cry of victory.

What exactly does Paul mean in saying **I have kept the faith**? The word "faith" (*pistis*) has so many different meanings in the Bible and even in Paul that it is not easy to decide which meaning is intended. The parallelism with the preceding two phrases and the overall tone of the Pastorals might suggest that he has kept the deposit of the faith and handed it on faithfully (2 Tim 2:2), hence "the faith" in its objective sense. This is what he has urged Timothy to do (1 Tim 6:20); thus Paul would again be pointing to his own example. However, Timothy surely knows that. Hence it may be preferable to understand the phrase in the sense "I have kept my pledge to the end," "I have been faithful

Fig. 7. The road into Corinth points toward the Acrocorinth. Aided by Timothy, Paul later sent Titus on a crucial mission to the community here.

to my baptismal commitment," or some equivalent. This would correspond to the widespread use of *pistis* in the Hellenistic world for fidelity to an oath or for trustworthiness. Josephus uses the word for marital fidelity.[2] It was also the supreme virtue of the soldier, bound by sacred oath (*sacramentum*) to the emperor. So highly was it held in esteem in Rome that a temple was erected to the goddess Faith (*Pistis*): Numa "was the first to build temples to Faith . . . and he taught the Romans their most solemn oath by Faith, which they still continue to use."[3] Of the three marks of triumph, Paul puts fidelity as the climax. In the Greek there is a beautiful rhetorical flourish in the similar sounding verbs *teteleka* ("I have finished") and *tetērēka* ("I have kept"). As Jesus having "loved his own in the world . . . loved them to the end" (John 13:1), so Paul has been faithful to the end.

The final outcome of this process is not Paul's death but **the crown of righteousness**, which the apostle awaits with utter assurance. He does not say "I hope that I will gain it" or "perhaps I will gain it." The present tense **awaits** indicates that the crown is unquestionably already there for him to receive. The Greek word is used for a deposit that waits to be retrieved or a treasure that is held in keeping, waiting to be claimed. As Paul has kept the faith, so the

4:8

2. *Jewish War* 2.121.
3. Plutarch, *Numa* 16.1.

reward is kept for him. Today we reward athletes with medals or silver or gold cups, and military honors are given with medals or pins. What is done at the Olympics by having the victorious athletes stand while their national anthem is played and the gold, silver, or bronze is draped around their neck was done in Hellenistic times by a crown. A leafy wreath was the usual crowning of athletes, but for more important occasions crowns of precious materials were used. For Christians the crown becomes a symbol of the reward of eternal life (James 1:12; 1 Pet 5:4; Rev 2:10).

The notion of reward implies merit on the part of the one rewarded. In this, Paul agrees with first-century rabbis. But for the apostle it is the merit of a righteousness that has been attained by faith in Christ (Rom 3:22), a faith that in Paul's case has also been manifested by a total commitment even unto imminent martyrdom. As Paul has been faithful, the Lord cannot be less so, for he is just to his own sworn word: "Remain faithful until death, and I will give you the crown of life" (Rev 2:10). As with Jesus, the injustice of the human court will be reversed by God through the gift of eternal life.

However personal his experience of the imminent end, Paul knows that he is not alone in his witness: **not only to me, but to all who have longed for his appearance**. He knows too that this letter will be read publicly, and thus he wishes to encourage the faithful of Ephesus to hold on to the faith they have received, whether or not it leads to martyrdom. That faith concretely looks to the **appearance**, the parousia, the manifestation of Jesus Christ, victor over death. More than simply a belief in his coming, that faith is an ardent longing for that day of consummation. The Greek word for **longed for** is literally "loved," which has here the meaning of an intense eagerness to encounter the beloved. From his earliest letter, Paul described this ardent hope (1 Thess 3:13; 4:13–18; 5:23), and here he voices his ardent desire for the imminent return of Jesus—another indication of the early rather than the later first-century dating of this letter. To be a Christian is to long for the return of Jesus in his glory—and to live in the bright hope of that final consummation.

Reflection and Application (4:6–8)

Paul's anticipation of his execution and his ardent assurance of eternal life has been echoed in the lives of hundreds of martyrs ever since. Blessed Jacob Gapp, a Marianist priest who spoke out against Hitler, was betrayed to the Nazi authorities by a couple posing as his catechumens and, after a trial in which he defended his faith, was guillotined on August 13, 1943. Hours before his death he wrote to his family: "At seven o'clock this evening I will go to our dear Savior, whom I have always ardently loved. . . . I am completely happy. . . . After such a difficult struggle, I am now at the point of my life where I consider the present day to be the most beautiful of my life. May God reward all that you have done for me since my childhood. . . . How often I have thought of you. Don't be sad. Everything passes; only heaven remains. . . . Please inform all of our relatives of my death. I have been condemned for treason. . . . Our mother is waiting for me. After a few hours I will be with her. What a joy!" He was beatified on November 24, 1996, by Pope John Paul II.

Home Safe (4:9–18)

[9]Try to join me soon, [10]for Demas, enamored of the present world, deserted me and went to Thessalonica, Crescens to Galatia, and Titus to Dalmatia. [11]Luke is the only one with me. Get Mark and bring him with you, for he is helpful to me in the ministry. [12]I have sent Tychicus to Ephesus. [13]When you come, bring the cloak I left with Carpus in Troas, the papyrus rolls, and especially the parchments.

[14]Alexander the coppersmith did me a great deal of harm; the Lord will repay him according to his deeds. [15]You too be on guard against him, for he has strongly resisted our preaching.

[16]At my first defense no one appeared on my behalf, but everyone deserted me. May it not be held against them! [17]But the Lord stood by me and gave me strength, so that through me the proclamation might be completed and all the Gentiles might hear it. And I was rescued from the lion's mouth. [18]The Lord will rescue me from every evil threat and will bring me safe to his heavenly kingdom. To him be glory forever and ever. Amen.

OT: Ps 62:12–13; Isa 53:3; Dan 6:21–24
NT: Rom 11:25; Col 4:10, 14; 1 Tim 1:20; Titus 3:12; Philem 24
Catechism: wounds to unity (817), apostasy (2089)
Lectionary: (4:10–17b) Feast of Saint Luke

Those who have attended the dying know how important it is for the terminally ill to be surrounded by loved ones. Paul feels the same human need Jesus felt in the garden when he told his three intimate disciples, "My soul is sorrowful even to death. Remain here and keep watch with me" (Matt 26:38). The Greek redundancy (literally "hasten to come to me quickly") puts the accent upon the extreme urgency of the need. **Demas** is listed as a companion of Paul

4:9–10

in his first Roman captivity (Col 4:14; Philem 24), but now, like the disciples of Jesus in the garden, he has abandoned Paul, either because he has found the secular life more appealing—**enamored of the present world**—or simply out of fear. The other two companions may well have been sent by Paul to continue the ministry, not that they have abandoned him (that would be particularly strange in the case of Titus, if this Titus is the same as Paul's trusted disciple to whom he addressed a letter).

The **Galatia** to which **Crescens** departs could be the Roman province in Asia, but it is just as likely Gaul, which in Greek was called Galatia, modern-day France. Crescens, a Latin name, suggests that he would have been an ideal missionary to that part of the empire, which had by the first century become thoroughly Latinized. **Dalmatia** corresponds roughly to Croatia on the Adriatic coast. It lay to the north of Nicopolis, where Paul told **Titus** to join him for the winter (Titus 3:12). If Titus had indeed made it to Nicopolis and had not thereafter returned to Crete, it would not have been far for him to travel to Dalmatia. This seems likely as the easiest travel plan, although it is not impossible that he had accompanied or visited Paul in Rome and went to Dalmatia from there.

4:11   **Luke**, assumed to be the companion of Paul on his journey to Rome (Acts 27:1–2), appears in Philem 24 with Paul in his Roman imprisonment, and in Col 4:14 he is described as "the beloved physician." The Muratorian canon adds, it seems, that he was knowledgeable in law. If so, this would be an additional reason why Paul, in the shadow of the Roman court, would want him at his side. As I pointed out in the introduction, there are many similarities in style between the Pastorals and Luke's two works, and this gives reason to believe that his hand is detectable in the composition of these letters.

The expression **Luke is the only one with me** has a sense of loneliness about it. Were the Christians of Rome afraid to be identified with Paul, or is he perhaps speaking only of his close collaborators who are no longer with him? The latter is possible, although it is also possible Paul means that all, except those of whom he has spoken favorably in the letter, deserted him. It is also suggested that Paul means those who had influence or legal expertise, whose help would have been crucial to his defense. In any case, Paul may well have been abandoned by those from whom he had every right to expect support (2 Tim 4:16), not unlike Jesus abandoned by his disciples at the hour of his trial.

Timothy is then asked to **get Mark**, either from Ephesus or to pick him up on the way. This Mark is probably the same Mark who appears in the Acts of the Apostles as the companion of Paul and Barnabas, his cousin, on their first missionary journey (Acts 13–14). Mark abandoned them halfway, so upsetting Paul that he would not take Mark on his second journey (15:36–41). If Paul is referring to the same Mark, there has obviously been a reconciliation by this time. It is not clear whether Mark's usefulness **in the ministry** means that Paul would be able to continue and extend his ministry in Rome through Mark or simply that Mark would be useful to Paul himself in his present need. If the former, then it is amazing that Paul, in imminent danger of execution, would still be vigorously carrying out an apostolate in his chains.

Tychicus, a native of Asia, was one of the trusted seven who accompanied Paul with the collection for the church in Jerusalem (Acts 20:4). He carried Paul's letters to the Colossians (Col 4:7) and to the Ephesians (Eph 6:21) and perhaps to other churches to which the circular letter was sent. Paul said he would send Artemas or Tychicus to replace Titus in Crete (Titus 3:12), and that was probably Paul's purpose in sending him now to Ephesus—to replace Timothy while the latter came to Rome. Obviously this disciple was a highly respected, responsible, and competent leader.   **4:12**

Was Paul kept in the kind of house arrest Acts describes as his first imprisonment there (Acts 28:16–31), or was he kept in the less hospitable prisons, which were bitterly cold in winter? Either way, arrested probably in more moderate temperatures, he did not think to prepare to spend a winter in Rome. He asks Timothy to pick up the **cloak** he had **left . . . in Troas**, the port city Paul had passed through on numerous occasions, where Luke records the story of the youth Eutychus falling out the window (16:8; 20:6–11). **The papyrus rolls** (*biblia*) are called "books" in some translations, but the book, or codex with leaves bound at the margin, did not become widespread until Christians began to bind the Scriptures that way (second- and third-century New Testament writings are virtually all bound that way). The *biblia* were originally papyrus scrolls, to be distinguished from **parchments**, which were leather. The expense of the latter explains why both sides were used and why words were written without spaces between them. *Biblia* got its name from the ancient city of Biblos, as parchment got its name from the city of Pergamum, for which it was famous.[4]   **4:13**

What did these scrolls contain? Surely they included Old Testament texts, probably those used as *testimonia*, that is, texts the apostolic preachers used to show their fulfillment in Christ. Also quite likely they contained some of the sayings of Jesus and perhaps copies of some of Paul's earlier letters or outlines of

---

4. Although the Greek and Latin word for parchment is *membrana*, the connection with Pergamum stuck in people's minds, as today "xerox" is often used for any photocopying machine. The church at Pergamum is one of those addressed in the Apocalypse (Rev 2:12–17).

Fig. 8. Fragment of the Scroll of Leviticus. Paul asked Timothy to bring him "the papyrus rolls, and especially the parchments" (2 Tim 4:13).

The Schøyen Collection MS 2649. Oslo and London.

his sermons. If he was about to die, why would he ask for reading matter? We can only speculate. Perhaps he hopes to have time to continue his ministry, however limited, perhaps for his own spiritual nourishment, perhaps both. Without friends, he might at least have the consolation of the word of God. My mentor in Pauline studies, Père Ceslas Spicq, who was interned with a number of other priests by the Nazis during the Second World War, later shared with his students that all he had with him was a Greek New Testament, but what a consolation that was!

4:14   Since **Alexander** was a common name in the Hellenistic world (Mark 15:21; Acts 4:6; 19:33), we should not conclude immediately that he is the heretic Paul says he excommunicated in 1 Tim 1:20. But the likelihood that there was some kind of betrayal or vindictiveness from within the Christian community or from someone who *had been* a member (as Alexander in 1 Tim 1:20 had been) is suggested by *1 Clement,* written to the Corinthians from Rome some thirty years later, saying that Paul (and Peter) were martyred "because of jealousy and envy," and for Paul he adds "strife."[5] That would have made Paul's suffering—like that of Jesus, who was betrayed and denied in his passion—doubly painful. In any case, either Alexander was involved in getting Paul arrested or he testified against him at his first hearing. The Greek verb most often translated **did me . . . harm** is used in the judicial language of the day for bringing proof, demonstration, testimony. Here it doubtless refers to the specific accusation and testimony against Paul.

5. *1 Clement* 5.2, 5.

Steps in Paul's Trial

Paul's mention of his "first defense" (2 Tim 4:16) invites us to consider what may have been the process of his trial and presumably his second imprisonment in Rome, which ended in his execution (assuming, of course, the authenticity of 2 Timothy). Although Roman trial practice evolved over the years, the following were the major steps:[a]

1. *A complaint* (*postulatio*) was brought by someone who would give the name of the accused (*nominis delatio*) to the praetor (a magistrate ranking below a consul and having chiefly judicial functions). The complainant in Paul's case could have been Alexander the coppersmith.
2. *Summons.* If the complaint seemed well founded, the praetor issued a summons (*citatio*) for the accused (*reus*).
3. *Interrogation.* When he appeared, the accused was given a preliminary examination (*interrogatio*). The purpose was to obtain as much information as possible and, if possible, a confession of guilt. If Paul was outside of Rome, in the provinces, as is likely, he would have been arrested by the imperial police (*milites stationarii*) for local interrogation first by a magistrate (*irenarcha*). It may have been at this time that "everyone in Asia deserted me," including Phygelus and Hermogenes (1:15). If there was not sufficient evidence for a trial, the judge would declare *non liquet*—meaning not that the accused was innocent but simply that there was not enough evidence to justify further action—and the case would be dismissed.
4. *Inscription.* Otherwise—and this must have been the case with Paul—the judge would have the charge put in writing (*inscriptio*) and signed by the accuser(s), known as *subscriptor(es)*. A first hearing would normally be presided over by a praetor representing the emperor, and if more evidence was sought (*ampliatio*), this could explain the delay that allowed Paul to write Timothy and urge him to come "before winter" (4:21). We do not know at what level Nero himself would have been involved. Given Nero's manic kind of administration, his declaration that profession of Christianity was a crime, his macabre glee at making a spectacle of Christians (he made torches of them for his gardens), and the fact that he had in his hands a major leader of the Christian movement, we have every reason to suspect that Nero would have presided at the trial himself, if not also at an earlier hearing.
5. *Trial.* The trial itself involved an address by the accusing party (this could have been Alexander, 4:14), an address by the defense, and the introduction of evidence, whether oral testimony, documents, or character witnesses.
6. *Verdict.* This was given by the presiding praetor or by the emperor himself.
7. *Sentencing.* Once a guilty verdict was pronounced, the sentence was announced and was usually imposed immediately. In Paul's case it meant execution (application of the *ius gladii*).

a. See William L. Burdick, *The Principles of Roman Law and Their Relation to Modern Law* (Holmes Beach, FL: Gaunt, 1964), 676–719.

What was the substance of the accusation? It could hardly have been a dispute between the non-Christian Jews and the Christian Jews, for cases like that would have been dismissed by the Romans, as they had been earlier (Acts 18:14–16; see also 26:30–32). So somehow the accusers must have managed to argue that Paul had committed a crime against the empire or the emperor, so as to deserve capital punishment. It would have been sufficient to claim that Paul's proclamation that Jesus is Lord (*kyrios*), the only Lord, implied that the Roman gods were naught and that the emperor was not a god either. The greatest crime was treason, but offending the honor of the emperor (called *majestas*) could also bring the death penalty. In the time of Tiberius (AD 14–37), the slightest affront or disrespect to the emperor constituted *majestas*. (Tiberius was the emperor and Pilate the procurator of Judea when Jesus was crucified.)

Paul is not in a position to avenge himself and, even if he could, he knows that "vengeance is mine, I will repay, says the Lord" (Rom 12:19). He does not even pray for vengeance, as Jeremiah did (Jer 20:12). But he knows that God is a just God whose eyes are too pure to countenance evil (Hab 1:13). Thus he refers to the psalm: "Lord, . . . / you render to each of us / according to our deeds" (Ps 62:13). If the just must receive their due (2 Tim 4:8), so must the wicked. The judgment is left to God, whether this be eternal punishment or the chastisements to which the excommunicated are liable (1 Cor 5:5).

4:15   Timothy himself is not exempt from the danger Alexander poses. The NAB says that Alexander **has strongly resisted our preaching** (literally "our words"). So what Alexander has opposed may not have been Paul's preaching but Paul's self-defense offered at his hearing.

4:16   At his **first defense** Paul was left without anyone to speak in his **behalf— everyone deserted me**! No doubt by this time association with Paul could have brought arrest, and the danger of a connection made any associate of Paul a candidate for execution. Paul experiences what Jesus experienced in the garden: "They all left him and fled" (Mark 14:50). But like Jesus, who asked the Father to forgive his enemies (Luke 23:34), and like Stephen, whose death Paul had witnessed (Acts 7:58–60), the apostle prays, **May it not be held against them!** Was Paul thinking of Stephen's prayer as he uttered this one? Or, if the writer of the letter is Luke, is there an intentional allusion to the martyr's prayer he recorded in Acts? In any case, there is a difference between the expectation of divine justice upon Alexander's malicious attack (2 Tim 4:14) and the prayer of mercy for those disciples who out of weakness and fear left Paul to face his accusers alone.

Paul Meets Nero

BIBLICAL BACKGROUND

The chronology of Paul's life makes it virtually certain that he was imprisoned during the reign of Nero (AD 54–68). Like emperors before and after him, Nero was known to be highly sensitive to the slightest whiff of *majestas*, offense to the honor of the emperor. Weaseled by his mother to the imperial throne at the age of seventeen (he would later murder her), he was arguably the worst emperor Rome ever saw. He murdered his younger brother, a rival to the throne. He killed his pregnant wife in a fit of rage, then castrated and married a young freeman because he resembled her. On a public stage he acted as a hero driven mad or a woman giving birth, and he raced a ten-horse chariot in the Olympic games. He probably was himself responsible for the burning of Rome. In search of a scapegoat, "Nero substituted as culprits" the Christians, subjecting them to torture, wild beasts, and even to burning as torches to light up his gardens at night. He ruled so shamefully and lasciviously that after his suicide at the age of thirty, by cutting his own throat at the approach of rebelling Roman soldiers, the Senate officially damned his memory.[a] He readily accepted the titles "lord," "savior," and "god," and in the eastern part of the empire there was a cult of Nero. An inscription on the island of Cos calls him "the good god."

Given the great interest that emperors took in capital cases, we can assume that Nero was no exception, particularly since Paul, a Roman citizen, was a Christian leader, although we have no text that says Nero presided over Paul's trial and condemnation. That the apostle proclaimed that Jesus was the supreme Lord who would destroy "every sovereignty and every authority and power" (1 Cor 15:24) would easily have threatened an emperor who gladly accepted the supreme, divine honors. It is likely, then, that it was Nero himself before whom Paul was summoned at some point in the trial, most probably toward the end.

a. Tacitus, *Annals* 15.44.

The absence of testimony in Paul's favor may have made his situation more critical, but there was one who **stood by** his side. **The Lord**, who had promised to be with his disciples, supplying them with wisdom for their defense at trials (Luke 21:15; see also 12:11–12), kept his promise in Paul's case. Like a defense lawyer, the Lord stood at Paul's side, giving him the strength not only to defend himself but to use the occasion to proclaim the gospel. We may infer that his defense was something like that recorded by Luke when Paul was brought before Felix and Agrippa (Acts 24:10–21; 26:2–23), that is, a report of the basic facts about Jesus Christ, including his resurrection from the dead—in short, the *kērygma*. But in this case, Paul sees his mission **completed**, brought to its consummation. It is

4:17

not just the end of his preaching career; it is the crowning of it, for Christ had called Paul to proclaim the good news before Gentiles and kings (9:15; 1 Tim 3:16). And if, indeed, it was before Caesar Nero himself that he spoke, it was a glorious finishing of the race (2 Tim 4:7), for when the emperor presided at court he was surrounded by a retinue of consuls, senators, women of honor, as well as by the Pretorian guard—representatives of "all" the Gentiles.

The outcome of Paul's first defense was not as bad as it could have been, for at least he was **rescued from the lion's mouth**, that is, from death. The proverbial phrase about the lion's mouth, found already in the Wisdom of Ahiqar (seventh century BC), here probably evokes Ps 22:22, the Passion Song in which the psalmist prays, "Save me from the lion's mouth." Paul was saved from execution—temporarily.

4:18   The Lord's recent saving act leads Paul to think of what might lie ahead. Here too his faith leads him to the assurance that **the Lord will rescue** him **from every evil threat**. This echoes the last petition of the Lord's prayer: "Deliver us from the evil one" (Matt 6:13). And it is also another echo of the Passion Song in which the psalmist repeatedly evokes God's deliverance:

> In you our ancestors trusted;
>> they trusted and you rescued them. . . .
> You relied on the Lord—let him deliver you;
>> if he loves you, let him rescue you. . . .
> Deliver me from the sword. (Ps 22:5, 9, 21)

It is likely that Paul murmured this prayer repeatedly as he recalled the last hours of Jesus on the cross and his use of the psalm.

Since Paul believes his death is near (2 Tim 4:6), it is unlikely that he thinks of deliverance from prison. The following sentence rather affirms that the Lord will literally "save me *into* his heavenly kingdom." This is yet another echo of Ps 22:29: "Kingship belongs to the Lord, / the ruler over the nations." The real ruler of the nations is not the one who holds the sword over Paul; it is the one whose heavenly glory Paul already glimpses, the one whose rule over the nations Paul has extended throughout the Roman Empire. Sirach said that no real harm can touch the person who fears the Lord (Sir 33:1). In that same vein Paul is living out what he wrote earlier to the church in Rome: "What will separate us from the love of Christ? Will anguish, or distress, or persecution, or famine, or nakedness, or peril, or the sword? . . . No, in all these things we conquer overwhelmingly through him who loved us. For I am convinced that neither death, nor life, nor angels, nor principalities, nor present things, nor future things, nor powers, nor height, nor depth, nor any other creature will be able to separate us from the love of God in Christ Jesus our Lord" (Rom 8:35, 37–39). That Paul expresses confidence in God's love even in the face of the sword is especially meaningful in light of the tradition that it was by the sword that he was executed.

To him be glory forever and ever. Amen. Paul closes with a doxology addressed to Jesus his savior. "At the threshold of the tomb, Paul begins to sing an eternal thanksgiving."[6]

Reflection and Application (4:9–18)

The picture of Paul proclaiming the gospel to the Roman Gentiles reminds me of a trial of some of my friends in Nepal who were brought to court on charges that they were evangelizing non-Christians. The trial gave them the opportunity to actually evangelize the judge and the people in the courtroom by telling them the gospel story. More people heard about Jesus Christ in the courtroom than in the marketplace.

Final Greetings (4:19–22)

[19]**Greet Prisca and Aquila and the family of Onesiphorus. [20]Erastus remained in Corinth, while I left Trophimus sick at Miletus. [21]Try to get here before winter. Eubulus, Pudens, Linus, Claudia, and all the brothers send greetings.**
[22]**The Lord be with your spirit. Grace be with all of you.**

NT: Acts 18:2; 19:22; 20:4; Rom 16:3–5
Catechism: communion of saints (946–48)

There are others besides Paul who long for the Lord's appearance and his   **4:19** reign (2 Tim 4:8). Having voiced his love for God, Paul turns to his close friends. **Prisca** (a shortened form of Priscilla in Acts 18:2) and her husband **Aquila** appear six times in the apostolic literature, and four of the six times Priscilla is named first. Scholars give various reasons for this preference: she was perhaps from a high Roman family, she was first or more outstanding in the faith, or she was the one whose hospitality was most manifest when Paul visited their home. It is more likely that she was more active in ministry than her husband. In any case, they were an outstanding apostolic couple in the

---

6. Spicq, *Épîtres pastorales*, 2.822.

Erastus the City Treasurer?

BIBLICAL BACKGROUND

Is this Erastus (2 Tim 4:20) the same Erastus mentioned in Rom 16:23 as the city treasurer of Corinth? The Greek word for "treasurer" is *oikonomos*, who was often a city-owned slave, even though holding a prestigious position. In that case, though, he would have been forbidden to travel. In 1929 an inscription discovered in Corinth mentions an Erastus who had the Roman civic office of aedile (*aedilis*), a Latin word for which the Greek equivalent would be *agoranomos*. The inscription says that Erastus paved the street in return for receiving the office of aedile. Did Paul (or Luke) simply mistranslate Latin *aedilis* by Greek *oikonomos* in Rom 16:23? Since the aedile was responsible for the public markets, it is not impossible that Paul met him when paying taxes on his work space and thus might have called him "treasurer." We will probably never know for sure. The ultimate prestige of Erastus was not any civic office that he may have held but that he was one of Paul's most trusted collaborators in planting the apostolic faith in Asia and Europe.

early Church, living in Rome until they were expelled by Emperor Claudius, then for a year and a half in Corinth, and next in Ephesus. They seem to have returned to Rome after the death of Claudius (AD 54), since Paul greets them in his letter to the Romans and refers to the church that meets in their house (Rom 16:3–5). But 2 Timothy seems to assume that they are in Ephesus or its environs, to which (assuming authenticity) they had returned. As mentioned in the commentary on 1:16–18, **Onesiphorus** by now may be dead; at least it does not seem that he is in Ephesus or Paul would have mentioned "Onesiphorus and his household."

4:20   **Erastus** was one of Paul's early collaborators, who was with him and Timothy during the third missionary journey (Acts 19:22). Preparing to leave Ephesus for Macedonia and Achaia, Paul sent the two of them on ahead of him. In our passage the situation is reversed: Erastus stays in Corinth while Paul moves on.

Trophimus was a native of Ephesus and a companion of Paul and Timothy on earlier journeys (Acts 20:4) and in Paul's final visit to Jerusalem (21:29). That he was sick, and not healed by Paul, is one of the rare mentions of illness in the apostolic workers of the New Testament. Paul himself seems to have suffered from some kind of eye infirmity when he was in Galatia (Gal 4:15), and the weakness, or "thorn in the flesh," of 2 Cor 12:7–9 may refer to an illness. It can be consoling to modern ministers to know that the early ministers were not supermen or superwomen, but, as St. John Chrysostom notes, were able to accept God's plan for them even if this includes illness.[7]

In 2 Tim 4:9 Paul urged Timothy to come quickly. He repeats the same request here, replacing "soon" with **before winter.** The letter must have been written in autumn, and few ships dared to face the storms that frequently rake the Mediterranean in winter. In the Roman winter Paul will need the cloak that Timothy is to pick up for him in Troas. The cloak he is speaking of was of heavy material shaped like a poncho, round, with a hole for the head in the middle. (A less likely suggestion is that the object was a container for the scrolls.)   4:21

Despite what Paul said earlier about being abandoned by everyone (4:16), friends in a less intimate circle than Paul's close collaborators send their greetings. None of them is mentioned elsewhere in the New Testament. We know nothing about **Eubulus** or **Pudens,** though later tradition said Pudens was a senator converted by Peter. Irenaeus (around 130–200) identifies **Linus** as the first successor of the apostles Peter and Paul, who ordained him as bishop of Rome: "The blessed Apostles, having founded and built up the church [of Rome], committed into the hands of Linus the office of the episcopate. Of this Linus Paul makes mention in the epistles to Timothy."[8] According to the *Apostolic Constitutions* (around AD 380), **Claudia** is mother of Linus.[9]

The letter concludes with a greeting so familiar to us we may overlook its impact: **the Lord be with your spirit.** It echoes an Old Testament greeting found already in Judg 6:12, where the angel greets Gideon with the words "the LORD is with you." And it is the greeting the angel gives to Mary (Luke 1:28). "With your spirit" is just another way of saying "with you." For the Lord to be with someone is to experience his presence in an effective way, strengthening, reassuring, and providing concrete help. And, as in the case of both Gideon and Mary, it announces a call to a critical mission for the people of God—a point that would surely not be lost on Timothy, to whom Paul had given the charge to stir up the Spirit of his call (2 Tim 1:6–7). Since the verb is missing in the Greek, the expression here can mean either "may the Lord be with you" or "the Lord is with you." In any case, Paul, knowing that he is soon to depart this life, whether before or after the arrival of Timothy, commends the life and future of his disciple to the Lord, the only one who will certainly remain.   4:22

After blessing Timothy, the direct addressee (**your** is singular in the Greek), Paul thinks of all those who may hear this letter publicly read: **grace be with**

---

7. *Homilies on 2 Timothy* 4:20.
8. *Against Heresies* 3.3.3.
9. *Apostolic Constitutions* 4.46.

all of you. "Grace" covers the whole of God's loving plan, but here it is the loving-kindness, the favor or blessing like that which the angels proclaimed to the world at the birth of the savior (Luke 2:14). We might gloss: "May God's love envelop all you who hear this letter read," and that would extend to the listeners and readers of today as well.

Reflection and Application (4:19–22)

One of the great witnesses to ministering in the midst of illness in our days was Pope John Paul II, who, in the midst of progressively debilitating Parkinson's disease, not only carried on a vigorous ministry traveling the world but in the process set a great example for ministers of all times who are afflicted with illness. He also wrote a *Letter to the Elderly*, in which he shared his reflections on aging and illness.

On the threshold of death, human consciousness is inevitably gripped by the thought of those left behind. Blessed Jakob Gapp, a Marianist priest who was martyred by the Nazis for his open condemnation of Hitler, wrote a letter on the eve of his going to the guillotine expressing his love for the members of his family. One of my mother's last gestures, when she could no longer speak, was to point to her heart and to all of us around her bed. When one is about to meet God, suddenly life appears in its brilliant simplicity: love God and love everyone; the two commandments that Jesus taught say it all.

The Letter to Titus

Titus was a Gentile disciple of Paul, whom Paul brought to the council of Jerusalem (Gal 2:1–3; Acts 15:1–35) and who is mentioned nine times in 2 Corinthians as Paul's delegate to the Christians in Corinth (7:6–14; 8:6, 16, 23). Neither the Acts of the Apostles nor the other New Testament letters give us any information about the evangelization of Crete or of Paul's or Titus's roles there. But, assuming the Pastoral Letters are authentically Paul's, the establishing of communities there was probably later than in Ephesus, as the church in Crete seems from this letter to be in an earlier stage of organization. It is possible that Jewish Christians coming from Jerusalem had brought the faith to the Jewish community there prior to the arrival of either Paul or Titus and that Paul sent or left Titus there to solidify the growing church over which they assumed apostolic authority. Following Paul's policy stated elsewhere (Rom 15:20), he would not have done so had another apostle first evangelized the area. Whether there were informal communities already there on Paul's arrival or he was the first to evangelize them, a major issue of the letter is the need for good leaders—presbyters or bishops—and Paul tells Titus to appoint them in every town with a Christian community.

Aside from the qualifications of ministers, Paul gives pastoral directives for the various states of the Christian life: older men, older women, younger men, slaves, and all Christians, grounding his counsels in the redeeming grace of Christ, who gave himself that his people might be holy. These counsels build to a climax in a hymn that traces the saving plan of God from its initial appearance, through baptism and the gift of the Holy Spirit, to the hope that leads to eternal life (Titus 3:4–7). Though it is the shortest of the three letters, the epistle to Titus provides a rich source of wisdom for all Christians, especially ministers.

Organizing the Church in Crete

Titus 1

After a lengthy greeting Paul launches immediately into directives for Titus, who has a daunting task before him. There are fledgling Christian communities throughout Crete, and Titus must organize them, appointing leaders who are solidly mature Christians. Although Paul addresses the letter to Titus personally, he knows that Titus will read it publicly. Some of his listeners, especially if they have come from the early Jewish-Christian communities in Palestine, may have some questions about either Paul's authority or that of Titus, who is, after all, a Gentile. That perhaps explains the rather long greeting in which Paul asserts his apostolic authority.

Address and Greeting (1:1–4)

[1]Paul, a slave of God and apostle of Jesus Christ for the sake of the faith of God's chosen ones and the recognition of religious truth, [2]in the hope of eternal life that God, who does not lie, promised before time began, [3]who indeed at the proper time revealed his word in the proclamation with which I was entrusted by the command of God our savior, [4]to Titus, my true child in our common faith: grace and peace from God the Father and Christ Jesus our savior.

OT: Num 23:19; Josh 1:2; 24:29; Jer 7:25
NT: Rom 1:1; 2 Cor 8:23; Phil 2:6–11
Catechism: eternal life (988, 1020)
Lectionary: Memorial of Saints Timothy and Titus

The first impression we get from the address and greeting is its unusual length.   **1:1**
In the Greek, 1:1–4 is one sentence. The compactness of the whole section is
compounded by the theological intensity of the terms, which are actually a
summary of Paul's apostolate.

In his earlier letters Paul called himself "a slave of Christ" (Rom 1:1; Gal 1:10;
Phil 1:1). In calling himself **a slave of God** here, perhaps he wishes to identify
himself with Christ in the state of a slave, which he embraced in assuming flesh
and being obedient even unto death on a cross (Phil 2:6–11). As Jesus did that
for the sake of **God's chosen ones**, so Paul has committed himself totally to the
same mission. However willingly embraced, slavery suggests a person without
the freedom to determine his or her own path, one whose life and work is totally
at the service of another. But this slavery is an honor, because it is also Paul's
vocation to be an **apostle of Jesus Christ**, one called and sent with authority by
the Son of God. It may even be that because Paul is God's slave, wholly God's,
he can be God's delegate. In the Roman world slaves could occasionally be
invested with full authority to represent their masters, and the more important
the master, the greater was the honor of the slave. Already in Greek thought,
to be a slave of the king was considered an honor. Even more, to be a slave of
a god, as prophets claimed to be, lifted one above one's fellow human beings,
including kings: "I live in no sense as a slave of yours but of Apollo."[1] But Paul
is a Jew, and he is placing himself in the long succession of those in the Old
Testament who were called to be God's slaves and delegates: Moses (Josh 1:2),
Joshua (24:29), and the prophets (Jer 7:25; Amos 3:7). To be also an apostle of
Jesus Christ would imbue Paul with even more authority—the power to speak
with the authority of the Son of God.

The goal of Paul's mission was to call forth, foster, and protect the faith of
those who, in God's mysterious providence, would say yes to the gospel. Recalling this apostolic mission echoes the opening address of Romans, where Paul
wrote that through Christ "we have received the grace of apostleship, to bring
about the obedience of faith . . . among all the Gentiles, among whom you also
. . . are called" (Rom 1:5–6). "Obedience" suggests an act of the will, but it is
not blind obedience. The gospel is also addressed to the mind; it makes sense
to the one whose heart is seeking the truth. Thus faith brings **recognition of
religious truth**. The Greek word for "recognition" (*epignōsis*) here refers not to
knowledge in general but to a perception of an aspect of an object one already
knows. Here that aspect of revealed truth is that it leads to a holy way of life.
The gospel transforms one's life!

1. Sophocles, *Oedipus Rex* 410.

Here we again meet *eusebeia* ("devotion, religion"). The Greek reads literally "the truth that is according to *eusebeia*." This term is difficult to render adequately in English, because it has both a vertical dimension (dedication or devotion to God or the gods) and a horizontal dimension (right relationship with one's fellow human beings). The Septuagint used the adjective form (*eusebēs*) to translate the Hebrew words *saddiq* ("just, righteous") and *hasid* ("loyal, devoted"), used for both dimensions. The Latin equivalent *pietas* connotes the same virtues. For Paul, then, the term was a happy convergence of the Jews' as well as the Gentiles' description of a person of highest virtue. For a Roman or Hellenist of Paul's day to hear that the gospel bore fruit in *eusebeia* would evoke admiration. The gospel makes men and women more devout and better neighbors and citizens! The truth of revelation, which bears fruit in this godliness, is not merely speculative; it is a truth that manifests itself in charity (Eph 4:15). We find here an echo of 1 Tim 1:4–7 and 4:7 and an anticipation of what is yet to come in Titus: the truth of the gospel is the opposite of speculation about genealogies and myths that has nothing to do with conversion and changed lives.

1:2   This godliness, which is the gospel lived, rests upon the **hope of eternal life**. In modern English "hope" can mean just wishful thinking, as in "I hope I live to be a hundred." But in Paul, when God or his gifts are the object, hope is the assurance in the present life of what is to come, which lasts forever. This, of course, does not justify presumption but rather is trust based on what God had done and promised.[2] It is this hope, generated by God's love, that fires the Christian to courageously walk the journey in this world, even in the midst of persecutions, trials, and temptations (Rom 5:5; 8:1–39). The apostle's preaching and the faithful person's response are simply instruments to bring people to the final goal, eternal life, which is not just the soul's union with God but a share in the bodily resurrection of Jesus Christ.

When did God make these promises that ground Christian hope? Elsewhere Paul speaks of the promise or promises made to Abraham (Rom 4:13; Gal 3:16) or to the fathers (Rom 15:8), but here it was something **promised before time began** or "before the foundation of the world" (John 17:24; Eph 1:4), that is, from all eternity. The sense, then, is that God determined from all eternity to bestow eternal life on those who would receive the good news. His saving plan was always in his heart. (In the Greek there is an intentional wordplay on the "eternal times" of the divine promise and the "eternal life" that is its goal.)

1:3   But God chose to reveal this promise **at the proper time**. That suggests that he chose to wait until "the time was ripe." In fact, he engaged his people in a long

---

2. 2 Tim 2:13; Rom 5:2–5; Gal 5:5; Col 1:5, 27.

pedagogy until he felt they were ready—and the world was ready too. Despite what
the Roman emperors did to impose the worship of the gods—and of themselves!—
there was widespread dissatisfaction with the old religions, as we know from
the multiplication of various cults and mystery religions, as well as philosophies
that were groping for a better way of life. Moreover, the *pax Romana*, the time
of relative stability imposed by the military power of Rome, made it possible for
missionaries to travel anywhere in the known world without hindrance. It was at
that time of world history that God sent his Son as the fulfillment of the promise
and the Spirit as the firstfruits (Rom 8:23), or first installment (2 Cor 1:22; Eph
1:13–14), of eternal life. Paul was now delivering both the message and the life.
The apostle's mission was not a personal initiative on his part but a sacred trust
and a command given to him by God for the purpose of carrying out his saving
plan. Indeed we have in these brief, compact verses the entire sweep of God's plan
of salvation, from its origin in the eternal heart of God, through its revelation in
Christ and the Holy Spirit, to the apostolic proclamation of the gospel, leading
to salvation and eternal life for everyone who believes (Rom 1:16).

Finally we come to the addressee of the letter, **Titus**. Who is he? When the   1:4
church in Jerusalem raised its eyebrows at Paul's not requiring circumcision
of his Gentile converts, Paul headed to Jerusalem and took with him an un-
circumcised Gentile convert, Titus. It was a bold strategy, for this Titus had
even become a trusted collaborator in Paul's mission. In the presence of such a
successful witness, the Jewish leaders would be hard put to object to the mission to the Gentiles as Paul understood it. The strategy worked. Titus was not
required to be circumcised, and Paul went on to insist, against opposition, that
the case of Titus must stand for all Gentile converts (Gal 2:1–5).

It is plausible that Titus was the same person called Titus Justus in Acts 18:7,
whose house in Corinth Paul used when forced to leave the synagogue. If so, Titus's
being a native of Corinth could have given him added influence in the church there.
Paul calls him his "partner and co-worker" and even counts him as one of the
"apostles of the churches" (2 Cor 8:23), who walks "in the same spirit," "in the same
steps" as Paul (12:18). Paul sent him to deal with a troublesome group in Corinth,
and Titus succeeded in bringing the factious party to repentance, which brought
great joy to Paul (7:6–7). He then sent Titus back to Corinth to oversee the collection for the poor in Jerusalem (8:6). Titus was a trusted collaborator indeed.

It is not surprising, then, that Paul, now in his elder years, calls Titus his **true
child**. The Greek phrase means literally "a legitimate child born in wedlock." In
the spiritual sense here Paul probably means that he was responsible for Titus's
conversion. In any case it certainly means that, like Timothy (1 Tim 1:2), Titus

has been a faithful disciple. He has walked in the same spirit as his mentor (2 Cor 12:18), so that Paul could send him to Crete not merely to preach the gospel but to show how it should be lived (Titus 2:7). Paul's ministry, threatened by his aging, will be carried on without compromise or deviance by his spiritual descendent, unlike others of Paul's associates, who have abandoned him and made a shipwreck of the faith (1 Tim 1:19).

It is important not to miss the communal thrust of this entire passage. With the other Pastorals, this passage is a primary witness to the handing on of the apostolic Tradition. The gospel will not end with the apostles. It will continue in those ordained and delegated to safeguard and proclaim it, and in the Church itself, which shares the **common faith**. In the usual greeting, **grace and peace**, Paul identifies Jesus by the same title he has just given to God: **savior**.

Reflection and Application (1:1–4)

Two things are important about this text. On the one hand, knowledge of the faith ("recognition of the religious truth"; 1:1) is important. One cannot survive spiritually if the only information one gets about the faith is the Sunday homily. Nor can the religious education we received as children suffice, for adults need adult food (1 Cor 3:2; Heb 5:12–14), and food must be taken regularly. On the other hand, a purely speculative knowledge of the faith can be disastrous, as Jesus himself said: if you do not live the word you have heard, your house will collapse in the flood (Matt 7:24–27).

The Church today continues to have the responsibility to hand on the apostolic Tradition. If that Tradition is authentically proclaimed and guided by the magisterium, it is also passed on by "the contemplation and study made by believers, who treasure these things in their hearts (see Luke 2:29, 51) through a penetrating understanding of the spiritual realities which they experience" (*Dei Verbum* 8). That means that whatever our state in life, if we are anointed by baptism and confirmation, we like Paul and Titus are stewards of a sacred Tradition (1 Pet 4:10) that we must contemplate, study, and live in order that we may pass it on in all its richness to the next generation.

What It Takes to Be a Leader (1:5–9)

[5]**For this reason I left you in Crete so that you might set right what remains to be done and appoint presbyters in every town, as I directed you,**

⁶on condition that a man be blameless, married only once, with believing children who are not accused of licentiousness or rebellious. ⁷For a bishop as God's steward must be blameless, not arrogant, not irritable, not a drunkard, not aggressive, not greedy for sordid gain, ⁸but hospitable, a lover of goodness, temperate, just, holy, and self-controlled, ⁹holding fast to the true message as taught so that he will be able both to exhort with sound doctrine and to refute opponents.

NT: 1 Tim 3:2–7, 15; 2 Tim 2:24–25; 1 Pet 5:1–4
Catechism: bishops in apostolic succession (1555–56), presbyterium (1567)

The challenge Titus faces is very different from that facing Timothy. The   1:5
latter is in charge of a relatively mature community, where leaders are already in place and where attention must be given to the qualifications of any new appointees. But in Crete the communities are without presbyters and the Church is a young, tiny seed planted in rough soil. Though we do not otherwise know of a visit by Paul to Crete, the situation presented in this letter is that he left Titus with much organizing work still to be done. Paul's directives in this letter tend therefore to be more forceful and urgent.

There is a play on words in the Greek between **I left** (*apelipon*) and **what remains** (*leiponta*), which perhaps explains the unusual idea of putting in order, perhaps also rectifying, the things that "remain" (to be done). This will involve, first of all, assuring that each community is provided with the necessary leadership. **Presbyters** in the plural probably means that Titus should assure that

Crete: Opportunities and Threats

BIBLICAL BACKGROUND

Situated at the maritime convergence of three continents—Africa, Asia, and Europe—and enjoying favorable winds from both north and south, Crete's many ports made it an ideal center of trade. Mythology enveloped its fabled King Minos, possessor of the first maritime empire with its hundred cities. The mountains were held to be the first dwelling place of the goddess Artemis on earth. They also hindered communication, a factor that Titus would have to contend with. By the second century BC the Jewish population there was so large that Roman historian Tacitus thought it was their original homeland.[a] In reality, the Philistines—who gave the name Palestine to the Jews' homeland—came from there.

a. *Histories* 5.2.11.

the church in each town has its "board of elders," as in the Jewish synagogues. This was no mean task, for the island is 156 miles from east to west and 35 from north to south, and mountains reaching to 7,882 feet run the length of the island (fig. 9).

1:6   Titus's authority derives from Paul, whose directives must be carried out. These directives concern primarily the qualifications for becoming a presbyter. These are virtually the same as in 1 Tim 3:2–4. Paul is obviously concerned about the good reputation of the leaders, and thus anything that would tarnish that reputation, and through it the Church, must at all costs be avoided in candidates for the presbyterate. To be **blameless** would not mean totally without sin, for as Augustine remarks, in that case nobody could ever be a presbyter. The word refers primarily to the absence of any public crime or dishonor. Leaders of the community are public persons, and they embody the Church's call to holiness in a special way.

This symbolic role goes beyond mere moral rectitude. It even means being **married only once**. The Greek literally says "a one-woman man" or "a one-wife man." Given that in Roman law, men were legally free to commit adultery, while women were not, this could mean that the presbyter-to-be should not have a reputation of being a womanizer. However, fidelity in marriage was expected of every Christian, so St. John Chrysostom and the Christian Tradition have understood the phrase in the sense of not remarrying after the death of one's wife.[3] To live celibately after the death of one's wife would be countercultural, for the Augustan laws, the *lex Julia de maritandis ordinibus*,[4] and other regulations penalized widowed men from the ages of twenty-five to sixty who did not remarry. It is likely that Paul's theological basis for this requirement was that Christian marriage is an icon of the marriage of Christ and his Church, with which the marrying of a second wife would conflict, for Christ never had any other spouse than his Church (see also the comments on 1 Tim 3:2). The pastor, or presbyter or bishop, is thus not only a shepherd; he is a symbol of Christ, as his marriage is a symbol of Christ's marriage to the Church.

The requirement of clerical celibacy in the West was still a long way off, though *Apostolic Constitutions* 6.3.17 (around AD 380) would require that a candidate unmarried before ordination must remain celibate. In the early Church, requiring celibacy would, from a purely practical point of view, have unduly limited the pool of available candidates. Today in many Eastern churches,

3. *Homilies on Titus* 1:6.
4. Under Caesar Augustus, these laws, instituted 18–17 BC with a view toward promoting morals and increasing population, encouraged marriage and having children. Celibates who did not marry were forbidden to receive inheritances or attend public games.

Fig. 9. The Askifou Valley on Crete.

including those united with Rome, married men may be ordained as priests, but unmarried priests may not marry after ordination, and celibacy is required of bishops. Thus in the Catholic Church the symbolic dimension of the priesthood, rather than practical considerations, continues to be the governing principle in the East, as it has been in the West for ten centuries.

The expectation of order in the family extends to other members of the household, particularly **children**. **Licentiousness** suggests unrestrained sexual activity, which Roman society, at least among the upper classes, tolerated in youth who had reached puberty, whereas being **rebellious** refers to disobedience. Children may indeed turn out badly through no fault of their parents, but then their father should not be placed in charge of the Church, lest the disobedience of his children give members of the Church license to disrespect the authority of their leader. It is clear, then, that the relationship between family and the Christian community is so intimate that the family can be called the "domestic church."

This is made clear in the following verse, for the Church is the household **1:7** of God. The **bishop**, or overseer, is the **steward** (*oikonomos*), a technical term for the person who manages a household for the owner—in this case, for the Lord (Luke 12:42; 1 Cor 4:1–2; 1 Pet 4:10). The conjunction **for** ties this verse closely to the preceding one and appears to equate the **bishop** (*episkopos*, "overseer") of 1:7 and the "presbyters" (*presbyteroi*, "elders") of 1:5. In Phil 1:1 Paul speaks of "overseers [*episkopoi*] and ministers [*diakonoi*]," both in the plural, with no mention of presbyters. Was "bishop" originally merely a synonym for "presbyter"? Saint Jerome thought so.[5] At any rate, at this stage of development the two roles seem intimately associated, if not identical.[6] Certainly we do not yet have here the clear delineation of bishop, priest, and deacon that we find in the letters of Ignatius of Antioch at the beginning of the second century. All of this argues for an earlier rather than a later date of the Pastorals. They certainly could not have been written after Ignatius, who died around AD 110. Whereas in 1 Tim 3:6 Paul says that the overseer should not be a recent convert, he makes no mention of that here, probably because nearly all the Christians in Crete are recent converts—all the more reason for being judicious in the selection and appointment of elders and overseers.

What does it mean to be **blameless**? In Titus 1:7 Paul returns to the word he used in 1:6 and now further details its meaning. First of all, he must **not** be **arrogant**. The one who is to be symbol and instrument of unity in the community must not act like a dictator, a bull in a china shop who cares nothing for others' opinions or ideas, who is not willing to listen, who is haughty or disdainful of others. Such an attitude shows no respect for those who, after all, are his brothers and sisters. Similarly, one who is **irritable**, who flies off the handle at the slightest provocation, has no place in leadership. Nor does one who is an excessive drinker (**a drunkard**) or one who gets into fights over trivia (**aggressive**) or uses his office to get rich (**greedy for sordid gain**). This list of gross vices is understandable in light of what Paul says later about the general reputation for vice among the Cretans. It suggests the challenge Titus faces in finding or forming qualified leaders among his recent converts.

1:8   On the positive side Paul lists seven qualities a bishop must possess. As manager of the house of God, he is to be **hospitable** (literally "a lover of outsiders"), that is, he should offer a welcoming embrace to those who knock at his door seeking spiritual or material help. This would apply first, of course, to needy members of the Church, those who have fallen through the cracks and effectively become outsiders even within the community. Christians, particularly the bishop, should not shrink from the sacrifice that hospitality entails. If the presbyter or bishop is supported by the community, as is called for in 1 Tim

5. *Letters* 146.1.
6. This text helps clarify the position of bishop in 1 Tim 3:1–7, which is probably no different from that mentioned here.

5:17–18, then he is actually representing the hospitality of the community as well as his own.

Lover of goodness is one of the twenty-one characteristics of the spirit of wisdom in Wis 7:22 ("loving the good"). Moved by God's love, one does not even think evil; one does not rejoice in wickedness but rejoices in the truth (1 Cor 13:5–6). The word **temperate** means to be reasonable, sensible, keeping one's head—particularly appropriate for a leader who is periodically confronted by groups or individuals pressing their often conflicting agendas. In other words, the bishop must be a person of good judgment, which would have been shown in his ability to govern his own household (1 Tim 3:4). To the quality **just** Paul adds **holy**. Holiness means living a life that manifests one's consecration by the blood of Christ. It is required of all the baptized (1 Cor 3:17) but is especially demanded of one who represents the holy community. The bishop is not to be merely an administrator; he is before all else a religious man, a man of prayer and worship, who models for the faithful what each of them should be. **Self-controlled** refers to regulation of the appetites in regard to food, drink, and sex. Hailed by the ancient moralists as a human virtue, self-control is for the Christian a gift of the Holy Spirit (Gal 5:23). A similar positive and negative description of the Christian steward is found in Luke 12:41–46, a further hint that this letter may have been composed by Luke under Paul's direction.

The last trait concerns the candidate's faithfulness to the apostolic Tradition that has been handed on to him. The **true message as taught** may indeed refer to an early form of the Apostles' Creed, since the word *logos* ("message") can also mean "pattern." Thus in 1 Cor 15:2 Paul says that to be saved his readers must "hold fast to the word" exactly as Paul preached it to them, which Paul then spells out in a series of propositions that seem to be drawn from an early Christian creed (15:3–5). In any case the candidate must have sufficiently precise knowledge of the faith in order to pass it on uncontaminated and undiluted, and he must be totally committed to the message. "Lack of education in a clergyman prevents him from doing good to any one but himself."[7]

1:9

Reflection and Application (1:5–9)

By the way he or she lives, every Christian is either a witness to the gospel or a counterwitness. When one is a public person, representative in a special way of Christ as a leader in the community, the honor of the Church is even more

7. Jerome, *Letters* 53.3.

critically at stake. In our day, when scandals among the clergy have rocked the Church, this passage of Paul's letter to Titus is as timely as ever. One need not be a priest or deacon, however, to find this reminder challenging. The multiplication of lay ministers makes Paul's concern widely applicable to anyone who functions in a public way in the community of Jesus.

Nor are the virtues specified by Paul limited to bishops or pastors. They are virtues for any Christian, particularly for anyone who would be a minister in the Christian community. They would also apply to whoever is head of the domestic church, the family. Note how much emphasis is placed in the Pastorals on teaching. The Christian cannot grow in depth and stability without an ever deeper understanding of the faith. And while this growth is not merely intellectual but should be accompanied by prayer and virtuous living, Paul's emphasis is a call today for ongoing instruction and study of the faith in its sources in the Scriptures and in the teaching of the Church. The proliferation of Bible study groups in the Catholic Church in recent years has made access to the Bible easier. The teachings of the Bible are well organized in the *Catechism of the Catholic Church*, which is a solid and easily readable exposition. In addition, knowledge of the history of the Church, particularly through the lives of the saints, fosters greater understanding and love of our inherited gift.

False Teachers (1:10–16)

[10]For there are also many rebels, idle talkers and deceivers, especially the Jewish Christians. [11]It is imperative to silence them, as they are upsetting whole families by teaching for sordid gain what they should not. [12]One of them, a prophet of their own, once said, "Cretans have always been liars, vicious beasts, and lazy gluttons." [13]That testimony is true. Therefore, admonish them sharply, so that they may be sound in the faith, [14]instead of paying attention to Jewish myths and regulations of people who have repudiated the truth. [15]To the clean all things are clean, but to those who are defiled and unbelieving nothing is clean; in fact, both their minds and their consciences are tainted. [16]They claim to know God, but by their deeds they deny him. They are vile and disobedient and unqualified for any good deed.

OT: Jer 9:2–5
NT: Matt 15:11, 18–20; 23:25–28; Rom 3:23; 1 Tim 4:1–5; 6:1–10; 2 Tim 3:1–9
Catechism: myths (285), the battle with evil (407–9)

This section is tied closely to the preceding one, giving the reason why it is im-   **1:10**
portant to appoint leaders who are virtuous, reliable, and faithful to the apostolic
Tradition: there exist already large numbers of self-appointed teachers filling the
air with vain speculations and deceiving the faithful. Most of these come from
among the **Jewish Christians**. The Greek literally says "the circumcision,"[8] so
one might ask whether these troublemakers are non-Christian Jews. However,
inasmuch as Paul orders Titus to discipline them, it seems that they fall under
his authority and hence belong to the Christian community. There was already
in the second century BC a large colony of Jews in Crete, and the earliest converts to Christianity would have been among them. They might be especially
prone to an anti-Paul attitude, particularly if they had been visited by Jews or
by Jewish Christians from Palestine whose spirituality was heavily influenced
by the law. That Titus was a Gentile may have made his authority over the Jewish Christians less acceptable to them, but if that possibility occurred to Paul,
he did not consider it worth mentioning.

They must be silenced (literally "muzzled, gagged")—language much stronger   **1:11**
than what is used in 1 Timothy. Paul doesn't say how this is to be done. If, as
seems likely, these "deceivers" are within the Christian community, a series of
interventions is possible—from admonition to excommunication. Paul leaves
the method to Titus, but he must exercise his authority decisively. The serious threat to the Church can be seen in the effect their **teaching** is having on
households—**whole families**—the pillars of the Christian community. Destabilize the family and you destabilize the Church.

The teachers, moreover, are not inspired by enlightened zeal but by love of
sordid gain, with which heretics are regularly stigmatized (1 Tim 6:5; 2 Pet
2:3). But Cretans generally had a reputation for greed and dishonesty, for being
an island of pirates: "Cretans and Aetolians consider piracy and brigandage
honorable."[9] "So common among them is sordid love of gain and lust for wealth,
that the Cretans are the only people in the world in whose eyes no gain is
disgraceful."[10] Plutarch records that Perseus was abandoned by all his soldiers
except for the Cretans, who followed him "not through good will, but because
they were as devoted to his riches as bees to their honeycombs."[11]

These references could be dismissed as the kind of ethnic slurs that might be   **1:12–13**
expected from non-Cretans, but even a Cretan himself attests to the characteriza-
tion. Poets in the Greek world were often called prophets, and, according to the

---

8. Compare "the circumcision party" (RSV) and "those of the circumcision" (NRSV and NJB).
9. Cicero, *Republic* 3.9.15.
10. Polybius, *Histories* 6.46.3.
11. *Aemilius Paulus* 23.4.

evaluation of ancient writers, Epimenides, whom Paul quotes here, deserved the title.[12] The reputation for lying could largely be traced to the Cretans' claim to have the tomb of Zeus, whereas everyone knew that Zeus was immortal! But the modern reader may wonder how this letter, meant to support the mission in Crete and intended for public reading, could possibly ingratiate Paul with the Cretan Christians.[13] Perhaps they would agree with Paul that such negative traits were common in their culture. It would be not unlike Christians today skewering the major faults of the culture in which they live. The aspect that Paul focuses on particularly is lying, which has infected the false teachers even in the Christian community, who are his real target. Titus is to act vigorously. The metaphor underlying Paul's command to **admonish them sharply**, so that they may be **sound**, or healthy, **in the faith**, is a medical one. "Sharply" in the Greek means literally "cutting off," like a surgeon who can restore the patient to health only at the expense of removing what is diseased. This could mean either convincing the erring parties of their errors or, if that proves unsuccessful, excommunicating them.

1:14   The specific target of the false teaching appears in Titus 1:14. The problem seems similar to that mentioned in 1 Tim 1:4, involving speculations about genealogies. **Myths** here, of course, has the meaning "unreal, imaginary, illusory." The Greek myths were often criticized even by Greek authors as projecting sexual misconduct onto the gods, but the myths here are said to be **Jewish**. They are probably tales created about biblical characters, such as we find in some of the noncanonical Jewish literature of the period. When these rob the attention Christians should be giving to the gospel, they become its enemies.

We are not sure what precisely the **regulations of people** (literally "precepts of men") **who have repudiated the truth** are, but they are likely some of the Jewish ceremonial practices, branded by Jesus as "human precepts" (Mark 7:7), that some Jewish Christians were trying to impose upon their Gentile peers. These would refer primarily to regulations concerning vessels or food that is clean or unclean, observances that one of the Dead Sea Scrolls calls "works of the law,"[14] a term Paul uses repeatedly in Galatians (2:16 [three times]; 3:2, 5,

---

12. Plutarch, *Solon* 12.7.

13. It is suggested that Paul is not condemning the Cretans but instead is using a literary paradox, quite common among the Stoics, as an illustration of the "vain dispute about words" that he is targeting. A common paradox was: "When I lie and admit that I lie, do I lie or speak the truth?" If a Cretan poet counts himself among the liars (1:12) and says that Cretans are liars, is he lying or telling the truth? "That testimony is true" could then be a continuation of Epimenides's remark, further leaving the question of whether it is true. See Patrick Gray, "The Liar Paradox and the Letter to Titus," *Catholic Biblical Quarterly* 69 (2007): 302–14. Targeting the Jewish group(s), however, the context makes this hypothesis less likely.

14. Martin Abegg, "Paul, 'Works of the Law,' and MMT," *Biblical Archaeology Review* 20 (Nov./Dec. 1994): 52–61.

10). To impose these as requirements for salvation or even for perfection is to deny the freedom of the children of God.

It is hard to decide whether the Greek term in Titus 1:15 should be translated **clean** (NAB) or "pure" (RSV and NIV), because the meaning slides from what is ritually clean to what is morally pure, but the careful reader will understand. The original audience of the letter would certainly have understood the saying, because, in one form or another, it was a proverbial principle in the Mediterranean world even before the first century. We find it on the lips of Jesus in the New Testament (Matt 15:11; Mark 7:15; Luke 11:41). While the principle of Christian freedom may have been misinterpreted by the Corinthians as licensing promiscuity (1 Cor 6:12–14), it clearly applies to the matter of foods, none of which is any longer unclean (Mark 7:19; Acts 10:14–15). What really matters is purity of heart (Matt 5:8). If foods or other material things cannot defile the pure of heart, the reverse is not true: the wicked can defile whatever they use. They themselves are first **defiled** by sin, and here Paul is thinking of the sin of disbelief. (A single concept is expressed jointly by the two terms **defiled and unbelieving** [the technical term for this literary feature is hendiadys], hence, "defiled by disbelief.") They contaminate whatever they touch.

It was a principle of Stoicism that the source of defilement was in the person: "Material things are indifferent, but the use one makes of them is not."[15] "Whatever good comes to the bad man is vitiated by his wrong use of it. Just as the stomach, when it is weakened by disease, gathers bile, and, changing all the food it receives, turns every sort of nourishment into a source of pain, so in the case of a perverse mind, whatever you entrust to it becomes a burden to it and a source of disaster and misery."[16] But even in Jewish ritual law, the one who is unclean renders unclean whatever he touches (Hag 2:13–14). Real pollution begins in the mind and the perversion of conscience. Paul applies this general principle to those who refuse the light of faith. To disbelieve is the defiling sin. That means that the issue of what is clean and unclean is not a matter of utensils or foods but of personal choice to believe or not believe in Jesus Christ. Believers' consciences have been purified by faith (Acts 15:9), and that renders them clean.

The problem with the false teachers is not that they verbally renounce **God**. The problem is that they **claim to know** him. To "know God" in the Bible means to confess him as the true God *and* to live according to his commandments, that is, living justly (see Jer 22:15–16: "Your father . . . / did what was right

15. Epictetus, *Discourses* 2.5.1.
16. Seneca, *On Benefits* 5.12.5–6.

and just. . . . / Is this not true knowledge of me?"). It means the confession of a good life more than a confession of words. "Just as deeds can deny, so deeds can profess."[17] That these teachers claim to know God poses a compounded threat to a religious community, for these wolves look like sheep (Matt 7:15). But their true character can be seen by their works, which in this case deny what they outwardly profess. We can extrapolate and say that just as truth bears fruit in every kind of goodness (Eph 5:9), so false teaching leads to sterility and rotten fruit.

Reflection and Application (1:10–16)

Paul's decision to quote a Cretan's criticism of his own culture, which echoes the judgments of some non-Cretans, raises the question of whether this is what today we would call ethnic labeling. Paul is obviously making a generalization. Surely he is not thinking of the blameless Cretans whom Titus should appoint as presbyters (Titus 1:5–9). On the witness of Epimenides, it is likely that such negative tendencies were widespread among the Cretans, which would explain why Paul stresses so emphatically that the Cretan converts be trained in the virtues. I have heard several visitors to my hometown, San Antonio, say, "The people here are warm and hospitable." Such a general impression does not mean there are no exceptions. By the same token, outsiders can have negative impressions of people in an area, impressions that may even be confirmed by locals like Epimenides. I have heard Indian Catholics criticize their own culture for its caste system and the unjust practice of the dowry, as American Catholics criticize elements of "the culture of death" in their own country. The context shows that Paul is applying this not to every Cretan but to the false teachers (1:13). But it is possible that the statement could be heard today not as a general criticism of a culture but as an ethnic slur, which would go against the norms for the Christian use of language elsewhere mandated by the New Testament and Paul himself (3:2; Matt 5:22; Eph 4:29). The danger of this misinterpretation is probably the reason why this text is never read in the liturgy.

"To the clean all things are clean" (Titus 1:15) does not mean that one can engage in sin and not be defiled—a splitting of body and soul that Paul condemned in 1 Cor 6:12–20. Nor does it mean that Christians can read or view just anything—pornography, for example—without defiling themselves. (Pornography is the fastest growing addiction today among men!) It does mean, though, that the more integrated our spirit and body are, the purer are our hearts, and

---

17. Augustine, *Sermon* 269.4.

the more we will be able to view the world, persons of the opposite sex, human sexuality, and the goods of this world with a contemplative, nonpossessive, loving embrace—in short, to see as God sees and to love as God loves.

To help preserve the purity of the faith, the Church at one time put some books on the Index of Forbidden Books. This is no longer the case, nor is a bishop's imprimatur required to assure the orthodoxy of a book's theological contents. All the more important, then, is good theological formation for the laity as well as the clergy, that they may discern the truth of claims that come today in volleys from so many sources.

Virtues for Different States of Life

Titus 2

The pastoral questions we examined in 1 Timothy return here. How do Christians in their different states of life live the gospel? What would daily Christian living mean for the elderly, the young, the married, slaves, and masters?

Older Men and Women (2:1–5)

> [1]As for yourself, you must say what is consistent with sound doctrine, namely, [2]that older men should be temperate, dignified, self-controlled, sound in faith, love, and endurance. [3]Similarly, older women should be reverent in their behavior, not slanderers, not addicted to drink, teaching what is good, [4]so that they may train younger women to love their husbands and children, [5]to be self-controlled, chaste, good homemakers, under the control of their husbands, so that the word of God may not be discredited.

OT: Ps 128; Prov 16:31–32; 21:9; 2 Macc 6:18–31
NT: Acts 5:33–39; 1 Cor 7:3–5, 33–34; Eph 5:21–32; Col 3:18; 1 Tim 2:8–15
Catechism: temperance (1809), moral life sustained by gifts of Holy Spirit (1831), chastity as self-mastery (2339)

2:1 To the modern reader, some of the counsels Paul now gives may seem so obvious as to be trite. But one must remember the raw condition of the Church in Crete, made up largely of recent converts who have come from a life infected by the loose morals of the surrounding culture (Titus 1:12). As appears so pervasively in the Pastorals, Paul's concern is to shore up and stabilize the lives of

Cicero on Vices in the Elderly

BIBLICAL BACKGROUND

Cicero, a Roman statesman, orator, and author of the first century BC, wrote: "The old should strive by their counsel and practical wisdom to be of as much service as possible to their friends and to the young, and especially to the state. But . . . luxury, a vice in any time of life, is in old age especially scandalous. But if they add excess in sensual indulgence to luxurious living, it is a twofold evil. For then old age not only disgraces itself; it also serves to make the excesses of the young less shameful."[a]

a. *De Officiis* 1.34.123.

families, the building blocks of the Church. The sound doctrine of the gospel is not mere intellectual truth; it affects the very structure of relationships in the home as well as in the Church. Neither can stand without the practice of virtue. Paul addresses those virtues that, from his own experience in Crete and possibly from what Titus has reported, he sees are most needed.

Even though many outside the community are infected by the vices of the culture, there are those who will judge Christianity by high moral standards. They will look for the fruits of the gospel (Matt 7:20) and judge it by the kind of behavior it produces. Thus Christians should live in a way "that the word of God may not be discredited" (Titus 2:5).

As for yourself indicates that Paul is returning to Titus's responsibilities, after having discussed the qualifications of presbyters and targeted the false teachers. Titus must teach **what is consistent with sound doctrine**. That is, in contrast to the disastrous effects of the false teaching that Paul has just discussed, Titus must draw out the practical consequences of the gospel for daily living. In a culture where Dionysus, the god of wine and revelry (like the Roman god Bacchus), was worshiped and where Paul has already painted gluttony as a common vice of the Cretans (1:12), Paul first counsels temperance.

In the Christian community, sobriety in the **older men** is important because of their roles as examples and leaders of households and also because it would normally be from them that the presbyters or elders (1:5) of the church would be chosen (the Greek words for "presbyters" in 1:5 and "older men" in 2:2 come from the same root). Saint Thomas Aquinas says that for the Greeks wine is the milk of the aged in their weakness, but it can easily lead to excess.[1] Paul does not

2:2

1. *Commentary on Titus* 2:2.

Paul and the Moralists

BIBLICAL
BACKGROUND

From Paul's major letters prior to the Pastorals, it is evident that for him the central event of the Christian life is the death and resurrection of Jesus and the gift of the Holy Spirit that, through baptism, brings one into intimate communion with the Father and the Son. From this new gift flows a life of virtue that transcends even the moral expectations of the old law. Much of Paul's discourse, especially in Romans and Galatians, puts this new life of grace in contrast with the Jewish legal system. But inasmuch as his ministry is not only to the Jews of the Diaspora but to the increasing number of Gentiles, the question arises as to how Paul's ethical teaching confronts the Gentile world.

On the one hand, the way many people lived in the Roman and Hellenistic world provided an immense challenge to the high moral standards of the gospel. Consider, for example, how Paul has to tell the Corinthians that incest is wrong and that tolerating it in the community is wrong (1 Cor 5:1–5) or that union with a prostitute profanes one's union with Christ (6:12–20). We know, too, that abortion and the abandonment of babies were not uncommon.

On the other hand, Paul's world was not without its moralists, particularly the Stoics, who promoted virtue and condemned vice. Emperor Augustus himself wanted to restore morality to his people and strengthen families. Many of Paul's lists of virtues and vices parallel those of the moralists of his day. Concerned to spread the gospel, he is keenly aware that the pagan world would judge the Christian message by the behavior of Christians. So, at one level, Paul joins hands with the contemporary moralists. But his motivation for living a virtuous life goes beyond that of the moralists. Theirs is a kind of commonsense morality, often motivated by the wisdom of consequences. Paul's derives from the consecration of baptism, the union of the Christian with the death and resurrection of Jesus Christ, and the presence within the Christian's body and soul of the sanctifying Holy Spirit. And the attending virtues in which the Christian is to grow are rooted in faith, hope, and charity, themselves gifts from God.

forbid wine; he even encourages Timothy to take some for his frequent illnesses (1 Tim 5:23); but for elderly Christians, being **temperate**, or sober, should also bear fruit in prudence, levelheadedness, and the ability to make sound decisions based on the life experience they have accumulated and on the transforming action of the Holy Spirit (2 Tim 1:7). **Dignified** and **self-controlled** means that they should be worthy of respect and honor not merely because of their age but because they are examples to the young and to non-Christians as well.

The combination **faith, love, and endurance** is very Pauline, endurance being the hallmark of hope (1 Thess 1:3). That they should be **sound** (literally "healthy") **in faith** reflects the doctrinal concern that runs through the Pastorals to defend the faithful against the threat of extraneous genealogies and myths. Those who are infected are "weak in faith" (Rom 14:1; see also 4:19), hence the importance of clarity in teaching. But mature faith is also marked by love, which is born of truth (Eph 4:15) and rejoices in the truth (1 Cor 13:6), and by perseverance, which alone guarantees fruitfulness (Luke 8:15) and even salvation itself (Matt 24:13). The particular witness that the aged can give is their lifelong fidelity. Such witness may not entail martyrdom, as it did for Eleazar (2 Macc 6:18–31), but it adds luster even to the witness of Jesus, who, dying young, was not able to show in his own body what kingdom living in advanced age would look like. That is the privilege of the elderly faithful.

The first three qualities—temperate, dignified, and self-controlled—come rather naturally to the aged, but the last three—faith, love, and endurance—are specifically Christian and, in fact, may become more difficult with age, since the experience of shattered dreams and broken promises can make the aged skeptical, and advancing weakness can make them impatient. That is why serenity, love, and joy in the aged are all the more powerful a witness to the presence and power of the Holy Spirit. Paul is thinking of the theological virtues—endurance being the typical manifestation of hope (1 Thess 1:3)—that give elderly Christians strength from a divine source. This addition of the theological virtues gives the lie to those who claim that the admonitions of the Pastorals are simply the moralizing of Greek philosophers.

The motivation for the behavior of Christian women, like that of the men, is a religious one. Since behavior, including dress, reveals who the person is (Sir 19:25–26), the **older women** should act with religious reverence in all they do, for they are holy. The Greek word *hieroprepēs* (**reverent**) is used outside the Bible for the conduct befitting a priest or priestess, one who serves in a temple. Used here, it suggests that women consecrated by baptism should manifest that consecration in how they dress, speak, and act, perhaps even suggesting that their role, especially in the household, is an act of worship, a liturgy, for wherever they are, they are part of God's temple (1 Cor 3:16).

2:3

Not slanderers: the Christian woman refuses to spread lies about others, a vice for which Greek women were frequently faulted in contemporary literature. So too drunkenness in elderly women, as even occasional epitaphs testify: "She wept on earth for only one thing, that the cup was empty."[2] Lest we think sobriety was recommended only to women, we need to recall Titus 1:7–8 and 2:2, where men are equally targeted. Addictions may not be limited to alcohol.

2. Cited by Spicq, *Épîtres pastorales*, 2.619.

In a *New Yorker* cartoon picturing mourners at a funeral, one lady whispers to another, "She was a great shopper!"

2:4–5   The older women are also called to teach virtue, especially to the younger women. That "teaching" of women is entrusted to women is probably just common sense, given the womanly roles in which the younger women are to be formed, but it is also a measure of prudence, avoiding even the possible appearance of any sexual irregularity if their formation were confided to men. The word **self-controlled** (also NRSV and NIV) can be translated "sensible" (RSV, JB, and NJB), "discreet" (KJV), or "temperate" (NEB). It is expected of bishops and older men as well (1 Tim 3:2; Titus 1:8; 2:2). **Chaste** implies sexual discipline and, more, an integrity of life. In the Greek culture of Paul's day, while a man's field of action was the exterior world, the wife managed the everyday affairs of the household. So the addition of the adjective **good** to **homemakers** probably means that they should exercise their authority not like tyrants but rather with gentleness and understanding. Jerome comments: "Let them not wish to give their husbands the illusion that they govern the household well because they make terror reign there."[3]

Paul had insisted that the gospel makes all equal, male and female (Gal 3:28). But he was also concerned for order within both the family and the Church (1 Cor 11:3–15; 14:34–35), and he does not see freedom in Christ as authorizing disturbance of antiquity's universal norm for domestic life, where women were supposed to be **under the control of their husbands**. This statement, which would be better translated "be subordinate to," as in Eph 5:21, stands in considerable tension with what Paul says elsewhere about marriage. He insists on mutuality of rights and duties in marriage (1 Cor 7:3–5), states that the husband is anxious to please his wife and the wife to please her husband (7:33–34), and frames the traditional family authority structure with a call for *mutual* submission in love (Eph 5:21–25).

This tension between cultural norms and the newness of the gospel underlines the necessity of an ongoing interpretation by the Church when it comes to the practical implications of the total biblical witness. If "authority" in marriage is conceived as competitive, then indeed for peace one of the two must have the final say. Such apparently was the wisdom of the Roman-Hellenistic world. But if there is true love, the kind of sacrificial love that Christ showed on the cross, then the two become not only one flesh but one spirit, and this demands a high degree of mutuality. The gospel should make better wives and better husbands! As Israel of old was, by its conduct, responsible for the honor of God's name

3. Cited in ibid., 2.621.

(Ezek 36:20–22), Christian men and women are responsible for the honor of the gospel they profess. Called to be the light of the world by their example and good works (Matt 5:14), Christian women will attract others to Christ.

Reflection and Application (2:1–5)

The United Nations declared 1999 the International Year of Older People, and to coincide with it in the same year the Pontifical Council for the Laity in Rome issued a document entitled *The Dignity of Older People and Their Mission in the Church and in the World*. That same year also Pope John Paul II wrote a pastoral *Letter to the Elderly*, sharing with them his own insights about the grace and challenge of old age. After reviewing the witness of Scripture on aging, climaxing with our text from Titus, the Pope adds:

> Thus the teaching and language of the Bible present old age as a "favourable time" for bringing life to its fulfilment and, in God's plan for each person, as a time when everything comes together and enables us better to grasp life's meaning and to attain "wisdom of heart." . . . Old age is the final stage of human maturity and a sign of God's blessing.
>
> In the past, great respect was shown to the elderly. . . .
>
> And what of today? . . . We see that among some peoples old age is esteemed and valued, while among others this is much less the case, due to a mentality which gives priority to immediate human usefulness and productivity. (*Letter to the Elderly* 8–9)

Younger Men (2:6–8)

⁶**Urge the younger men, similarly, to control themselves, ⁷showing yourself as a model of good deeds in every respect, with integrity in your teaching, dignity, ⁸and sound speech that cannot be criticized, so that the opponent will be put to shame without anything bad to say about us.**

OT: Prov 4; 5; 7; Sir 6:18–37
NT: 1 Cor 6:12–20; 1 Tim 4:6, 12–13; 5:1–2
Catechism: scandal (2284–87)

While Titus was to "say" to the older men and women what they should do (2:1), he is to **urge** the **younger men**—notice the slightly stronger verb here, delicately nuancing the method of instruction appropriate to the difference

2:6

of age. But his flock will be more influenced by Titus's personal example (2:7) than by his speaking and exhorting. Let them see in him what they should become. Here is another example of Paul's repeated anxiety that the beauty and success of the gospel not be compromised by bad example, whether by Christians in relation to nonbelievers or by the pastor in relation to his flock.

2:7   What **good deeds** might Titus be urged to do? As leader of the churches in Crete he would no doubt be called upon to aid the poorer members, just as pastors today are often approached by the needy of their parish. But Paul probably considers the ministry of teaching to be the primary good work that Titus should be doing, as the next phrase indicates. The **teaching**, faithful to the apostolic Tradition, should be presented without corruption or frivolity, for the word of God is healthy both in itself and in its effects.

2:8   **Speech that cannot be criticized** incorporates a legal term, which can also be translated "free from censure," appearing only here in the New Testament and meaning that an accused person is declared innocent. The Roman courts may find Christians guilty of atheism, that is, refusal to worship the Roman gods. But the Christian message itself must not be corrupted by infidelity to the apostolic Tradition and thus incur the censure ultimately of Christ as judge. The **opponent** here may mean Satan the accuser of old (Rev 12:10), the Roman authorities, or the false teachers who could find a weak spot in Titus's teaching should it depart in the least from the apostolic Tradition and the word of Jesus.

Slaves (2:9–10)

⁹Slaves are to be under the control of their masters in all respects, giving them satisfaction, not talking back to them ¹⁰or stealing from them, but exhibiting complete good faith, so as to adorn the doctrine of God our savior in every way.

OT: Exod 12:43–44; 21:1–11; Deut 16:11–12; 23:16–17
NT: Eph 6:5–9; 1 Tim 6:1–2a; Philem 16–17
Catechism: slavery (2414)

2:9   Finally, Paul turns his attention to **slaves**. The institution of slavery was so common in the ancient world that it is estimated that at one time Corinth's population was two-thirds slaves (see the commentary on 1 Tim 6:1–2a). Neither the preachers of the gospel nor the laity in Paul's days sought to eliminate the institution. Their focus was rather the transformation of the heart and mind, as slave and master met at the same Eucharistic table and worshiped the same Lord, who became a slave for the sake of both. Or, as Augustine remarks, Christ paid the same price for both master and slave.[4] So, in keeping with the same concern for order, Paul advises Timothy to exhort the Christian slaves to voluntarily submit to their masters. The NAB's **under the control of their masters** tends to limit the relationship to merely external obedience. Other translations render the Greek word as "submission," which is more than servile obedience.[5] If it implies keeping one's place (1 Cor 14:34), it also connotes an attitude of respect and charity toward all those in authority.

In light of modern abuses of authority and the heinous crimes of blind obedience to unjust orders (the Nuremberg trials: "I was just following orders"), "obedience" and "submission" have become neuralgic words to many contemporaries. And indeed, the New Testament knows that there is a time when one must obey God rather than humans (Acts 5:29), and Jesus himself challenged the authorities not only in word but in the dramatic deed of cleansing the temple (Matt 21:10–17). Even so, the Bible makes it clear that the universe is ordered hierarchically, and Christians must be outstanding in respect for that order (Titus 3:1; 1 Pet 2:13–14), for they follow him who submitted himself to authorities, whether his parents (Luke 2:51) or the religious authorities (Matt 17:24–26) or civil authorities (22:15–22).

But was slavery a just institution? Paying off debts rightly incurred is, of course, a matter of justice. In the ancient world one of the ways of doing this was by selling oneself into slavery, usually for a determined time. Even so, it gave the master more power than we would consider conscionable today. Other situations were even more unjust. The question here, however, is what the Christian slave should do in this situation. Paul does not counsel or approve running away or rebelling against one's master. From a practical point of view it would have been folly for the tiny Christian minority to undertake such a universal reform. Christians had a more immediate and urgent agenda: to proclaim the gospel and convert hearts. That also involved the practice of virtue by everyone, master and slave. It must be admitted that in the Pastorals Paul does not address the masters, as he does in Col 4, only the slaves. Why this omission? We don't know. Perhaps it is simply that there were no slave owners among the Christians of Crete, all the converts having come from the lower strata of society (1 Cor 1:26). In light of the continued existence today of slavery, we wish he had said more. But it is clear that he wants the slaves to be virtuous, so as to make the gospel more attractive to all, slaves and masters.

---

4. *Sermon* 94.
5. Other translations are "be subject" (NIV), "be obedient" (JB, NJB), and "be submissive" (NRSV).

They are to give their masters **satisfaction**, to please them. Just as Christian spouses should do positively what pleases the other (7:33–34) and as Paul sought to please others in order that they might be saved (10:33), Christian slaves must seek to please their masters as a testimony to their faith in him who did not please himself (Rom 15:3) and came not to be served but to serve (Mark 10:45). In so doing they please God, and this is a very different kind of posture than the kind of "pleasing men" elsewhere condemned when it goes counter to what pleases God (Gal 1:10).

2:10   As a social class, slaves were proverbially thought to be pilferers, so that if one could testify that a slave had never stolen, that sufficed to classify him as a good slave. One could object that slaves had had their freedom stolen from them, so why not compensate for it? No doubt many a slave thought that way. But Paul insists that they not steal from their masters but instead exhibit **complete good faith**, that is, be totally trustworthy. Within the system, unjust though it was, the slave is not excused from virtue. On the contrary, as a Christian the slave should behave in a way to become more endeared to his or her master. Why? To win the master and others to the gospel. Choosing a beautiful metaphor already used in the Greek world for endowing something with elegance, Paul says that slaves will thus **adorn** the teaching of Christ. Polybius speaks of augmenting the honor of cities "by adorning them not with paintings and reliefs, but with dignity and greatness of soul."[6] Similarly, the virtue of Christian slaves will make the gospel shine before the pagan world, increasing its attractiveness. Ceslas Spicq concludes: "Those who are at the bottom of the human hierarchy, deprived of public and private rights, and who ordinarily obey out of fear of punishment, are not only capable of living the purest gospel ideal but can also add to the splendor of the collective Christian life, to increase its attraction to the pagans. No Christian is so insignificant that he cannot honor God in this way."[7]

Reflection and Application (2:1–10)

Being a Christian is not merely a matter of saving one's soul but of living in such a way that the beauty of the gospel shines forth in word and action. Jesus said of his disciples, "You are the light of the world. A city set on a mountain cannot be hidden. . . . Just so, your light must shine before others, that they may see your good deeds and glorify your heavenly Father" (Matt

6. *Histories* 9.10.12.
7. Spicq, *Épîtres pastorales*, 2.626.

5:14–16). But in the same gospel Jesus warns that we are not to perform good deeds "to win the praise of others" (6:2). How do we reconcile these passages with one another and with this counsel to Titus? Obviously, if we act just to look holy to others we fall into hypocrisy, but if we do the right thing because it is the right thing to do, whether we are seen or not, we will give glory to God, and our good works cannot be hidden long (1 Tim 5:25). Our example will preach louder than words. By the same token, non-Christians can be scandalized and turned away from the faith by the disorderly behavior of Christians.

Doctrinal Foundation for the Transforming Virtues (2:11–15)

[11]For the grace of God has appeared, saving all [12]and training us to reject godless ways and worldly desires and to live temperately, justly, and devoutly in this age, [13]as we await the blessed hope, the appearance of the glory of the great God and of our savior Jesus Christ, [14]who gave himself for us to deliver us from all lawlessness and to cleanse for himself a people as his own, eager to do what is good.

[15]Say these things. Exhort and correct with all authority. Let no one look down on you.

OT: Exod 19:5–6; Deut 7:6; Ezek 37:23
NT: Eph 5:25–27; 1 Tim 2:1–6; 4:11–12
Catechism: God desires all to be saved (851), training in virtues (1810–11)
Lectionary: Christmas Mass at Midnight; (2:11–14; 3:4–7) Baptism of the Lord (C)
Lectionary (Byzantine): Theophany

Why should Christians of the different states of life just mentioned live virtuously? Not because of some Stoic or other philosophy, but rather because of what God has done. Such is the meaning of the simple introductory conjunction **for**. The motivation is essentially theological. The switch from the catechesis of virtues to **the grace of God** is abrupt, suggesting the very surprise of the appearance, like a meteor from outer space. "Grace" appears sixty times in Paul's undisputed letters. In the Greek Bible it most frequently translates *hen* ("favor, mercy") and occasionally *hesed*, the Hebrew Bible's most frequent characteristic of the Lord: "merciful, beneficent love" shown to his covenant people. But it also would be meaningful to the Hellenistic readers of the letter, for the Greek word *charis* was frequently used of favors granted by the emperor on the occasion of his visit to a city. The †aorist tense of the verb **has appeared**

2:11

(*epephanē*) signals a discrete moment in the past,[8] referring to the incarnation but more particularly to the saving death of Jesus upon the cross and the kind of blinding glory of the risen Lord that Paul experienced on the road to Damascus. Paul considers all these moments as one revelatory event. The Greek word used here, *epephanē*, is related to the Greek term *epiphaneia*, which has given us the English word "epiphany." Describing God's action in Christ as an epiphany appears in 2 Tim 1:10 (rendered "appearance" in the NAB). There it is further described as bringing life to light.

The difference between this grace and the "grace" of the emperors is that it offers eternal salvation—**saving all**. That does not mean that all people are automatically saved, but, because of God's desire to save all people (1 Tim 2:4), salvation is now available to all, Jew and Gentile alike. There is a hidden criticism here against the frequent hailing of the emperor as an "appearance" of the divine and of his "grace" as "savior."

2:12   In the Old Testament **training** most often meant educating children in the law of God and disciplining them, even punishing them (Deut 21:18; Sir 7:23), something that God himself does for his children (Deut 8:5; Prov 3:11–12; Heb 12:5–11). In the opinion of some authors, Paul is thinking of the severe physical discipline accompanying education in the Greek world and implying that the cross and suffering is the way Christians get trained. But here it is grace that educates. The thought is very Pauline: in the face of God's overwhelming kindness shown in Jesus Christ, one cannot help but be transformed, for one is gazing on his brilliant glory through the power of the Holy Spirit (2 Cor 3:18). The energy comes more from awareness of God's love than from his commands or the trials he sends. Suffering itself is of no avail for transformation unless its darkness is bathed in the overwhelming light of God's love and grace.

The effect of this transforming light is first of all to bring about in the believer a decisive rejection of its opposite: **godless ways and worldly desires**, the rebellion against God so characteristic of pagan life (Rom 1:18) and the accompanying passions, which Paul earlier calls the flesh (8:3–8; Gal 5:16) and 1 John 2:16 calls the lust of the flesh, the lust of the eyes, and worldly pride. Titus 2:12 may echo a baptismal formula recited by converts in the rite of initiation; it is similar to 2 Pet 1:4: "escaping from the corruption that is in the world because of evil desire."

---

8. The aorist tense in Greek generally signals a discrete past act, once done, as distinct from other past tenses, e.g., "did" instead of "was doing" or "has done." The NAB nevertheless translates it here as "has appeared," indicating the ongoing effect of the appearance.

The positive effects of God's training grace are threefold, expressed by three adverbs that, interestingly, address the three objects of charity: (1) Oneself: **live temperately**—temperance or self-control, highly regarded among the Greek ethicists, was also listed by Paul via another Greek word as one of the fruits of the Holy Spirit (Gal 5:23). (2) Others: **justly**—justice regulates one's relationships with others. (3) God: **devoutly**—devotion or piety directs one's relationship with God. That God's grace could accomplish this in those who must live in this world corrupted by sin and ruled by Satan (2 Cor 4:4; John 17:15–16) is amazing indeed.

But Christians are not just incarnations of the high ethical standards of the Greek philosophers. Like the source, which is "the grace of God," the goal of our transformation is the return of Jesus, which, like the grace of his first coming, will be an **appearance**. Christian life is framed by two epiphanies: the past coming of Christ and the future coming. God's grace makes Christians grow in the virtues in order to be ready for the Lord's return (1 Thess 3:12–13). They await the day of the Lord with eager expectation, for it will not pounce on them as a thief in the night but will be welcomed as the light that has made them children of the light (5:4–5). Hence this **hope** is a **blessed**, happy one that prompts the faithful to cry out, "*Marana tha!* Come, Lord!" (1 Cor 16:22; see also Rev 22:20). Unlike the first coming, which was humble even to death on a cross (Phil 2:7–8), the final one will be glorious.

2:13

Great as an epithet for God was commonly used for the pagan gods, particularly Zeus. Hence, Paul's use of **great God** would be familiar to his Greek readers or listeners, obviously replacing the Greek gods. Do the words **God** and **savior** both apply to Jesus, or does the first refer to the Father? By translating **the glory of the great God and of our savior Jesus Christ**, the NAB takes "God" as referring to the Father rather than to Jesus.[9] But "God" and "savior" stand spatially closer together in the Greek than in the English translations, so it is equally possible that Paul is calling Jesus both God and savior. Aside from the grammatical uncertainty, another factor favors the second option. The Pastorals repeatedly borrow language from the Hellenistic world, and there in the royal epiphany it was not unusual to speak of the emperor as "god-savior." Paul would then be throwing an intentional polemic against the idolatry of the pagan world. Jesus will appear as both God and savior.

9. Other translations are "the glorious appearing of our great God and Savior, Jesus Christ" (NIV), "the appearing of the glory of our great God and Saviour Christ Jesus" (JB, NJB), and "the manifestation of the glory of our great God and Savior, Jesus Christ" (NRSV).

2:14   Having evoked the future, Paul now evokes the past. A Christian looks to
the coming glory because he or she stands on the glorious past. Jesus **gave himself for us**. He "has loved me and given himself up for me," Paul wrote to the
Galatians (2:20). What made it a sacrifice was that Jesus chose to give himself
freely—and that because he loved us.

Christ's death on the cross freed us from the powers that held us bound,[10]
powers he lumps here under the term **lawlessness**. The image is one of being
tied up like a captive or being under a superior power, like a slave. The image of
liberation from this lawlessness differs considerably from the liberation from
the "works of the law" that Paul develops in Galatians. There the love of Christ
manifested on the cross frees one from the need to seek salvation in the Jewish
observances of circumcision and food laws—a temptation the Judaizers were
presenting to the Gentile Christians. In the Galatian context freedom meant
finding salvation in the gracious gift of God in Christ rather than in the works of
the law. There, of course, Paul headed off the objection that such freedom would
lead to license by stating that the freedom he was talking about is the freedom of
love, which fulfills the law by going beyond it in loving service to neighbor (Gal
5:13–15). Here in Titus, in the context of the untamed character of the Cretans,
it is this latter sense of freedom that Paul must insist on: freedom from license
or, as he says, "lawlessness." One can be chained by either compulsion—that of
the rigid legalist or that of the heedless prodigal. In either case, whether one is
slave to the law or to lawlessness, it is the unimaginable love of Christ carried
to his death on the cross that sets the captive free.

The price of that liberation was the blood of Jesus (Rom 3:25; 1 Cor 6:20),
which cleanses from sin and claims a people for himself. The link from deliverance to cleansing to making a people of his own is probably the author's
recollection of that sequence in Ezek 37:23, which speaks of deliverance and
cleansing, producing a people belonging to God: "No longer shall they defile
themselves with their idols, their abominations, and all their transgressions.
I will deliver them from all their sins of apostasy, and cleanse them so that
they may be my people and I may be their God." Beneficiaries of the elective
grace of God, Christians should not presume on this grace to remain idle
but should be **eager to do what is good** (literally "to pursue good works").
The Greek verb for "be eager" means to pursue with energy and eagerness. It
implies that those who are delivered and cleansed by Christ will experience
an interior delight and will be motivated not by fear or even by the promise

---

10. This is Paul's favorite way of understanding the redemption; see Rom 3:9; 6:18–22; 8:37–39;
1 Cor 15:24–27; Gal 4:3–7.

of a reward but simply because of the overwhelming love with which they have been graced.

Following his style elsewhere, Paul concludes this little section with a direct   2:15
exhortation to transmit to the faithful what he has just elaborated to Timothy. There is a progression here from **say** to **exhort** to **correct with all authority**. Some will respond to simple teaching, others to preaching, and some only when corrected. The shepherd is not to cave in before the obstreperous demands of any individual or clique. He should not fear to use the authority he has been given. Like a good parent he will correct and reprimand those who deviate from the truth of the gospel or its discipline. **Let no one look down on you.** Obviously, Titus cannot control how others speak or even think of him, but, anchored in the divine commission he has been given, he can refuse to be cowed by such opposition.

Reflection and Application (2:11–15)

In Nepal, where I lived for six years, the king was held by many to be an incarnation of the god Vishnu, and when the streets were cleaned and readied for his passing, many Nepalis would line up to be divinely blessed by a glimpse of the monarch. Similarly, when the king or queen would "appear" at a performance of their daughter at the school where I taught, the students would shout: "Hail to the five times glorious king," repeating the same for the queen. I recall these events when I think of how we as Christians look forward to the "appearance of the glory of the great God and of our savior Jesus Christ."

In his earlier letters Paul presents God's love as the source of our transformation. It empowers us to overcome any obstacles, even persecution and death itself (Rom 8:31–39). It is the soil in which we are rooted, enabling us to know what is beyond knowledge (Eph 3:17). It is the source of holiness (1 Thess 3:12–13) and knowledge and discernment (Phil 1:9–11). These texts and others of Paul are reminders that spiritual growth is, in the last analysis, letting oneself be loved. Externally, God's love appeared in the self-gift of Christ on the cross ("who has loved me and given himself up for me"; Gal 2:20), but then this very love enters us personally through the gift of the Holy Spirit, which fires us with hope for the journey (Rom 5:5). That is why our most basic self-awareness, prior to any other consideration and never to be forgotten, is that we are "the beloved of God" (1:7).

Some of the virtues that Paul recommends here were those likewise recommended by the philosophers of his day. So what is particularly Christian about all this? Plenty. The difference lies in the motivation the Christian and the Christian minister bring to their practice of these virtues, as well as the inner power of grace. It is not for mere inner tranquility or peace with others (encouraged by the Stoics) that the Christian undertakes the process of transformation. It is because of the prior love of God shown by Jesus on the cross and the power of the Holy Spirit given already as a foretaste of glory ("as we await the blessed hope"; Titus 2:13).

How We Should Live—and Why

Titus 3

The Christian life involves many expectations. Paul's directions for Christian conduct, which he continues here, would sound like the old law all over again were it not for the powerful motivation he finds in the grace of Christian baptism. He will then conclude the letter with some final directives and a blessing to all who hear the letter read.

Living in This World by Baptismal Grace (3:1–8)

¹Remind them to be under the control of magistrates and authorities, to be obedient, to be open to every good enterprise. ²They are to slander no one, to be peaceable, considerate, exercising all graciousness toward everyone. ³For we ourselves were once foolish, disobedient, deluded, slaves to various desires and pleasures, living in malice and envy, hateful ourselves and hating one another.

⁴But when the kindness and generous love
　　of God our savior appeared,
⁵not because of any righteous deeds we had done
　　but because of his mercy,
he saved us through the bath of rebirth
　　and renewal by the holy Spirit,
⁶whom he richly poured out on us
　　through Jesus Christ our savior,
⁷so that we might be justified by his grace
　　and become heirs in hope of eternal life.

⁸This saying is trustworthy.

I want you to insist on these points, that those who have believed in God be careful to devote themselves to good works; these are excellent and beneficial to others.

OT: Wis 11:4–8; Sir 7:1–17; Isa 32:15; Joel 3:1

NT: Matt 28:19–20; Rom 12:18; 13:1–7; Eph 2:3–10; James 2:24; 1 Pet 2:13–17

Catechism: washing and renewal (1215), prefigured in Old Covenant (1217–22), obedience to authority (2242)

Lectionary: (3:4–7) Christmas Mass at Dawn; Catechumenate and Initiation of Adults apart from Easter Vigil

3:1   Those who gathered around Titus to hear him read this letter from Paul have just heard the apostle demand respect for Titus's authority, a fitting transition to the present section, which begins with a reminder to submit to **magistrates and** civil **authorities** as well. There is, in fact, a transition here to the social life of Christians—how they are to behave not merely in the Christian community but in the world outside. These counsels have close affinities with those Paul gave in Rom 12:17–13:7, but here one finds a more explicit theological and even sacramental basis for them. Christians who have claimed Christ as their Lord and King could easily be led to think they were thus freed from obedience to the emperor and even to local civil authorities. In some cases they could use the righteous disobedience of the martyrs as an excuse to disobey in other circumstances. The Palestinian Jews revolted against Rome in AD 66–70, and Acts 5:37 recalls the revolt of Judas the Galilean, who refused to pay taxes to the Romans. There were a large number of Jews in Crete, many among them having become Christians. How would they have felt about their restive Jewish brothers in Palestine? Polybius, writing some 150 years before Christ, may be reflecting a Greek prejudice that was either unfounded or outdated by Paul's time, but he says this: "Cretans, owing to their deep-seated lust for wealth, are involved in constant quarrels both public and private, and in murders and civil wars."[1]

In this environment Paul evokes the teaching spoken by the Master, that civil authorities have their rights, that authority in civil society is willed by God (John 19:11). More than being subject and obedient to the civil order, Christians should be ready to cooperate in whatever project will promote the common good. Today we might say they should be willing to take the leadership in such projects. Obviously, not **every . . . enterprise** may merit the title **good**. Tertullian warns the faithful against following the principle of obedience

1. *Histories* 6.46.9.

to authority if it leads to idolatry,[2] and the apostles said that in certain cases "we must obey God rather than men" (Acts 5:29). Even so, Christians should be exemplary citizens, building a better world.

To slander no one is literally not to "blaspheme," but the context makes   3:2
it clear that what is meant is malicious speech against either the authorities mentioned (the Christian should pray for them; 1 Tim 2:1–2) or anyone else. Similarly, the preferred approach of the Christian is not to be litigious or quarrelsome but conciliatory, that is, seeking to reach agreement and, as much as possible, hanging in there until unity is achieved. There are, in fact, two ways of approaching disagreements. The first is to try to browbeat the other into submission; the second is to assume the other person's good will and search together for a solution. Although this supposes the other's willingness to do the same, which is not always the case, such is the preferred approach. This assumes a balanced sympathy, an ability to stand in the other's shoes, an inclination born of charity to yield to the other's preferences. All of this demands a good measure of Jesus' humility, patience, meekness, and gentleness (Matt 11:29) or, as our text says, a disposition **to be peaceable, considerate, exercising all graciousness toward everyone.**

Two reasons are given why Christians should have this humble, gentle at-   3:3
titude toward outsiders. **We ourselves were once** where Gentile sinners are. Paul associates himself, Titus, and his readers with the sins of the Gentile world, though he would not excuse the Jews of sin either (Rom 2:21–24; 3:9–20; 1 Tim 1:15). This awareness of one's former state urges an attitude of humility and gentleness in addressing those still blinded by sin and unbelief. I once heard a twenty-two-year-old former drug addict lecturing a fifteen-year-old about the dangers of certain rap music the teenager was listening to. It was advice of tough love but couched with both humility and experience, as he said, "I was once where you are." Spiritual blindness, indeed, seems to be the sense of the Greek word *anoētos*: **foolish,** mindless, unable to perceive and appreciate spiritual values. It is the confession of every convert: "I was blind but now I see." **Disobedient** refers to an attitude of rebellion—against God and against earthly authorities, whether parents (Rom 1:30; 2 Tim 3:2) or the state. "Led astray and straying" would best capture the next Greek word, translated **deluded** in the NAB ("misled," JB, NJB; "deceived," NIV; "led astray," NRSV), because ordinarily one is not only seduced by evil but one also chooses to follow the seduction. In Matt 18:12 the sheep is not lost but straying, the metaphor suggesting that there is strong hope for an imminent return, but this demands on

2. *On Idolatry* 15.

the part of the Church a willingness to reach out to the sinner and lead him or her back to the fold.

Paul agrees with the Stoics that being controlled by one's passions is the worst kind of slavery (Rom 6:6, 12; Gal 5:13). Augustine would speak of the passions that claimed him before his conversion as the sweet chains from which he wrestled to free himself, though he was still bound by them.[3] From the perspective of the convert, the time in sin was a way of living, a habitual commitment to wickedness, to which the vice of **envy**, or jealousy, is added, as in Gal 5:21, where it joins the squadron of vices that trigger conflicts.

Finally, in place of the unifying power of charity, the unredeemed state is described by a Greek word that can be taken both passively and actively: **hateful ourselves and hating one another**. This list could be described as the photographic negative of redemption. If one would list the opposite of each vice, one would have the portrait of a holy person, the culminating virtue being charity, the love of God and neighbor.

3:4   The positive motivation for Christian behavior, however, is not a list of virtues or good works. It is rather what God has done to deliver us from the life of darkness. It is as if the wretched prisoner just described is suddenly bathed in the light of an opened door. God's saving action manifested two facets of his divinity. His **kindness** (*chrēstotēs*) appears multiple times in the Psalms as the reason for the people's worship and thanksgiving. The second attribute, translated **generous love**, is expressed by the Greek word that gives us the English word "philanthropy." The Greek word *philanthrōpia* ("love of humankind") was common in the Hellenistic world and among the Stoics, for whom it described a friendly relationship in dealing with others. Sometimes such kindness comes unexpectedly, as when the centurion treated his prisoner Paul in a gentlemanly manner (Acts 27:3) or when the native Maltese showed the shipwrecked apostle and his companions "extraordinary hospitality" (28:2). It was especially used of rulers regarding their subjects and thus was fittingly used of the gods in their benevolence toward human beings. That is the sense here. But in the context, this **kindness and generous love of God our savior** is equivalent to the love by which he sent his Son (John 3:16).

3:5   Nothing on the part of human beings could have merited this grace. It is not the works of human "righteousness" but the overwhelming **mercy** of God—a strong Pauline theme. **He saved us** refers to the once-done act of God in Christ that is past, though there is also a present dimension ("the gospel" through which you "are . . . being saved" in 1 Cor 15:1–2) and a future ("in hope we

---

3. *Confessions* 8.11.25.

Augustine on the Bath of Rebirth

Augustine refers to this passage in one of his baptismal homilies: "Look, you are going to come to the holy font, you will be washed clean in baptism, you will be renewed in the saving 'bath of rebirth.' When you rise from these waters, you will be without sin. All the things that were haunting you from the past will be blotted out. Your sins were like the Egyptians in pursuit of you, but only to the Red Sea."[a]

a. *Sermon* 213.8.

were saved" in Rom 8:24). Here, though, the mention of Jesus Christ and grace is delayed to permit salvation to be directly linked to **the bath of rebirth**, obviously baptism. The word *palingenesia* is usually translated **rebirth** but sometimes "regeneration." It is a theme that runs through the Gospel and Epistles of John (John 1:12; 3:5–8; 1 John 3:1). Paul, too, holds that Christians are made children of God, but in his early and undisputed letters he never speaks of baptism in terms of regeneration. He speaks instead of "adoption" (Rom 8:15; Gal 4:5), perhaps reflecting the Jewish resistance to anything that would risk equating human beings to God by nature. Paul does speak of the Christian life, however, as a "new creation" (2 Cor 5:17), a theme that appears already in the baptism of Jesus, where the dove recalls either the hovering wind/spirit of Gen 1:2 or the dove that announces to Noah the regeneration of the world after the flood (8:11). In any case, in one stream of the New Testament tradition, there is a cosmic dimension to baptism; that is, with the baptism of Jesus and the baptism of each Christian, God is creating the world anew. This cosmic sense of rebirth or regeneration appears in a saying of Jesus in Matt 19:28, where it is translated "new age" (NAB) or "new world" (RSV): "In the new age, when the Son of Man is seated on his throne of glory." Here in Titus, though, the meaning is certainly rebirth, a usage that could argue for a post-Pauline hand. Perhaps this indicates that, by the time the Pastorals were written, theological sophistication was sufficiently developed to be able to affirm rebirth or even to affirm that we are "share[rs] in the divine nature" (2 Pet 1:4), without compromising God's transcendence.

The question now comes whether **renewal by the holy Spirit** is to be connected with the "bath" or whether it is a subsequent moment or grace, such as might be connected with the sacrament of confirmation or with what those in the Charismatic Renewal call "baptism in the Holy Spirit." In the adult rite of initiation in the early Church, baptism and the laying on of hands were intimately associated (as even today in the Byzantine rite, "chrismation"—the sacrament of confirmation—immediately follows baptism), without the kind of delay between one ritual and the other that happened later in the Church in the West. Thus in the early Church, initiation meant both the water rite and the laying on of hands assuring the gift of the Holy Spirit (Acts 8:17; 9:17; 19:6). Grammatically, too, the single preposition **through** (*dia*) governs both **bath of rebirth** and **renewal by the holy Spirit**. So it is best to see the two together.

However, **renewal** is not a mere synonym for **rebirth**. As R. C. Trench pointed out a century ago, rebirth is an image taken from nature, renewal from the realm of art.[4] And if rebirth is unusual for Paul, renewal certainly is not. In fact, it is one of his favorite words for the *process* of transformation in Christ. The inward person is being *renewed* day by day (2 Cor 4:16), and thus one must be *renewed* in the spirit of one's mind and put on the *new* person (Rom 12:2; Eph 4:23–24), who is being *renewed* (Col 3:10). Like an artist carefully restoring a faded or damaged masterpiece, the Holy Spirit works upon the Christian until the divine image is restored (2 Cor 3:18). The bath, then, is both a new beginning and an ongoing process, for once given, the Holy Spirit is continually *being given* to the Christian (Gal 3:5; 1 Thess 4:8).

3:6   This Spirit was **poured out**. The image comes from Isa 32:15 ("until the spirit from on high / is poured out on us") and Joel 3:1:

> I will pour out
>   my spirit upon all mankind.
> Your sons and daughters shall prophesy.

Peter affirms that the latter promise was fulfilled on the first Christian Pentecost with the gift of the Holy Spirit giving birth to the Church (Acts 2:17–21). Since God gives the Holy Spirit without measure (John 3:34), it can only be **richly**, or lavishly, that he pours out the Spirit. God does the pouring out, but he does it **through Jesus Christ**, to whom is now clearly given the title **savior** (Titus 2:13), earlier given to God (3:4). We have then, here, a marvelous Trinitarian wrapping for the rites of initiation: God, the Holy Spirit, and Jesus.

3:7   The aim or purpose of this entire process is now given. **So that we might be justified by his grace** (a very Pauline term; see Rom 5:1) is equivalent to the new birth, but it highlights the prior state of sinfulness in which we found ourselves and thus underlines how unmerited the gift was. It is because of

---

4. R. C. Trench, *Synonyms of the New Testament* (London: Kegan Paul, 1894), 65–66.

the state of sonship that we **become heirs** (Gal 4:7), no longer of the land of Canaan but of **eternal life** itself. **In hope** is less a caution than an assurance. Although hope would not be hope if it already possessed what it hoped for, yet "if we hope for what we do not see, we wait with endurance" (Rom 8:25). Titus 3:7 is a kind of condensation of Rom 5:17: "How much more will those who receive the abundance of grace and of the gift of justification come to reign in life through the one person Jesus Christ."

Whether the entire passage (Titus 3:4–7) comes from a liturgical hymn or from the catechesis of an early Christian community or from the author of the letter, it is something worth basing one's life on. This seems to be the sense of Paul's statement at this point: **this saying is trustworthy**. The saying refers to the previous hymn and grounds the consequent expectation of **good works**. And thus the pastor must preach and **insist** with all firmness, for it is from the revelation of God's saving grace that sinners are not only transformed into children of God and heirs of eternal life but also become fruitful in good works. From sinner, to son or daughter, to servant—that is the effect of the gospel. Not only are these good works **excellent**, good, and beautiful in themselves, they are also **beneficial**, or useful, to all human beings. Thus the gospel will become attractive to those yet to be evangelized precisely because of the good works that Christians perform. "Your light must shine before others, that they may see your good deeds and glorify your heavenly Father" (Matt 5:16).

3:8

Reflection and Application (3:1–8)

"The devil can cite Scripture for his purpose," wrote Shakespeare in *The Merchant of Venice*. That truism, illustrated in Satan's tempting of Jesus (Matt 4:1–11), can be applied when evaluating Scripture's witness concerning civil authorities. On the one hand, there are clear passages in which the New Testament counsels obedience to those in charge of the civic order: "Let every person be subordinate to the higher authorities, for there is no authority except from God, and those that exist have been established by God. Therefore, whoever resists authority opposes what God has appointed, and those who oppose it will bring judgment upon themselves" (Rom 13:1–2). Jesus said Pilate's authority was given by God (John 19:11; see also 1 Pet 2:13–17 and Titus 3:1). However, other texts sound a different note. I have already mentioned the apostles saying that they must obey God rather than human beings (Acts 5:29). And Jesus does not deny Satan's claim that all the kingdoms of the world were in Satan's possession (Matt 4:8–9), for they have been handed over to him and he gives them to whomever he wishes

The Catechism on Authority and Obedience

LIVING TRADITION

The duty of obedience requires all to give due honor to authority and to treat those who are charged to exercise it with respect, and, insofar as it is deserved, with gratitude and good-will. (Catechism 1900)

The citizen is obliged in conscience not to follow the directives of civil authorities when they are contrary to the demands of the moral order, to the fundamental rights of persons or the teachings of the Gospel. *Refusing obedience* to civil authorities, when their demands are contrary to those of an upright conscience, finds its justification in the distinction between serving God and serving the political community. . . .

"When citizens are under the oppression of a public authority which oversteps its competence, they should still not refuse to give or to do what is objectively demanded of them by the common good; but it is legitimate for them to defend their own rights and those of their fellow citizens against the abuse of this authority within the limits of the natural law and the Law of the Gospel." (Catechism 2242, emphasis original)[a]

a. *Gaudium et spes* 74.5.

(Luke 4:5–6). And what are we to say of the despotic regimes that have slaughtered thousands, even millions, in our own recent history? Was their authority willed by God? The Church has clear guidelines on this matter.

Violence today. We can detect here Paul's awareness of the negative tendencies of the Cretans, but who is to say we do not find these same virtues hard to practice today, when new forms of hostile interaction are at hand—like road rage! In reflecting on Titus 3:3 and the kind of violence that erupts on our streets, I recall a Catholic judge telling me that when two young men have been in a fight and their case is brought before him, he will call them to his office privately and try to get them to deal directly with their issues and show them how much they really have in common, and frequently they will end up shaking hands, with no need for further litigation.

Renewal. One of the initiatives taken by Pope John Paul II was the restoration of Michelangelo's paintings in the Sistine Chapel. Centuries of dust, candle smoke, and incense had dulled the magnificent works of art. Cleansed and renewed, they became brilliant. Similarly, though created in the image and likeness of God, the human is heir and accomplice of sin that sullies the divine image. But the Holy Spirit, the divine artist, cleanses and renews the divine image and conforms it no longer to the old image of God, Adam, but to the new image of God, Jesus Christ: "All of us, gazing with unveiled face on the glory of the Lord, are being transformed into the same image from glory to glory, as from the Lord who is the Spirit" (2 Cor 3:18).

Faith and works. We should also note the important relationship in Paul between faith and good works that is highlighted in Titus 3:8. Certainly we are saved or justified by faith (Rom 3:28; Eph 2:8), and our calling is not according to works previously performed (2 Tim 1:9), but there is also an expectation that this faith be active and manifested in works (Eph 2:10; 1 Thess 1:3). Matthew records Jesus saying that to enter the kingdom it is not sufficient to call him "Lord, Lord," but one must do the Father's will (Matt 7:21), and in Matthew that involves good works (5:16; 25:31–46).

As a Last Resort (3:9–11)

⁹**Avoid foolish arguments, genealogies, rivalries, and quarrels about the law, for they are useless and futile. ¹⁰After a first and second warning, break off contact with a heretic, ¹¹realizing that such a person is perverted and sinful and stands self-condemned.**

OT: Prov 22:10, 24–25; Sir 11:33; 12:10–18; 13:1
NT: Matt 18:15–17; Rom 12:18; 1 Cor 5:3–5; 1 Tim 1:3–4; 6:20–21
Catechism: excommunication (1463)

In the concrete situation in Crete, it is not sufficient to insist on preaching the   3:9–11
true and "healthy" doctrine. The pastor must be aware of elements that would gnaw away at the deposit of faith. A remarkable order is given here. First, Titus should himself avoid getting involved in the speculations and **arguments** in which some of the Cretan Christians are getting involved (the situation sounds very much like that in 1 Tim 6:20–21). The monotonous Greek "and . . . and . . . and" (literally "argument *and* genealogies *and* rivalries *and* quarrels") suggests how numbing is the variety of these **useless and futile** conflicts. But then, if the person is "factious" (RSV) or "divisive" (NIV; "disputes what you teach," JB, NJB; "causes divisions," NRSV), the matter is more serious. As the alternative translations indicate, this person may not necessarily be a **heretic** according to our modern understanding, though that is not ruled out either. The basic issue is whether he or she is open to correction. If a **first** warning is effective, the issue is settled. If a **second warning** fails, then the shepherd responsible for the flock will **break off contact**.

Does this mean excommunication? A lot depends on what "heretic" means here. If it means simply a troublemaker, a divisive person who refuses correction, then some kind of avoidance by Titus and his community may be intended. But if it means a denial of the faith and the propagation of false teaching in obstinacy to correction, formal excommunication is meant. In that case, excluding the person from the community is done not only to protect the Christian community from corruption by false teaching but also for the ultimate benefit of the recalcitrant, by what might be called the therapy of privation: "That his spirit may be saved on the day of the Lord" (1 Cor 5:5). After repeated attempts, truth and charity require that the individual's rejection of the Christian community, its doctrine, and its standards be openly recognized. Such is the nuance of the word **perverted**. The original meaning of the Greek verb is "to turn inside out," to make what is interior become exterior, that is, to show it for what it really is. It is not the Church or the shepherd who condemns; the person **stands self-condemned**. Obviously, Paul is viewing the matter in terms of objective error or sin. He does not consider the possibility of a malformed conscience or the heretic's possible action under inculpable ignorance.[5]

Reflection and Application (3:9–11)

Every institution must have means to preserve its identity, not least the Church. If moral lapses mar the beauty of the bride of Christ, false teaching threatens her life. The Church is a community of love, but one that is based on truth (Eph 4:15). And so it is with every relationship within the Church. Love must guide the pursuit of truth and the preservation of it as well.

Final Instructions, Exhortation, Greetings (3:12–15)

[12]**When I send Artemas to you, or Tychicus, try to join me at Nicopolis, where I have decided to spend the winter.** [13]**Send Zenas the lawyer and Apollos on their journey soon, and see to it that they have everything they need.** [14]**But let our people, too, learn to devote themselves to good works to supply urgent needs, so that they may not be unproductive.**

[15]**All who are with me send you greetings. Greet those who love us in the faith.**

Grace be with all of you.

---

5. Inculpable ignorance, sometimes called "invincible ignorance," is present when a person, through no fault of his or her own, has no awareness of the wrongness of an action. Canon Law equates error and inadvertence to this kind of ignorance: "Ignorance means lack of knowledge about an issue, error refers to a false judgment about the matter at hand, and inadvertence implies a lack of attention to an issue" (*The Code of Canon Law: A Text and Commentary*, Study Edition [Mahwah, NJ: Paulist Press, 1985], commentary on Canon 1323).

OT: Isa 1:17; Mic 6:8
NT: Acts 18:24–28; 20:4; James 2:14–26
Catechism: good works and God's grace (2009)

Preparing to conclude the letter, Paul gives some concrete directives. **Ar-**   3:12
temas is a contraction of Artemidorus ("gift of Artemis"), obviously a Gentile
convert who had been named after a pagan divinity. Paul did not require any
of his Gentile converts to change their pagan theophoric (god-bearing) names.
Perhaps the contractions, which obscured their meaning, made them more acceptable. Artemas is not mentioned elsewhere in the New Testament, though
Tychicus is mentioned four other times (Acts 20:4; Eph 6:21; Col 4:7; 2 Tim
4:12). Paul is not certain which of his disciples he will send to replace Titus,
nor exactly when he will be able to do so. That Paul later sends Tychicus to
Ephesus, presumably to replace Timothy (2 Tim 4:12), suggests that he finally
decided to send Artemas to Crete to replace Titus.

The location of **Nicopolis** ("Victory City") is not certain, because there
were a number of cities bearing this title in the empire at this time. Yet what
we otherwise know of Paul's travels and the desirability of a moderate winter
sojourn makes the choice easier. Most authorities follow Jerome in identifying
this Nicopolis with the city whose ruins lie on the shores of the Ionian Sea in
what is northwestern Greece today. It lay on a peninsula with the sea to the west
and the Ambracian Gulf to the east. The closeness of the two bodies of water
would have made for a milder **winter.** (Why winter in Alaska if you can winter
in Florida!) We know from Rom 15:19 that Paul had reached that area already
by AD 58. Winter was less suitable for sea travel, but we can assume that Paul
also expects to exercise a vigorous evangelizing activity there. Titus's presence
would help in this work as well as provide the opportunity for Paul to form his

Nicopolis and Actium

BIBLICAL BACKGROUND

The southern tip of the peninsula on which Nicopolis lay pairs with
a similar tip jutting from the south, where the ancient city of Actium
lay. This forms a strait giving entrance to the Ambracian Gulf. Here
Augustus defeated Antony and Cleopatra in the crucial naval battle
of 31 BC. To commemorate that victory, Augustus not only founded
the city of Nicopolis as a Roman colony but erected a monument
to Neptune and Mars made of the battering rams from the prows of
ships captured in the battle.

disciple further. It may well have been at Nicopolis that Paul was later arrested and returned to Rome for his second Roman imprisonment.

3:13   Like Artemas, **Zenas** bears the contracted name of a pagan god (Zenodoras, "gift of Zeus") and is unknown to the rest of the New Testament. No doubt a Gentile convert, he was a member of a profession esteemed in the Hellenistic world, and by identifying him as **the lawyer** Paul probably means to distinguish him from other disciples who have the same name. The mention of the two names, Zenas and Apollos, otherwise unknown in the New Testament argues in favor of the letter's Pauline authenticity, for an imitator would understandably mention Paul's well-known disciples, but why would he mention obscure ones unknown in the rest of Paul's letters?

Apollos is undoubtedly the disciple well known for his eloquence (Acts 18:24; 19:1) and mentioned multiple times in the Corinthian correspondence.[6] The arrival in Crete of such prestigious missionaries would incline the local community to keep them there as long as possible to benefit from their ministry. Thus Paul urges Titus not to delay their traveling to their next destination, but to **send** them **on their journey soon** and to provide them with **everything they need** for it. This was the customary exercise of hospitality in the early Christian communities: "Beloved, you are faithful in all you do for the brothers, especially for strangers; they have testified to your love before the church. Please help them in a way worthy of God to continue their journey" (3 John 5–6). It was customary to send voyagers on their way by accompanying them for a short distance before taking leave of them: the Ephesian presbyters escort Paul to his ship (Acts 20:38), the Christians of Tyre to the outskirts of the town (21:5). I experienced this cultural practice in south Asia frequently. The first time it happened I was confused by it, because I thought the villagers were going to walk the entire journey with us; but after escorting us far enough along the road, they bade a final farewell. Perhaps the practice was meant to tell the visitors, "We are sorry to see you leave, and we would really like to go the whole way with you."

3:14   That Paul reinsists on **good works** at the last minute may seem disconnected from what he just said, like a concern that recurred as he was ready to finish dictating the letter. But his mention of the duty of the local pastor to see to the needs of his guests may well suggest that every Christian is called to do works of this kind, especially hospitality and ministering to **urgent needs**. In fact, they should be outstanding in such devotion of charity. "What does it mean, 'devote themselves to good works'? It means that they should not wait for the

6. 1 Cor 1:12; 3:4, 5, 6, 22; 4:6; 16:12.

needy to come to them but that they seek out those who need their help. . . . In doing good deeds, it is not those who receive the kindness who are benefited, so much as those who do the kindness."[7]

The final phrase, **so that they may not be unproductive** (literally "without fruit"), may seem redundant and anticlimactic, but it is in fact a principle repeatedly stressed in the Gospels. The good tree bears good fruit (Matt 7:16–20); those who abide in Jesus bear much fruit (John 15:5). The sterile fig tree withers (Matt 21:18–22). It is God, of course, who is the ultimate judge of the tree's fruitfulness, but, as Paul says elsewhere in these letters, the outside world too can be attracted or repulsed by the gospel because of what they see in Christians. Thus Tertullian addressed the pagan world: "We serve as sailors and soldiers, we live in the country and trade [in the city], we share our talents with you, we do our works publicly to be of service to you."[8]

The final greeting, in contrast to the lengthy initial greeting (Titus 1:1–4), is unusually brief (compare Rom 16), as if written in haste. **Those who love us in the faith** may target the faithful as opposed to the heretics excoriated in the letter. But the verb for "love" here is not *agapaō*, the usual word for divine charity. It is *phileō*, which suggests friendship, even acquaintance, as if Paul were saying, "Greet all who know us" (Paul and his companions). And then he adds: **Grace be with all of you**. Here again, as in 1 Tim 6:21, it is obvious that, although the letter is addressed to him personally, Titus will read it publicly, both as mandate for the decisions he is authorized to make and for the obedience of the faithful that, on Paul's authority, he may expect.

3:15

Reflection and Application (3:12–15)

The letter to Titus echoes major themes of the Pastoral Epistles. Some of these themes pick up points emphasized in Paul's earlier, undisputed letters, though at times the vocabulary is different:

- the importance of evangelization by example and attraction, thus showing that the gospel promotes and even surpasses the highest ethical ideals of the Roman-Hellenistic world
- baptism as rebirth (called "new creation" in 2 Cor 5:17)
- the Holy Spirit as the agent of renewal

7. Chrysostom, *Homilies on Titus* 3:14.
8. *Apologia* 42.

- the necessity and importance of presbyters-bishops for shepherding the faithful
- the qualities expected of presbyters-bishops and deacons
- their solid formation, the importance of solid teaching, and the danger of false teaching
- perhaps most important of all, Tradition as the handing on of apostolic teaching to the next generation

These directives have the ring of apostolic authority, but they all derive from the prior unmerited mercy of God revealed in Jesus Christ (Titus 3:4–7).

The tone of the letter to Titus gives us the impression that the fledgling church in Crete is sailing through rough seas, where it is important for Titus to exercise his authority firmly. The pastoral leader is told to "refute" (1:9) and to "admonish sharply" (1:13). He is to "correct" (2:15) and "insist" (3:8). What is more, the people creating problems for the implantation and development of the church are characterized as "rebels" (1:10), "deceivers" (1:10), "liars . . . beasts . . . gluttons" (1:12), "vile . . . disobedient . . . unqualified for any good deed" (1:16), "perverted . . . sinful . . . self-condemned" (3:10). This kind of labeling is balanced, of course, by statements that the pastoral leader should be "hospitable, a lover of goodness, temperate, just, holy, and self-controlled" (1:8) and that the faithful should be "peaceable, considerate, exercising all graciousness toward everyone" (3:2)—virtues that would be expected even more so of a leader of the community.

The pastoral leader today should not take the authoritarian tone of this letter, proper and acceptable from an apostle, as a model for his or her ministry. Rather, as 1 Pet 5:3 says, "Do not lord it over those assigned to you, but be examples to the flock." A very important trait is to be a good listener with collaborative skills, developing the gifts of others and seeking unity in a common mission (Eph 4:7–16).

Suggested Resources

Note: commentaries by non-Catholic authors are marked with an asterisk (*).

From the Christian Tradition

Gorday, Peter, ed. *Colossians, 1–2 Thessalonians, 1–2 Timothy, Titus, Philemon.* Ancient Christian Commentary on Scripture: New Testament 9. Downers Grove, IL: InterVarsity, 2000. This series offers rich selections from patristic writings on every passage of the biblical text.

John Chrysostom. *Homilies on Timothy, Titus, and Philemon.* Translated by Philip Schaff. Nicene and Post-Nicene Fathers of the Christian Church 1.13. Edinburgh: Clark, 1819–93. Also available online.

Thomas Aquinas. *Commentaries on St. Paul's Epistles to Timothy, Titus, and Philemon.* Translated by Chrysostom Baer. South Bend, IN: St. Augustine, 2007.

Scholarly Commentaries

Fiore, Benjamin, SJ. *Pastoral Epistles.* Collegeville, MN: Liturgical Press, 2007. Good for parallel literary forms in Greek and Latin literature. Views the Pastorals as written later than Paul but clearly within the Pauline tradition.

*Houlden, J. *The Pastoral Epistles.* Philadelphia: Trinity, 1976. Argues for pseudonymity.

Johnson, Luke Timothy. *The First and Second Letters to Timothy*. New York: Doubleday, 2001. An excellent and readable commentary, supporting Paul's authorship of the Pastorals.[1]

*Marshall, I. Howard. *The Pastoral Epistles*. New York: T&T Clark, 1999. Holds to pseudonymity.

*Mounce, William D. *Pastoral Epistles*. Nashville: Nelson, 2000. A 641-page scholarly commentary with copious bibliography, accessible to the non-Greek reader. Holds to Pauline authenticity.

Quinn, Jerome D. *The Letter to Titus*. New York: Doubleday, 1990. Holds to pseudonymity of the letters. Maintains that Titus was written first, with the letter's long introduction serving to introduce all three letters.

Spicq, Ceslas, OP. *Les épîtres pastorales*. 2 vols. Paris: Gabalda, 1969. Those who read French will find this work enlightening and pastorally sensitive. Defends Pauline authenticity.

Wild, Robert A., SJ. "The Pastoral Letters." In *The New Jerome Biblical Commentary*, edited by Raymond E. Brown, Joseph A. Fitzmyer, and Roland E. Murphy, 891–902. Englewood Cliffs, NJ: Prentice Hall, 1990. This short commentary is especially useful for summarizing the arguments in favor of pseudonymity, which the author supports. Traces the sequence of movements of Paul, Timothy, and Titus supposed by the letters.

*Witherington, Ben, III. *Letters and Homilies for Hellenized Christians*, vol. 1: *A Socio-Rhetorical Commentary on Titus, 1–2 Timothy, and 1–3 John*. Downers Grove, IL: InterVarsity, 2006. Argues for authenticity.

Midlevel Commentaries

Johnson, Luke Timothy. *Letters to Paul's Delegates*. Valley Forge, PA: Trinity, 1996. A short, easy-to-read commentary supporting Paul's authorship.

*Kelly, J. N. D. *The Pastoral Epistles*. London: Black, 1960. Reprinted Peabody, MA: Hendrickson, 1993.

*Oden, Thomas C. *First and Second Timothy, Titus*. Louisville: John Knox, 1989. Excellent pastoral resource.

*Stott, John R. W. *The Message of 1 Timothy and Titus: God's Good News for the World*. Bible Speaks Today. Downers Grove, IL: InterVarsity, 2001.

---

1. Although in some of his writings Johnson rejects various aspects of the Church's teaching on sexuality (e.g., his article entitled "Homosexuality and the Church," *Commonweal*, June 15, 2007), he does not express those problematic views in his works on the Pastorals.

Popular Commentaries and Study Bibles

*Barclay, William. *The Letters to Timothy, Titus, and Philemon.* Philadelphia: Westminster, 1956. A popular, insightful, pastoral commentary, to be used by checking exegesis against more recent scholarly commentaries.

Hahn, Scott, and Curtis Mitch. *Thessalonians, Timothy, and Titus.* Ignatius Study Bible. San Francisco: Ignatius, 2007. Includes study questions.

Glossary

Ambrosiaster—an anonymous fourth-century commentary on all the epistles of St. Paul (excluding Hebrews), so called because it was for some time thought to be written by St. Ambrose.

aorist—the simple past tense (e.g., "did") as distinct from the continuous past ("was doing"), the present perfect ("has done"), or the past perfect ("had done").

bishop (*episkopos*)—literally "overseer," from *epi-* ("over") and *skopos* ("one who watches or looks out"). Used synonymously with "†presbyter" in Titus 1:5–7 and probably throughout the Pastorals and in Phil 1:1. Member of a board of elders charged with oversight of the community. Not to be identified with modern-day bishops, who, like Timothy and Titus, ordain and exercise authority over priests but for the most part are territorially based. In terms of their succession to Paul by ordination and being authorized to ordain, Timothy and Titus correspond to modern bishops and continue the sacramental and authoritative apostolic Tradition.

charism—a gift of God for the building up of the Church, either given directly by the Holy Spirit or mediated by the laying on of hands; unlike the grace that saves and is common to all, charisms differ according to individuals.

chiasm—a symmetrical arrangement of words, phrases, or ideas, as a-b-c-b-a.

conscience—the faculty of moral judgment by which a person recognizes the rightness or wrongness of actions.

deacon (*diakonos*)—literally "servant," an office subordinate to †presbyter. In the Pastorals deacons are appointed by Timothy or Titus for a variety of services in the community. From later sources we know that they were involved in the baptismal rite and in distributing the goods of the community to the poor. Women deacons also appear in the Pauline letters.

devotion—the usual NAB translation of the Greek word *eusebeia*, which can also be translated "religion, godliness, piety"; used in the Greek Bible not only for the duties of humans to God but also for a corresponding moral life.

Diaspora—Jews dispersed outside Palestine.

Didache—short for "The Teaching of the Apostles," an early handbook of Christian ethical and liturgical community instructions, concluding with a chapter warning about the final times.

eschatology—having to do with the "end times," which can be understood either as still coming or as the final times ushered in by Jesus Christ. Thus the New Testament can say we are living "in these last days" (Heb 1:2), introduced by the resurrection of Jesus Christ and the sending of the Holy Spirit (Acts 2:17). Still, Christians look forward to a final consummation with the return of Christ.

eusebeia—used ten times in the Pastorals. *See* **devotion.**

gnostic, gnosticism—a second-century movement that posed a threat to Christianity by assimilating Christian elements into its ideas of a secondary creator god responsible for the mistake of material creation, from which the gnostic sought to be delivered by a process of ascent to the supreme god. See also the sidebar on p. 94.

mandata principis—a letter form known already prior to Paul in which a superior gives directives to his delegate or subordinate. This seems to be the literary template followed in the letters to Timothy and Titus, explaining in part the difference of these letters from Paul's earlier letters addressed to the churches.

Muratorian canon—an incomplete listing of New Testament books discovered by Lodovico Antonio Muratori in Milan in 1740 and until recently thought to be the earliest listing of books accepted by the Church as inspired, dating to the late second or early third century. Several scholars date it as a fourth-century list from Syria or Palestine.

mystery—in Paul, the plan of God for the salvation of the world in Jesus Christ, now revealed in the gospel. For further background, see the sidebar on p. 88.

parousia—literally "presence or arrival." Used of the ceremonial entry of emperor or king upon visiting a city, for which the officials and populace go out to meet him. In the New Testament the word is used as a technical term for the second coming of Christ.

presbyter (*presbyteros*)—literally "elder." Not necessarily an older person but one who would be appointed or ordained because of his maturity and gifts for leadership. Our English word "priest" is a contraction of "presbyter." *See* **bishop**.

pseudonymous, pseudonymity—writings attributed to someone who is not their real author.

Septuagint (abbreviated LXX)—Taken from the Latin *septuaginta*, meaning seventy, the title Septuagint refers to a Greek version of the Jewish Scriptures produced in the third and second centuries BC by Jewish scholars, traditionally numbered at seventy, and used by Greek-speaking Jews and Christians. It departs considerably from the Hebrew version known today as the Masoretic Text, but scholars believe that at times it reflects a more original version of the Hebrew. It is quoted frequently in the New Testament.

Index of Pastoral Topics

This index indicates where the letters to Timothy and Titus provide material related to topics that are useful for evangelization, catechesis, apologetics, or other forms of pastoral ministry.

mediator, uniqueness of Christ as, 1 Tim 2:5–6

mentoring, 2 Tim 2:2

mercy, 1 Tim 1:13–16; 2 Tim 1:16–18; Titus 3:5

money, love of, 1 Tim 3:3; 6:10; 2 Tim 3:2. See also "wealth"

newly ordained, 1 Tim 4:11–5:2; 5:19–23

older men, 1 Tim 5:1; Titus 2:2

older women, 1 Tim 5:2; Titus 2:3–5

Paul's example, 1 Tim 1:1, 12–16; 2:7; 2 Tim 1:11–12; 3:10–12; 4:6–8, 16–18

perseverance, necessary for salvation, 1 Tim 4:10; 2 Tim 2:12

physical training and devotion, 1 Tim 4:7–8

prayer, 1 Tim 2:1, 8; 4:5; 5:5; 2 Tim 1:3

prayers for the dead, 2 Tim 1:16–18

prophecy, 1 Tim 1:18; 4:14

qualifications of ministers, 1 Tim 3:1–13; Titus 1:5–9

religious debates, 2 Tim 2:14–19, 23–26; Titus 3:9–11

salvation, 1 Tim 1:15; 2:4, 15; 4:16; 2 Tim 1:9; 2:10; 3:15; Titus 3:5. See also "savior"

salvation of all, God's will for the, 1 Tim 2:4; 4:10; Titus 2:11

Satan, devil, evil spirits, 1 Tim 1:20; 3:7; 4:1; 5:15; 2 Tim 2:26

savior, God or Jesus as, 1 Tim 1:1; 2:3; 4:10; 2 Tim 1:10; Titus 1:3–4; 2:10, 13; 3:4–6

Scripture, inspiration and usefulness of, 2 Tim 3:16–17

secular society, Titus 3:1–2

sin, sinner, 1 Tim 1:15; 5:20, 24; Titus 3:10–11

slaves, 1 Tim 6:1–2a; Titus 2:9–10

suffering for Christ, 2 Tim 1:8–12; 2:3, 8–13; 3:11–12; 4:5, 16–18

teaching, sound, 1 Tim 1:5; 4:6; 6:1–2a; 2 Tim 1:13; 2:2, 15; 3:14–15; Titus 1:9; 2:1

teaching and authority of bishops and priests (presbyters), 1 Tim 4:11; 6:2b–4; Titus 2:15

teaching/teachers, false, 1 Tim 1:3–7; 4:1–3; 6:3–5; 2 Tim 2:18; 3:6–9, 13; 4:3–4, 14–15; Titus 1:10–16; 3:9–11

Tradition, 2 Tim 1:13–14; 2:1–2; 3:14–15

vices, lists of, 1 Tim 1:9–10; 3:3, 8, 11; 5:13; 6:4–5, 9–10; 2 Tim 3:1–9; Titus 1:10, 15–16; 3:3

vices, of the last days, 2 Tim 3:1–9, 13; 4:3–4

virtues, lists of, 1 Tim 1:5, 14; 3:2, 4, 8–9, 11–12; 5:10; 6:11, 18; 2 Tim 1:7, 13; 2:22; 3:10; Titus 1:6–9; 2:2–10, 12; 3:2

virtues for different states of life, Titus 2:1–10

wealth, desire for, contentment, 1 Tim 6:5–10

wealth, right use of, 1 Tim 6:17–19

widows, 1 Tim 5:3–16

wine, 1 Tim 5:23

witness, exhortation to, 2 Tim 1:8

women, 1 Tim 2:9–15; 3:11; Titus 2:3–5. See also "widows"

young men, Titus 2:6–8

youth, message to, 1 Tim 4:12

Index of Sidebars

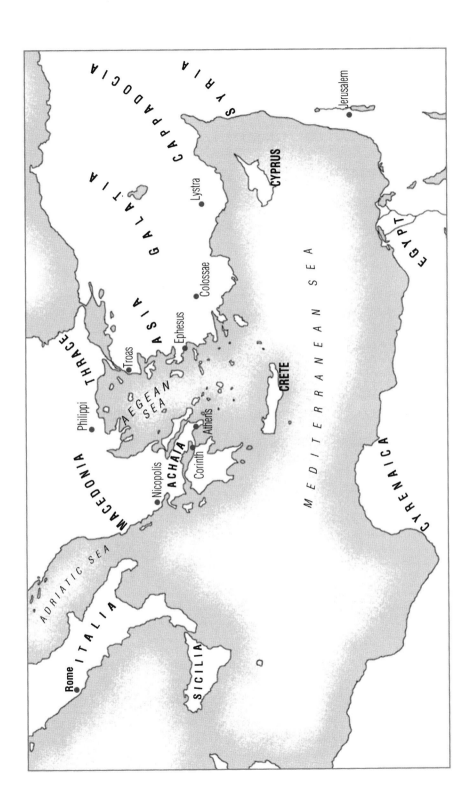